Canada and Citizenship Education

Edited by Keith A. McLeod
Faculty of Education
University of Toronto

Some of the articles in this book were originally presented at the Forum on Citizenship and Citizenship Education in Schools and Communities, sponsored by the Canadian Education Association and the Department of the Secretary of State, in Edmonton, November 1987

**Canadian Education Association /
Association canadienne d'éducation**
Toronto, Ontario, Canada

Acknowledgement

The Canadian Education Association and those who assisted in organizing the National Forum on Citizenship and Citizenship Education would like to thank the Department of the Secretary of State, Citizenship, for their support of the Forum and for their assistance in the publication of this volume.

Our appreciation is also extended to those who made presentations at the Forum, those who participated in it, and those who have contributed subsequent to the Forum to this volume on citizenship and citizenship education.

Thank you on behalf of the Canadian Education Association.

Keith A. McLeod, Forum Chairman

© 1989
Canadian Education Association/
Association canadienne d'éducation
Suite 8-200, 252 Bloor Street West,
Toronto, Ontario M5S 1V5

ISBN: 0-920315-37-2

Printed in Canada

Cover design by Fred Huffman

This volume is dedicated to the
original organizers of the
Canadian Education Association,
then called the Dominion Education
Association, which was formed in 1891 to
encourage the growth and development
of Canadian education and
Canadian citizenship.

K. A. M.cL

Contents

Part I: Past, Present and Future

Exploring Citizenship Education:
Education for Citizenship
Keith A. McLeod — 5

Canadian Citizenship for a Progressive State
B. Anne Wood — 19

The Current Status of Teaching about
Citizenship in Canadian Elementary
and Secondary Schools
Vandra L. Masemann — 27

Canadian Society in the Year 2000
Ronald C. LeBlanc — 53

Part 2: Citizenship, Schools and Teaching

The Charter and the Teaching of
Human Rights and Citizenship
Edwin Webking — 73

The Charter of Rights and Freedoms
and Legal Literacy
Michael E. Manley-Casimir, Wanda M. Cassidy,
and Suzanne de Castell — 83

Literacy for Citizenship:
The Literacy Role of the
Secretary of State Department
Brad Munro — 101

Ways of Teaching Values: An Outline
of Six Values Approaches
Ian Kupchenko and Jim Parsons   *107*

Theories and Attitudes Towards
Political Education
Marshall W. Conley   *137*

Thoughts on Education for Global Citizenship
Patricia and George W. Schuyler   *157*

Role-play and Citizenship Education
Moira Fraser Juliebo   *169*

Horizon Canada: Une collection unique
de l'histoire du pays
Benoît Robert   *175*

Co-operative Learning:
Active Citizenship Education
Daniel McDougall and Karen Annon   *181*

Selecting a Capital for Canada -
An Exercise in Simulations and
Citizenship Education
Charles Hou   *189*

Part 3: Recommendations and Suggestions

Recommendations and Suggestions from
the Forum on Citizenship Education   *195*

Part 1:
Past, Present and Future

Exploring Citizenship Education: Education for Citizenship

Keith A. McLeod
Faculty of Education, University of Toronto

IN THE FOLLOWING paper I will briefly examine not only the origins of education for citizenship within modern states but I will examine the phenomenon within the context of the development of Canadian thought and of schooling. More particularly I will analyze in some detail the thinking underlying the Canadian Studies Movement. I shall conclude with my own observations as to some of the basic needs in education today for citizenship for today and tomorrow. By the end of the paper it will be, I believe, clear that I think that some fundamental reorientations are necessary in our thinking about schooling and education for citizenship.

The essence of my perspective is that narrower concepts of citizenship education, as civics or as political education or socialization, are but a particular part of a broader and more complex concept of education for citizenship. This broader concept of citizenship education is not the equivalent of education per se, rather it is that all aspects of schooling can be seen in the context of citizenship and that all aspects of schooling can help to form citizens. Thus civics or political education is a particular but not a special part of education for citizenship. However, both the broader concept and the civic focus need to be planned for and developed as part of the program of studies within schools.

> *Afin de donner une orientation toute nouvelle à notre conception de l'instruction civique, l'auteur examine les origines de cet enseignement au Canada de même que les courants de pensée qui ont fait naître le mouvement en faveur des études canadiennes. Il termine son article par des commentaires sur certains besoins essentiels en éducation à la citoyenneté : un plan d'études global; un enseignement de connaissances sur le Canada et la citoyenneté qui ne soit pas limité aux cours de politique ou d'histoire; de meilleures méthodes et techniques pédagogiques; l'apprentissage de valeurs et d'attitudes; plus d'attention portée aux questions internationales; et la formation de citoyennes et citoyens instruits et capables de prendre part à la vie du Canada.*

Keith A. McLeod

States, Nations and Schooling

It is not a coincidence that public education was advocated by proponents of nation-states. The alterations in allegiance and even the promotion of change in allegiance of individuals and groups from simply local or parochial and provincial loyalties to states and most especially to the nation-state brought with it a demand for a system of education through which that new allegiance could be promoted, maintained or recognized. The nature of the culture and unification of the nation-state in large part determined the kind of political socialization the state authorities and society mandated. A common element was that people were to be educated to their passive role as subjects, that is, to be allegiant and to fulfil their responsibilities as "subjects."

The development of democratic states has added an important role - people as *active* participants in the state, as "citizens." Thus citizens not only continued to have parochial or provincial affinities and national functions and responsibilities as subjects of the state, but they now added their role as active participants in governing. This right to active participation in governing was seen as a part of a social contract or compact. Consequently, the political education of people in this context was a much more complex process. Not only had people to be educated for their role as parochial or provincial, and for their functions as national subjects, but for active participation in governing, thus they were to fulfil their rights as citizens. The schools' functions were to not only teach for parochial, provincial and national interests, and the subjects' responsibilities, but for the citizens' rights.

Coincidental with the growth of states and of democratic states was the phenomenon of nationalism and the concept of the nation-state. Sometimes in reaction to local allegiances, nationalism was a means to overcome the pluralism and diversity that was manifested in or through parochial and provincial allegiances (e.g., Germany prior to unification); sometimes it was a reaction to the pluralism and diversity within large polyglot states (e.g., The 19th century Austro-Hungarian Empire). Political economists and polemicists conceptualized the nation-state. They combined the idea of state allegiance, the phenomenon of the subject's patriotism and loyalty, with the concept that the development and the viability of a nation was dependent upon the extent of the cultural uniformity and conformity within the boundaries. Thus a nation, in classic terminology, came to be defined as a state composed of a single nationality. A nationality, in a similar classic sense, was a group of people bound together by ties of mutual interest such as common language, customs, laws, history, values, religion, economics, and institution. Above all, they had a feeling of being one-people, different from all other people. Advocates of this conception of nation-states, therefore, were also advocates of uniformity or the creation of uniformity. To nationalistic advocates the schools were the logical institutions to teach the requisite culture; the schools would maintain or create the cultural uniformity and conformity - symbolicly, attitudinally, and institutionally or behaviourally. Obviously, when the democratic state and nationalistic patterns are combined very complex political, socio-cultural, educational combinations can be present. For example, there can be democratic claims by competing nationalisms for different educational goals

Exploring Citizenship Education

and content. Or there may be democratically expressed but differing emphases among people: those who wish the school to emphasize parochial and provincial interests; those with state-subject interests (responsibilities), or those who wish to emphasize democratic-citizen functions (rights and participation). The formulations and complexities increase as the number of interest groups multiply in terms of what people see the functions or purposes of schooling to be.

Several typologies or characterizations have been devised by which to analyze the variety of images or purposes underlying schooling. I shall here simply list a variety of purposes or reasons for schooling. First, some see schooling as the extension of the family where the teacher works with the children in *loco parentis* at the school "house." Others, second, look to the economics of schooling. That at the individual level persons become economically useful through education or that at the national level increasing the standard of education will increase the productivity (GNP). Religious motivations form a third category of rationales: the school teaches, reflects or reinforces the religious precepts of a church or religion. Fourth, political socialization is seen by some as the main purpose: the education of citizens. Fifth, others may believe social control is of paramount importance: children are placed in the protected environment or alternatively they are taken into custody to keep them out of ignorance, poverty, and crime. Sixth, another set of rationales are clustered around the concept of cultural reproduction. The physical community, the collegial group, or the cultural community utilize schools to perpetuate the collectivities' way of life.

All of these purposes have some relevance to citizenship education in the sense of educating the citizens of today or tomorrow. They also have relevance to political socialization, an alternative name for what has been referred to as civics or civic education, the narrower concept, of preparing persons for actually taking part in the political system.

Canada

It was in the midst of 19th century thinking about states, nation-states, and nationalism that Canada was confederated in 1867. The Confederation Debates clearly indicate that there was general agreement that what the leaders were creating was a political structure, a "political nationality." There is also evidence within these Debates of an acknowledgement or awareness of pluralism in terms of languages, religions, and cultures. The constitutional proposals, worked out at the Charlottetown and Quebec conferences, and the *British North America Act* itself clearly demonstrate the attempts to synthesize parochial and provincial interests with the needs of a state and of a democracy, albeit 19th century style. Confederation produced provincial governments and a national government. The division of powers was along parochial/provincial and national lines. I am not going to pursue the constitutional history of Canada except to indicate that the federal system has been a matter of lively debate and a balancing act ever since.

What is germane to the line of thought I wish to pursue is that within a short time there was not only competition between the provincial and national interests and governments but between different forms of nationalism. All these competing interests and forms of nationalism found

Keith A. McLeod

expression in education and schooling.

First of all education, at Confederation, was made a provincial responsibility — in large part to recognize and to placate the fears of parochial (including religious parochialism) interests. Moreover, within the provinces, religious diversity, in the form of Protestantism and Roman Catholicism, was constitutionally entrenched in the educational systems. The provincial systems were also there to take into account the cultural and linguistic differences at the local level. The federal government was to express the new political nationality but it was primarily limited to just that, expressing a political commitment or allegiance.

Within a few years of Confederation, competing forms of nationalism, based in large part on the two linguistic-cultural traditions, came to the fore. They have been there ever since. Sometimes that divergence has been significant enough to bring about "separatist" political movements. Nor have these nationalisms been the only divisive forces. Parochial/provincial forces appeared before the ink was dry on the *British North America Act*. There have been parochial/provincial separatist movements from the east coast to the west coast based upon a variety of economic, political, and cultural interests.

The concepts people have had of Canada have not been static in other senses either. There have been many debates and discussions along the way from colony to nation. Should Canada be part of an imperial system or independent? Should Canada strengthen the British connection (1958) or the Commonwealth associations? Should Canada see herself as a North American nation or become even more closely associated with the United States through for example, "Reciprocity" (1911) or through "Free Trade" (1988)? Should Canada participate in la francophonie? Should Canada be involved in internationalism?   Should Canada be stolidly and stoicly independent?

At the same time that the debates over the status and relationships of Canada have taken place, and not divorced from the issues of status and relations, there has also been within Canada periodic movements to stress various forms of pan-Canadianism. The Canada First Movement (1868) wished to boost Canadian nationalism within the context of the Empire. The Imperial Movement saw the international involvement of Canada within an Imperial Federation as a further indication of the growth of Canada. Canadian involvement in World War I was also seen as further evidence of development; Prime Minister Borden's insistence upon independent Canadian participation in the peace treaty and in the League of Nations further enhanced for many the status of Canada.

Within Canada, and even within the field of education, there was a growth of pan-Canadianism. The formation of a national education organization, the Dominion Education Association in 1891 (now the Canadian Education Association) and the launching of the Dominion History Textbook contest in 1894 to find a pan-Canadian text that would downplay provincialism, were but two examples. The development of the Commonwealth concept in 1926 gave further impetus to the status of Canada.

However, the divergent views of Canada and its future that were found within pan-Canadianism also indicated divergence of national views. Was the increasing importance of Canada to be seen within the British

Exploring Citizenship Education

system, within a North American context, or as an independent nation? And was this nation to be unicultural, bicultural or pluralistic? The growth of immigration both before and after World War I had brought many new cultures to Canada.

Canada's leading role in World War II and her independent role in world or external affairs, including the United Nations, helped to decide the course of international status. It took a bit longer for internal settlement, for bilingualism and multiculturalism to emerge as national policy. However, on January 1, 1948, we became Canadian citizens. But what did that mean? There was for many years a "characteriscally Canadian" search for *the* Canadian identity. It became somewhat reconciled in bilingualism and multiculturalsim but only after a Royal Commission, a major separatist movement in Quebec, a mature realization and recognition of the cultural and racial pluralism, and a resurgent interest in pan-Canadianism based upon new or renewed premises.

The Canadian Studies Movement of the 1970s and '80s followed the exposés of the inadequancy and neglect of "what it means to be Canadians." For others the internal division within Canada, of English and French, of regionalism and provincialism was the stimulus for Canadian Studies. Also promoting Canadian Studies were those who perceived American economics and culture as an external continentalist threat. Multiculturalism also became part of the thrust for Canadian Studies. All these forces tended to focus on Canadian Studies. However, before dealing with Canadian Studies a brief historical analysis of education for citizenship is warranted.

A Brief Overview of Education and Citizenship: The 19th Century

The idea of educating people for their political as well as social roles was embedded in education in Canada even before Confederation. Egerton Ryerson, the man who took control of the fledgling system of education in Upper Canada had definite ideas on the subject. The predominant rationale for public education was that ignorance was a social evil, education a public good. In short, ignorance bred poverty and subsequently crime. Education was of "civil interest," of importance to a "free people" interested in maintaining their freedom and it was a requisite to social well-being. Ryerson outlined his reasons in a lengthy address on education from which I will quote parts at length because of their clarity and relevance.

> I. I observe then, in the first place, *that public education and public liberty stand or fall together*. Public liberty involves a state of society, as well as a system of government. The very terms "free people" suppose the existence of laws enacted by the consent of the people, and in the administration of which they participate. This supposes a knowledge of the principles of law on the part of the people, and their ability to aid in sustaining and administering those laws. Hence writers on government and statesmen have advocated or opposed the education of the mass of the people, just in proportion as they advocated or opposed their enfranchisement in regard to legislation and government. When kings only were regarded as legislators, they and the instruments of their will were

9

alone regarded as the proper subjects of public education.[1]

He went on to a second reason:

II. ... education, and even some general knowledge, is necesalsary to enable the people to discharge and exercise judiciously the first duty and most valued privilege of a free-man - the Elective franchise. The possesion of this right is a practical recognition that every freeholder is entitled to a voice in the enactment of laws which affect his person or property, or by which he is governed. This is one of the most essential conditions of a free government, but it involves corresponding duties and supposes corresponding qualifications on the part of electors. It is one of our dearest and justly cherished tenets, that the people of Canada make their own laws; but if they are the source of the law, ought not that source to be pure, intelligent and enlightened?[2]

Ryerson's third reason was equally clear:

III. ... the people are not only called upon to take a part in making laws, but also in administering them. The trial by jury not only confers upon the people a valued privilege, but imposes upon them a solemn and responsible duty. As jurymen they are often called to decide upon your character, your fortune, and even upon your life.[3]

Fourth, Ryerson deals with executing law.

IV....the education of the people is of the greatest importance in order to fulfil the various official trusts which a system of free government creates. The duties of the franchise and the jury box are only two out of many civil duties which must be performed in a free country. In administration of the law, both criminal and civil, there must be constables, clerks, magistrates, sheriffs and judges as well as jurymen. In the execution of the school law, there are required teachers, trustees, visitors and superintendents. In our system of municipal institutions, there must be collectors, clerks, councillors, wardens and mayors. In our militia system we require officers, from the corporal up to the adjutant-general and in the legislative system, we must have legislators from every district in Upper Canada.[4]

Thus Ryerson concluded that one of the most important duties of government was to provide for the education of the people. With reference to what might be referred to civic education he added "...the school does not teach political science; but it may and ought to teach those elements of it which are within the limits of school teaching, and within the time of school attendance, and within the capacity of youth: and the application of which involves their several duties as members of the State. And in the mastery of these elements youth acquire that mental discipline, and those aids and directions in the acquisition of knowledge which prepare them to act the part of intelligent free men, and to erect a superstructure of varied knowledge and usefulness."[5] Ryerson went on to list the required educational basics - the principles of grammar, the four fundamental rules and two simple operations of calculation, a few definitions and axioms, the

Exploring Citizenship Education

fundamentals of science, the principles and features of government; and a few other basics.

Ryerson's concept of education was based on the concept of the people having made a social compact. Children were to be taught industry and economy, virtue and knowledge for themselves and for society. Thus ignorance, poverty, and crime would be overcome. Christianity, to Ryerson, would, of course, be central to moral education and an essential element in schooling; non-sectarian Christianity would be found in the schools.

The school texts, the teaching, and the discipline and methods reflected the didactic nature of thought. The readers were moral tracts; schooling trained the mental faculties, and provided the basic knowledge that prepared one for life. Schooling initiated, but life taught and developed the youth beyond the basics including the moral injunctions. Only gradually at the end of the century when more children began to stay in school longer, sometimes even acquiring a year or two of high school did the curriculum become somewhat more elaborate. Even then the teaching, courses, and texts in Canadian history,for example, remained didactic and continued to stress the basic of government (including the Canadian system) and to teach *about* the principles and practices of democracy.

The 20th Century

As Canada grew, as international involvement broadened the scope of Canadians, as industrialization and urbanization became more obvious, as immigration increased, the stress and the shifts that had become evident in the late 19th century continued. There were many statements and demands about the need for a "new education" in the late 19th century and these continued into the 20th. Attempts were made to change education - to introduce technical and industrial education, home economics, civics, occupational guidance, improved science courses and Canadian literature. There were also attempts to introduce new educational innovations like guidance, intelligence tests, child centred education, and even experiential learning through the school gardening movement and laboratories. However, the methodology and character of schooling did not change. Didactic thought, recitation, memorization, and largely passive learning remained the rule and by overwhelming agreement, the norm. Citizenship remained where Ryerson and the like minded had placed it. Faith in basic education for life and for citizenship continued to be the standard, albeit basic education was becoming somewhat more lengthy.

Only gradually did the the idea of education through participation, as practice of life and even of democracy, take its place in Canadian schools. Calls for reform even in the 1920s saw only moderate success in reducing physical punishment, rule by principal and teacher martinets, introducing student councils, and in developing instructional methods that were student-centred and learning oriented. The depression of the 1930s and World War II delayed and retarded educational development. Reconstruction following World War II left primary and secondary education in the doldrums, and citizenship education with it despite the adoption on Janurary 1, 1948, of Canadian citizenship. Only a few calls for reform were heard; the trend was to provide more of the same as the growing population strained the educational systems.

Keith A. McLeod

The most significant calls for reform in the 1950s and '60s often came from within the organizations of the teaching profession. Teachers maintained that the quality of education depended in large part on the quality of the persons attracted to teaching and that was governed in large part by the adequacy (or inadequacy) of the renumeration. The single most important reform of these two decades was the significant improvement in teachers' salaries and benefits.

By the later '60s the calls for reform had multiplied. There were demands for better schools, better teachers, more and better Canadian Studies in a variety of subjects, more democratic educational practices, less reliance on physical punishment and penalities, more student centred learning and instruction, alternative schools, access to bilingual education, and even the first rumblings of multicultural and non-sexist education. Reform, however, quickly became formalized. If rote learning had been characteristic of the 19th and early 20th century the new formalism's was "process." There *was* strong de-emphasis in many quarters on sequential learning and teaching; what was learned was now secondary to the process, to how the content and skills were learned. For the academic student (notice the retention of the status word) the knowledge learned through "process" became more understandable, the skills learned indeed provided for continued learning. The whole context of schooling as well as the learning environment became more democratic. But for the non-academic student the emphasis on process too frequently hinged on teaching students social skills, fraudulent self-esteem, and self satisfaction: "s/he is working up to her/his interests/abilities/capacity." Moreover, if a student from a "poor background" was unlucky enough to be in a large school, with "many levels of courses" it was all the more likely that marking time would be the norm.

The emphasis on "social passing" became so normal that many of the students reaching grade 9 were reading at some four levels below that. Even with the so-called reforms in secondary education 40% who entered grade 9 dropped out before they achieved junior matriculation. The reform of education did not fulfil the promise of equality of educational opportunity for many potential citizens; they were participants in a political system but they remained and continued to remain unable to enjoy their full potential as persons, as citizens. Equity remained elusive; decades of promises for equality of educational oportunity remained unfulfilled.

However, along with the new math, the new science and the other reforms came a renewed emphasis on citizenship education in the form, this time of Canadian Studies and even Canada Studies. The idea was to help students to come to terms with the Canadian identity, even a new Canadian identity for it was undergoing a metamorphasis as Canada came to terms with French-Canada and pluralism. Emphasis on citizenship education is not an unusual phenomenon in times of stress and change.

Canadian Studies

The report of the National History Project, *What Culture? What Heritage?* states that the project's main interest was civic education which is defined as "the influence of formal instruction in developing the feelings and attitudes of young Canadians towards their country and its problems, and the knowledge on which these attitudes are based. Our interests in the

Exploring Citizenship Education

three subjects... [of Canadian history, social studies, and civics], stems solely from the fact that they are regarded in Canada as the traditional academic areas in which civic education takes place." [6]

Civic education was to be "closely geared to 'the pluralistic, multi-racial nature of our society'; it recognizes that Canada is not only a North American country but also is becoming more involved with the world community of nations; it seems to answer the objections of those who fear excessive nationalism; it offers a completely new, valid and perhaps even an exciting approach to the frustrating, much-abuse search for a Canadian identity." [7]

The Report's author, writing in 1968, certainly believed that Canada faced problems of size, regionalism, languages, and of having a large neighbour. Canada's existence was a problem: "Closely related to all of these problems, and making their solution more difficult, is the fact that we originally built a nation-state without firm foundations. In 1867, we created a political regime - a set of federal and provincial institutions - without a stable political community to support it." [8] The writer then cited ethnic pluralism as the Achilles heel. He was referring to the English-French Canadian cleavage and to the multicultural population. However, the Report's writer suggested that conciliation is possible and probable because he believed that free societies thrive on dynamic tensions. He believed civic education in the past has been too conerned with consensus. "Civic education in a democracy ... should not only consider areas of agreement, but also ... the inevitable differences of opinion that have always been and will continue to be an essential part of free societies." He adds " ... a stable democracy also requires a minimum ability among its citizens to resolve conflict with tolerance, understanding and knowledge of opposing viewpoints." [9]

Implicit in this concept of civic education is the teaching of the cognitive knowledge and skills associated with the existence and importance of the very survival of Canada. Skills and thought - appropriate to a democracy — should be imparted, learned, and utilized to develop appropriate attitudes.

The key recommendation was the establishment of a Canadian Studies Consortium:

> *The impetus for creating the Consortium should come from the Council of Ministers of Education, Canada. The Consortium should be based on the following principles. ONE: It should be designed to function as an interprovincial organization. TWO: It should be a completely independent organization, free of all political influences. THREE: It should consist of strategically located regional centres, with a national executive committee to serve as a data bank and clearing house for all its activities. FOUR: Its exclusive purpose should be to develop and distribute Canadian Studies materials and teaching strategies for use in elementary and secondary schools. FIVE: It should initiate and then work from position papers based on the findings and recommendations of this Report and other related studies. SIX: Final decisions regarding the selection and use of the materials should*

Keith A. McLeod

remain with the individual provinces. [10]

The Report rejected the idea of a standardized history or social studies program designed to encourage national unity. The belief was made clear that Canada had had too much nationalism, not too little and that an attempt to create uniformity and conformity was an ill-conceived reaction to a crisis. Rather, the pluralism and diverstiy of Canada was to be recognized as a basic premise. National understanding rather than national unity should be the fundamental objective of the new program.

New materials and strategies were to be designed to give students a "much greater understanding of their country and its problems." The tools were to be the intellectual disciplines and Canadian history was to be the key. The content would be based upon past and present problems, issues, principles and values that Canadians, as a result of research, were deemed to consider crucial. However, prescribed unrealistic attitudinal and behavioural aims for history or social studies courses were eschewed; the new program was to be "value-free." Students were to be free "to discover a real and vital Canada for themselves". [11]

Subsequently the Canada Studies Foundation was established. Teachers and the Foundation promoted Canadian Studies. Following nearly a decade of work, A.B. Hodgetts (the man who had established the National History Project) and Paul Gallagher (the director of the Foundation) published an up-date of Canadian Studies *Teaching Canada in the 80s*. The privately funded Foundation had worked to improve the quality of Canadian Studies. The result they announced was that "the present Canadian Studies movement has tended to emphasize regional, provincial, or ethnic issues and concerns, in-depth historical or microsociological investegations of one particular group, area, or activity as well as curriculum models and other strictly pedagogical considerations." [12] Also included was this analysis tucked in an epilogue: the "rapid pace of change" has "resulted in a severe down-grading of content and knowledge and an inordinate amount of time spent on skills to help students adjust to change without considering what standards might be used to judge the desirability of change."[13] In other words, there had been an undue emphasis on local studies and on *process* to the detriment of knowledge and value-oriented critical appraisal.

The writers set out a new agenda: "we have found that the normal social process by which our young people develop their values, attitudes, and standards of judgement through strong regional and ethnic forces is not yet balanced in formal education by sufficient opportunities to study, to know about, and to understand Canada as a whole. We believe that *Canada* studies - as distinct from all other more restricted *Canadian Studies* - should deal with our society as a totality, in country-wide, interlocking perspectives that can be shared by all Canadians wherever they may live. Otherwise, as the National History Project and many others have emphasized, this area of education will continue to be another division force in our society." [14] There was a clear shift to recognizing that the *content* and the *thrust* of Canadian history courses (and by implication other subjects) were important; that local and regional studies were reinforcing parochialism and provincialism. However, the authors still rejected a standardized course. "The Canadian Studies movement, in all its variety of techniques and products, should be sustained and nourished. What is needed now, however, is a common framework of ideas that educators in all provinces should use in the development of Canada studies that will be country-wide in perspective and objective." [15]

The authors then went on to outline what young Canadians should understand about their country. Two basic premises were stressed: (1) "That conflict of opinion, controversy, and stress are not only inevitable in all socities but are also within broad limits, a constructive force leading to human betterment"; and (2) "that an overemphasis on our differences may obscure the fact that along with people from all other countries, Canadians together face some gigantic, world wide problems in which we all have a stake." The first premise recognized and even made a virtue of the cracks in Canadian unity but the second outlined a crucial shift from "problems" to "issues," to examining the commonalities at least as a countervailing force to problems, differences and provincialisms. The new emphasis was to be on intellectually balanced Canada studies that were to be designed "to provide opportunities for our young people to acquire the knowledge and understandings to respect the values, viewpoints, and interests of Canadians from other groups and regions." [16]

The scope of their interest was still primarily if not exclusively with history and social studies. The stress was to be on "citizenship education and the study of Canadian communities" [17] in the elementary school and on four areas at the secondary level: the Canadian Environment, the Canadian Political System and the Canadian Economic System would be studied for three years followed by a year's study of Canadian Public Issues. To potential charges that this might be too political their response was that participative citizenship had to be encouraged. To fears that the new program was too national they replied that Canada must always be seen in a world context.

Despite efforts to secure continued support from the Government of Canada, from private sources, and even from the Council of Ministers of Education, the Canadian Studies Foundation was unable to secure sufficient funding to continue past 1986.

The extensive effort to reorient citizenship education and education for citizenship through the Foundation had come to an end and Canadian Studies were again left to the occasional conference, interest group, department of education, board, or teacher. The effort to promote citizenship education as Canadian Studies, or Canadian political education had lost its promoting interest group.

Where does citizen education as education for citizenship need to be in the remainder of this century? I would suggest the following:

(1) In all education we must again redress the imbalance and stress not only skills but knowledge that has some comprehensive plan. In historical studies sequential development has many merits - the flow of history and understanding the basis of change. Fragmented units of study that focus on micro-issues or local studies certainly have a place but the student must be able to place these in a context of time and space.

(2) A knowledge of Canada and even of citizenship is not to be found in the study of Canadian politics or history alone, although these are important in relation to political education for participation, but in many subjects, including Canadian literature, art, music, languages, family

studies and even science. There is no question of teaching for indoctrination or for nationalism in any narrow or uncritical sense but there is a strong case for teaching for and through participation. As the Symons report[18] noted at the post-secondary level our Canadian identity may be simply the lens through which we view science or the world environment.

(3) Teachers' instructional methods, strategies, and techniques must be broadened and strengthened. We must continue to strengthen discovery methods, group methods, including co-operative learning, and individualized programs and instruction. There are also times for didactic methods and even memorization (i.e., to insure remembering). Each child has a variety of ways in which she or he learns; each teacher must have a variety of methods. In life as in school "I" am not always central; society has priorities and needs too. Child-centred education has a fundamental pedagogical value but that pedagogy can not be exclusive. I would argue that "learning-based" pedagogy is also an appropriate pedagogical concept and it encompasses learning that may be teacher developed, community or socially based, child oriented, or even nationally or internationally based. Content, skills, and attitudes and values must all be present. We have been giving insufficient attention to *all* children adequately learning the basic skills of reading, writing, and arithmetic in the elementary school. There are far too many children accumulating deficits. At the secondary school too much attention is given to skills such as "research methods" and not enough attention to well planned content that gives the student a context for living and further learning. In an age of information the information the consumer absorbs needs context as well as skills.

(4) The neglect of value and attitude learning must be remedied. There have been some efforts at value clarification and moral education. These need not be parochial. I would in fact suggest that students and teachers through principle testing, and through the exploration of moral issues utilizing universally held values as epitomized for example, in the United Nations Declaration on Human Rights, address values and attitudes in many areas of the school program - in classrooms and courses and in student based activities.

(5) Humankind must be a more clearly stated focus of education for citizenship. There should be greater attention given to international interests and concerns, and common issues and patterns of behavior. The now trite phrase, the earth as a global village, is still valid. Citizens need knowledge, values, and skills by which to function as members of the international community.

(6) Last but not least, it is basic that education for citizenship must produce persons who are literate and capable of participation. School that produces an accumulation of failure in some students such that by grade 9 they are still illiterate or reading below grade 6, for example, is a travesty. Bureaucratized education has within it a built-in momentum, but that thrust forward for any child must be questioned when that child is not succeeding. Labelling the students has not helped but hindered. On the other hand there has been some success where teachers and systems avoid bureaucratized accumulated failure and attend to the below standard needs of the children, including the knowledge and skills they require to participate as citizens. Teachers can build broad and engaging programs around the

fundamentals for continued learning - reading, writing, arithmetic, thinking, analyzing and the desire to learn more. In an age of information can they be neglected?

Citizenship education I chose to interpret as education for citizenship, thus the basis for living in the world of today and tomorrow must be reflected in knowledge, values and attitudes; and skills.

---

1 Egerton Ryerson, "The Importance of Education to a Manufacturing and a Free People," *Journal of Education for Upper Canada*, vol. 1, no. 10, October 1848, p. 290.

    2 *Ibid.*, p. 290.
    3 *Ibid.*, p. 294.
    4 *Ibid.*, p. 296.
    5 *Ibid.*, p. 298.
    6 A.B. Hodgetts, *What Culture? What Heritage? A Study of Civic Education in Canada* (Toronto: OISE Press, 1968), p. 1.
    7 *Ibid.*, p. 10.
    8 *Ibid.*, p. 11.
    9 *Ibid.*, p. 11-12.
    10 *Ibid.*, p. 118.
    11 *Ibid.*, p. 121.
    12 A.B. Hodgetts and Paul Gallagher, *Teaching Canada for the '80s* (Toronto: OISE, 1978), p. 2.
    13 *Ibid.*, p. 132.
    14 *Ibid.*, p. 2.
    15 *Ibid.*, p. 2.
    16 *Ibid.*, p. 3-5.
    17 *Ibid.*, p. 16.
    18 T.H. B. Symons, *To Know Ourselves: The Report of the Commission on Canadian Studies* (Ottawa: Association for Universities and Colleges of Canada, 1975).

"The right ordering of our several loyalties"
Canadian Citizenship for a Progressive State

B. Anne Wood
Department of Education, Dalhousie University, Halifax

> *Society subsists through the faith and trust that its members place in one another. Further, there are various loyalties — to State, to Church, to home, to school. But the most fruitful idea in the definition is the **ordering** of our loyalties, the balancing, the nice adjustment, the rendering unto Caesar the things that are Caesar's and unto God the things that are God's. ...The study of citizenship, stated broadly, is the story of how men can best learn to live together well.*[1]

IN HIS ADDRESS on "Normal School Courses in Citizenship" delivered to the Canadian Education Association at Montreal on 7 November 1929, the superintendent of education for Nova Scotia, Henry F. Munro, captured the essence of progressive thought concerning citizenship. At that time, many urban English-speaking Canadian leaders would have agreed with Munro's analysis of the concept of citizenship. In itself this degree of consensus in

---

Dans cet historique de l'instruction civique, Mme Wood étudie le rôle que les éducateurs progressistes ont joué dans la mise en valeur de la citoyenneté. Elle cite l'exemple des écoles de la Nouvelle-Écosse et du système d'enseignement public de la ville d'Ottawa qui illustre de façon très concrète combien ce modèle progressiste et précurseur de consultation était efficace. Bien que les idées des progressistes se soient répandues partout au pays, elles n'ont eu que peu de répercussions. Mme Wood s'intéresse aux effets de cette idéologie sur la perception de la citoyenneté par les enfants. Parce que l'enseignement progressiste a été appliqué de façon conservatrice et que le gouvernement fédéral a tendance à glisser sur les questions controversées, l'instruction civique est fade et sans effets. Hodgetts, dans Quelle culture? Quel héritage? paru en 1972, s'est attaqué à ce programme scolaire en démontrant que les écoles canadiennes ne disposent pas de programmes d'instruction civique efficaces.

Anne Wood

the new nation was a major achievement of middle-class Protestant reformers. Within six decades they had transformed the political allegiance of many Canadians away from local and regional loyalties towards a national ideological consensus. The public schools in every province had played a key role in this transformation.

Central to Munro's notion of citizenship was its relationship to an ordered state. The teacher-in-training and later her students should understand not only the political structures and social organization of the state, but should delve into the chief economic and social factors underlying both. Tied into their understanding was a comprehension of the ethical purposes which should govern the behaviour of every member of the state. Specific social science courses should be taught in post-secondary institutions — history, anthropology, government, economics and sociology — to gain this understanding. But this exploration of ideas and meanings was not to be an open-minded, scholarly one. Munro quite candidly admitted that "Our object ...in such courses as we have in mind, is to indoctrinate the teacher-in-training with a certain total impression of society and human relationships." In the hands of a skilful instructor, Munro explained, a mental picture of "the great society of men" and the splendid vision "of the steady march of mankind from strength to strength" was to be imparted to the young teacher, who in turn would "transmit this vision to those who came under her." History was to be interpreted with a progressivist slant and biographies were to serve as role models for correct social leadership. The institutional practices of the public school and the teacher's inspirational personality were also key factors in the development of a progressive ideology of democratic citizenship. Munro believed that "the capacity and integrity of our democracy depend on the public school" and that "the ideas and ideals of citizenship must come home to men's bosom through the heart and conscience as well as the processes of the mind." The major function of the public school was to "arouse the social conscience, to challenge the latent power of youth in socially correct directions."[2]

The study of citizenship, therefore, involved the inculcation of a number of general principles on which Canadian youth in the 1930s were to base their social behaviour. Although society and public opinion were in a state of constant change, through their study of citizenship students could gain a feeling that the historical process had been fruitful and had led to major improvements in standards of living and social understanding. For instance, the "supplanting of the personal by the territorial principle of allegiance," Munro affirmed, had led to the abolition of slavery, the invention of parliamentary government and the idea of world co-operation. Munro also stressed the difference between liberty and licence. With the power of modern civilization came the need for social control. Democracy meant not only a progressive trend towards social freedom but entailed increasing social obligation. "In proportion as we get a society imbued with a sense of moral necessity of discipline," Munro stated, "shall sound and enlightened views of public duties prevail."[3]

Implicit in Munro's rhetoric was the belief of progressivists in North America that public schools should be a means of inculcating a common morality in the populace in order to promote a modern society. John William Dawson, Nova Scotia's first superintendent of education in 1850, laid the guiding principles for the *Free and Common School Acts* of 1864-1866. State

Canadian Citizenship for a Progressive State

schooling should be based on elements commonly accepted among cultural groups. Moral education and public financial support were major ways in which the state asserted its new "positive " role. A system of common schools, Dawson believed, would help to overcome Nova Scotia's localized political interest groups.

By 1910 the common school movement in Nova Scotia had achieved limited gains but had suffered also from major difficulties. One hundred and eleven out of 1,804 sections were without schools. The average daily attendance of pupils was a mere 64.3 per cent. Only one-third of the 2,723 teachers had Normal School training. There were wide curricular offerings, however, pioneered by Superintendent A.H. MacKay, many of them designed to promote a higher form of citizenship. Subjects such as callisthenics and military drill, vocal music, hygiene and temperance, moral and patriotic duties were offered in most schools, and manual training, domestic science, nature study in some schools. Rural gardens and a rural science summer school at Truro attempted to inject a new country life ethic into a demoralized population.

Since 1890 Nova Scotia had suffered from a serious economic slowdown as the region's major industries were increasingly taken over by Montreal and London financiers, and as national transportation policies favoured central Canada. Maritimers began a great western or New England emigration to seek new farmland or work in industry. Rural schools were left vacant, inadequately supported by local assessment and staffed by poorly paid, unqualified teachers. In 1921, the Carnegie Report concluded that "the widespread apathy toward public education in Nova Scotia ... chills one like an east wind. 'Let the government do it' is the universal attitude, instead of the healthy threat to 'put in' the people who will do it."[4]

In contrast, the Ottawa Public School Board between 1910 and 1937 presented an "object lesson" for progressive education in Canada. Under the capable leadership of John Harold Putman major structural changes in administrative procedures, an increased tax base, as well as a unique political situation enabled Putman to fulfil Munro's dream for Canadian citizenship. Within a year of his appointment Putman won control of school policy from the conservative, ward-heeling trustees and established his professional hegemony. A centralized School for Higher English and Applied Arts replaced scattered commercial classes. Expenditures for new buildings erected between 1910 and 1914 rose by 570.3 per cent over expenditures in the previous ten years. It was argued that new features, such as landscaping, new ventilation and sanitary systems, fire doors, assemblies, specialized art, manual training and domestic science rooms, and kindergartens, would cultivate a group ethic and improve school attendance.[5]

The School for Higher English reached out into the community and invited working class adults, parents and new immigrants to participate in evening classes, lectures, school exhibitions, art shows, and courses in English or citizenship. Through these programs, Putman hoped to transform the public school into a community centre. School leaders would mediate between the newly emerging middle class and the more alienated working class and immigrant groups. In a similar manner, Putman attempted to use the Ottawa schools as an instrument to solve the serious bilingual problems between English and French separate school supporters.[6] His sweeping structural solutions, however, were not acceptable either to Ottawa separate school supporters or to Ottawa Orange Order adherents.

In a 1917 survey of the Ottawa public schools, C.E. Mark compared the taxable assessment of the Ottawa separate school board with that of the public school board.[7] In 1911 Ottawa's taxable assessment amounted to $111,322,235 (in Ontario nearly 90 per cent of educational costs were raised locally). Only $18,620,479 were available for separate school expenditure. The Ottawa Public School Board had 8,867 pupils, 23 buildings, 250 teachers and supervisors paid a total of $265,957.37, but the Roman Catholic Separate School Board had 9,416 pupils, 33 buildings, nine annexes, and 191 teachers who were paid only a total of $96,937. The separate schools had no kindergarten, manual training or domestic science classes, and no supervisors of art, writing, music or physical education. The Ottawa public schools, on the other hand, equalled Vancouver, a city with twice the number of teachers, in having the highest number of supervisors of special subjects, a total of six in art, music, manual training, household science, physical culture, and writing. By 1917 Putman had centralized his purchasing, had hired clerical assistants and was shortly to hire a junior inspector. Putman believed these measures would cut down on waste and guarantee a quality product from each pupil derived from this more efficient administrative system.

Both Putman and Mark, as well as many progressive Canadian educators, believed that their efficiency model would co-opt the support of minority groups. For instance, both suggested that the solution to Ottawa's serious bilingual school troubles was the formation of a single board of education. In a plan outlined to Deputy Minister A.H.U. Colquhoun in January 1918, Putman proposed that this single, efficient board would guarantee a higher standard of instruction both in English and in French.[8] He recommended that a professional training school be established for French-speaking teachers and that sectarian religious instruction be allowed after school hours to any child whose parents desired it. If the Ottawa Public School Board took over the property and liabilities of the Separate School Board, within five years with qualified French and English teachers, Putman believed, separate school supporters would be satisfied with the education given to their children. He thought that with a public campaign through the newspapers, a majority of progressive people in the community would rally to his viewpoint on the merits of one board of education. Efficiency and a high-quality education would smooth over troubled racial waters, would take over sectarian control of separate schooling and would lead to a more broad-minded citizenry in Ottawa.

Both the French-speaking parents of the Ottawa Separate School Board and the Orange Lodge trustees on the Ottawa Public School Board were not convinced of the merits of what would amount to a loss of their control in this more professionally managed single board. In 1920 the Ottawa Separate School Board divided into English and French sections. A teachers' college for French-speaking students was established at the University of Ottawa in 1923; subsequently this was accepted into the provincial system and authority was given the university to administer its own examinations. The English-French controversy was therefore resolved by bureaucratic means. But the separate schools remained distinct from the public board, allowing more scope for the latter greatly to increase its expenditure for school property and safeguarding the public school children from an influx of children with different linguistic and denominational backgrounds. A secular public system reflecting Protestant Anglo-Saxon values remained intact.

Similar efficient models were advocated for both urban and rural boards in the 1930s right across Canada. A large number of middle-class reformers supported the progressive school leaders. Women members of such groups as the Local Council of Women, Young Women's Christian Association and the Imperial Order of the Daughters of the Empire promoted domestic science classes, supplied library books and other materials and lobbied for progressive school reforms.[9] Leading schoolmen exchanged ideas at the annual meetings of the Canadian Education Association and the National Council of Education.[10] Business leaders, representatives of American foundations, such as the Carnegie Foundation,[11] and city boosters met frequently with progressive schoolmen at meetings of the Rotary Club, Canadian Club, university alumnae associations, and fraternal organizations, such as the Scottish Rite Masons. Through their Protestant church affiliations these leaders imbibed the ideas of the social gospel movement and many became actively engaged in the Social Welfare League. Government commissions, such as the 1910 Royal Commission on Industrial Training and Technical Education, or Putman's 1925 survey of education in British Columbia,[12] broadcast these progressivist ideas and helped to form public opinion. By the 1930s a remarkably similar ideology was being preached by reform schoolmen across Canada.

What effects had this ideology on the notion of citizenship held by children or reflected in their view of Canada? Although this is difficult to assess, three authorities have attempted the task, a British observer in Canada during the 1930s, historian Robert Patterson, and a Canadian critic of the 1960s. Fred Clarke, professor of education at McGill in 1935, considered that education across English-speaking Canada conveyed "a common countenance,[13] and was distinguishable from American education. Secondary education with its graded structure and examination control still held sway. In the rural areas the local school districts with their concomitant parochial interests and control were far more widespread than the newer urban models, or the larger administrative units. Clarke was surprised at the "entrenched conservatism which prevails in many parts of Canada in matters of educational usage, particularly where the ideal of the 'average' or the exercise of local rights is concerned."[14] As a result of their concentration on passing examinations, Clarke concluded that "many Canadian schools at present seem to succeed in imposing upon the pupil a severe demand for sheer laboriousness with a very low demand for genuine, spontaneous, intellectual effort. The effect of such a condition in dulling the finer sensibilities, in retarding the growth of real powers, and in encouraging a heavy and conformable mediocrity, needs no emphasis."[15]

Robert Patterson has explored the impressions held by teachers during the progressive era and has reached a number of conclusions about why, at the practical level of the classroom during the period 1930-45, many of the progressive policies of educational leaders failed to be implemented. He notes that Canadian administrators were well aware of the weaknesses attributed to progressive education in the United States and retained the examination system to counter this. Programs of study and curricular guides, however, described at length the new progressive ideas promoted by educational leaders.

These ideas were widely used in the evaluation of individual differences in children, as a basis for establishing special classes, and as rationales to abandon practices of corporal punishment. Educational literature and in-service courses promoting learning by doing, activity methods, concern for the whole child, individual differences, mental health, student interest and democracy were widespread during these years. Course outlines for citizenship and character education explained how these new methods and attitudes would help implement the new progressivist philosophy. But at the same time, Canadian educators continued to be primarily concerned that the skill subjects — reading, writing, arithmetic and language — should not suffer. Formal or drill methods continued to be advocated across Canada. As Patterson concludes, "at the level of curriculum policy across Canada, the support given to progressive education was conditional in nature. In all provincial jurisdictions ... statements frequently indicated the Canadian avoidance of extreme progressivism, and the blending of the old and new in education." [16]

Patterson cites a number of reasons why the impact of progressivism across Canada was so muted. During the Depression and the Second World War there was a severe teaching shortage. The skilled teachers required to implement these sophisticated pedagogical ideas were not available. Normal school formal practices did not encourage creativity. Unable to cope with the newer ideas in large classes with limited facilities and library resources, teachers demanded textbooks and definite course outlines, indicating their preference for the formal methods of the past. Many Alberta teachers experienced confusion, fear, lack of understanding and reluctance to change in the face of strong departmental promotion of the new methodology. The changes introduced were not outgrowths of professional grass-roots agitation nor of effective in-service programs. Most of the effort to educate the profession and the public came after the announcements of formal program changes, as the result of regulation. Despite the urban models presented in a few Canadian cities, then, progressive school practices would not have been widespread in Canadian schools even by 1945.

In fact, the curious effect of the conservative implementation of progressive education in Canada, coupled with our national political policy of glossing over controversial issues, resulted in a bland, ineffectual form of citizenship. In a sweeping condemnation of Candian studies, A.B. Hodgetts's 1960s polemic *What Culture? What Heritage? A Study of Civic Education* described the labyrinth of confusion and inefficiency that prevailed in school systems across the country. By this time the monolithic ideology of the progressives was so entrenched in the curriculum that Hodgetts thundered,

> *The courses of study in Canadian history are based on the interests and concerns that preoccupied academic historians of the 1920s. These courses lack any contemporary meaning. They continue to be narrowly confined to constitutional and political history. Such things as protest and minority movements, class developments and issues, the influence of art, literature and ideas, education and religion, industrial*

Canadian Citizenship for a Progressive State

growth and a great many other aspects of human endeavour which should be an integral part of history are virtually ignored in our schools. We are teaching a bland, unrealistic consensus version of our past. [17]

Ironically, what progressive educators had been promoting 40 years earlier as a more vital, community-oriented view of citizenship now had become an authoritarian model. During times of industrial strife, massive immigration and bicultural problems, school leaders had used management techniques and progressive curricular reforms, both state incursions into the previously voluntaristic models of schooling, to produce a homogeneous Canadian form of citizenship. They believed that efficient administrative practices, more practical programs of study and an English Protestant vision of nationality would win allegiance from disparate ethnic, regional and class groups. Their paternalistic indoctrination of this monolithic viewpoint became increasingly inappropriate for Canadian citizens in the 1960s. A pluralistic society demands a more effective form of citizenship training, a deeper understanding of civic culture. Out of Hodgetts's trenchant criticism the Canadian Studies Consortium was formed. It took up the challenge of improving the quality of civic life and of "reversing the trend toward a monolithic conforming society, capable of being manoeuvered and misled, and of bringing the democratic ideal closer to fulfilment through reforms in the educational system and other social institutions." Like the progressive educators before them, these neo-progressives promised to "not only improve the quality of individual and civic life but also help to determine the future and possibly the survival of this country." [18]

---

1 H.F. Munro, "Citizenship," *Journal of Education* 2 (1929), p.126.

2 *Ibid.*, p. 126-127.

3 *Ibid..*, p. 128.

4 K.C.M. Sills and W.S. Learned, *Education in the Maritime Provinces of Canada* (New York: The Carnegie Foundation for the Advancement of Teaching, 1922), p.7.

5 B.A. Wood, *Idealism Transformed: The Making of a Progressive Educator* (Kingston and Montreal: McGill-Queen's University Press, 1985).

6 L.-P. Audet, R.M. Stamp, and J.D. Wilson, *Canadian Education: A History* (Scarborough: Prentice-Hall, 1970), pp. 281-287.

7 C.E. Mark, *The Public Schools of Ottawa. A Survey* (Ottawa: Pattison Printers, 1918).

8 J.H. Putman, letter to A.H.U. Colquhoun, 29 January 1918, Archives of Ontario RG3, Cody Papers.

9 V. Strong-Boag, *The Parliament of Women: National Council of Women in Canada 1893-1924* (Ottawa: National Museums of Canada, 1976).; D. Pederson, "Building Today for the Womanhood of Tomorrow: Businessmen, Boosters and the YWCA 1890-1930," *Urban History Review* 15 (1987), pp.225-242; N. Sheehan, "The IODE, the Schools and World War I," *History of Education Review* 13 (1984), pp. 29-43.

10 A. Chaiton, "The History of the National Council of Education of Canada," unpublished M.A. thesis, University of Toronto, 1974.

11 J.G. Reid, "Health, Education, Economy: Philanthropic Foundations in the Atlantic Region in the 1920s and 1930s," in *People and Places, Studies of Small*

Town Life in the Maritimes, ed. L. McCann (Fredericton: Acadiensis Press, 1987), pp. 101-122.

12 G.M. Weir and J.H. Putman, *Survey of the School System* (Victoria: Banfield, 1925).

13 F. Clarke, "Education in Canada —an Impression," *Queen's Quarterly* 42 (1935), pp.313.

14 *Ibid.*, p. 319.

15 *Ibid.*, p. 321.

16 R.S. Patterson, "The Canadian Response to Progressive Education," in *Essays on Canadian Education*, eds. N. Kach *et al.* (Calgary: Detselig, 1986), p. 87.

17 A.B. Hodgetts, "What Culture? What Heritage? A Study of Civic Education in Canada," in *The Best of Times/ The Worst of Times*, ed. H.A. Stevenson (Toronto: Holt, Rinehart and Winston, 1972), p.244.

18 *Ibid.*, p. 247.

The Current Status of Teaching about Citizenship in Canadian Elementary and Secondary Schools

Vandra L. Masemann
Masemann and Mock, Consultants, Toronto

THIS REPORT provides a summary of the current state of citizenship education in Canadian elementary and secondary schools. All of the Ministries and Departments of Education in Canada were contacted for up-to-date materials and information in the summer of 1987, and all contributed. Provincial officials supplied further insights in telephone interviews. In several provinces, the social studies curriculum is under review, and the most recent information available is included here. Provincial officials and Canadian Education Association personnel referred us to further sources of information in various school boards regarding innovative programs in citizenship education.

Definition of Citizenship Education
The School Curriculum

The definition of citizenship education in the various school systems across Canada is incorporated in the general goals for education itself and

> *Ce chapitre présente, province par province, l'instruction civique telle qu'on l'enseigne actuellement dans les écoles élémentaires et secondaires du Canada. Tous les ministères de l'Éducation ont fourni, au cours de l'été 1987, de la documentation et des renseignements à ce sujet et plusieurs commissions scolaires ont également apporté des informations sur des programmes innovateurs. Les réponses indiquent que même si les modèles en instruction civique au Canada se ressemblent, les variantes régionales sont notables. Autrefois, on enseignait le fonctionnement de « l'appareil gouvernemental », aujourd'hui on s'intéresse aux aspects sociaux, culturels et géographiques de l'instruction civique et au rôle des citoyens et citoyennes, êtres responsables et humanistes dans une société multiculturelle et bilingue. On constate également une sensibilisation aux affaires internationales et à la paix dans le monde. L'auteur donne, pour chaque province, les buts; les connaissances, les aptitudes et les attitudes recherchées; les méthodes et les mesures entreprises dans les écoles; et les différences entre les régions.*

Vandra L. Masemann

within the social studies curriculum specifically. For example, one of the Goals for Public Educaion in Nova Scotia is "to provide opportunities in school programs and activities for students to develop civic, social and moral responsibility and judgement." The definition of citizenship and citizenship education pervading the entire educational curriculum is wide and may not be explicitly expressed in a particular course. However, the goals of education in each province and territory allude to this very general function of the schools in producing future citizens. As the specific examples from each area of Canada show, there is much in the way of knowledge, skills, and attitudes that are considered important in forming Canada's future citizens.

The underlying pedagogical assumption in social studies and citizenship education is that the child learns first about the phenomena which are closest to home and then gradually extends his or her interests outward to the neighbourhood, the community, the province, the country and the world. In the elementary grades, the focus is on the family unit, the roles of family members and the functioning of the group. The focus then shifts to the functioning of the community, and the role of local government and volunteers in the community. The values associated with this approach are that Canadian citizens are like a family or close-knit community and that through hard work and co-operation the good of the whole will be furthered. On a level appropriate for the age of the child, there is an emphasis on the "helper" in the classroom and in the community. In many elementary classrooms in Canada can be found on decorated bulletin boards a list of "helpers" who are responsible for various classroom duties. Even in the early grades, there is an emphasis on organization as a way of solving problems and avoiding conflicts.

Beginning in the junior grades (4-6), there is an emphasis on developing and exploring the students' personal view of the community and discussions on how the neighbourhood could be improved. Students begin to develop a general knowledge of Canada, its geography, its people and its economy.

At the end of this period and into the intermediate level (grades 7-9), students begin to study the three levels of government. This is the level where several provinces and territories have explicit curriculum material on civics or government. There is also a focus on the growth of Canada as a nation and the events and people that influenced its development. There is an emphasis on Canada's cultural diversity, an examination of the Canadian identity and an overview of the rights of citizens. The theme of co-operation and working together is now extended to a larger Canadian community.

Within the Quebec curriculum, there is also an emphasis on moral development at this period. There is an explict linkage with moral development, the community, and the growth of the individual with the eventual focus on the development of the citizen.

As one advances into the secondary grades there is a trend towards opinions and ideas based on facts learned earlier. The facts serve as a foundation to further understanding. Students' experience and involvement in school clubs and government are used in the study of politics.

There is a study of the process of politics. There is analysis of the Constitution and the Canadian *Charter of Rights and Freedoms*, their meanings and implications. There is a study of the rights, freedoms and

The Current Status of Teaching about Citizenship

responsibilities of Canadian citizens.
There is an emphasis on the conflict between ideals and realities of democracy in Canada. Textbooks stress a need for interest in Canadian issues. Through case studies, simulation games and further study, students learn how citizens, by exercising their powers, can change the system if they become informed and involved. They learn about the role of citizens in politics and government, in order to make government work for its citizens. There is a stress on the need for informed and active citizens, on active interest through participation and critical inquiry. The emphasis is on politics and government, but the texts also encourage citizens to participate and become active in other Canadian issues and causes. Through student exchange visits, leadership camps and language programs in both offical languages and in heritage languages, students are expected to gain a wider vision of what it means to be a Canadian.

The main ideology that seems to run through citizenship education is the importance of citizen action and participation. This begins with involvement in the family unit, then expands to the neighbourhood. In secondary school, it is encouraged through school clubs and government. Educators hope that it is embedded in their minds enough to continue throughout their lives.

School Practices

The symbolism of Canadian citizenship at the elementary level is somewhat remote from the home and community-based world of the child. The Canadian flag is in evidence in books and on special occasions. However, observances such as school assemblies, singing the national anthem or saying the Pledge of Allegiance are generally now done at the discretion of local educational officials. Some schools have a regular routine of flying the flag and singing the national anthem. There is a great range of variation in local practice.

The provincial ministry or department of education may provide suggestions and materials for special days, but the initiative is local. Section 92 of the *School Act* of British Columbia is very explicit about school assemblies:

> 92 (1) *The principal of every public school shall establish a program, to be approved by the board, of school assemblies to be conducted at appropriate times during the school year.*
>
> *(2) Assemblies shall be held at least three times in a school year, including the school day immediately preceding Remembrance Day, shall promote loyalty to the Queen, respect for Canadian traditions, laws, institutions and human values, and shall include observation of occasions of historic or current importance to Canda and the Commonwealth, as well as appropriate references to the Canadian flag.*

As students progress through secondary school, their understanding of the institutions of govenrment and of democracy becomes more vivid through the use of parliamentary procedure in school clubs and student councils, through student leadership programs, and through simulations of such processes as elections. The flag and the national anthem are linked with an understanding of the complexities of the federal-provincial relationship and Canada's place in the world.

However, the less abstract forms of school practice also play a role in citizenship education. As is described in the section on *Innovative Models*, schools such as Harold J. Barrett Junior High School in Halifax County, Nova Scotia, or Alex Taylor Community School in Edmonton, Alberta, and the C.A.R.E. Program in Saskatoon are all based on a philosphy of citizenship that pervades every aspect of school life. The everyday courtesies and respect that students show for one another, the relationship to the surrounding community, and the willingness to give of oneself for the greater good are all evidence of citizenship-in-the-making.

School practices that refer to the multicultural nature of the school population are also assisting in the development of citizenship education. The example of holding a citizenship court in a Winnipeg high school and the multicultural policies and practices of the Vancouver School Board are both cases of citizenship education that reaches out to encompass the diversity of Canadians.

The definition of citizenship education that emerges from this brief review of curriculum and school practices is one that goes beyond a recitation of the mechanics of government. It seeks to ensure that Canadian citizens of tomorrow possess the knowledge, skills, and attitudes to practise their responsibilities and to exercise their rights.

Citizenship Education in the Provinces and Territories

General Impressions

The summary of responses from the provinces and territories indicates that there are broad patterns of similarity in citizenship education across Canada, and some notable regional variations. There has been in the past 20 years a shift away from the "mechanics of government" approach to a more broadly-based social, cultural and geographical approach. The role of the citizen as a responsible caring individual living in a distinct niche in Canadian society is stressed. In accordance with the concept of Canada as a "multicultural society within a bilingual framework," there is an emphasis on accommodating regional and cultural variations. There has also been a shift outward to an awareness of world affairs, the global community, and issues of peace. Finally, the rights of particular groups such as women, native people, and the physically challenged are acknowledged and discussed. The impact of the *Charter of Rights and Freedoms* is beginning to be felt in citizenship education across the country, and doubtlessly new generations of school children will learn to think about the rights and responsibilities of Canadian citizenship in ways that previous generations never envisaged.

The facts concerning each province and territory are presented here as they were sent in from each deputy minister's office. However, the very dryness of some of the material is belied by some of the conversations held with officials. There is a great sense of quiet loyalty and pride in being or becoming Canadian expressed from coast to coast. The "hidden curriculum" in citizenship education is that Canadians do not wish to sound too strident

The Current Status of Teaching about Citizenship

or boastful in their love of country, but that they wish to pass onto their children their joy in being able to express their heritage, in being able to speak one or several languages, in standing firm in their institutions of democracy, in cherishing the freedom to vote, and in taking their place in the world community of nations.

Ontario

Goals

The history and contemporary studies programs in Ontario in grades 7-13 assist and encourage students to develop skills and attitudes that will enable them to participate and contribute as members of their families and citizens of their school, community, province, country and the world and develop an appreciation of their rights and responsibilities as Canadian citizens.

Knowledge, Skills and Attitudes

Knowledge. Ontario students acquire knowledge of humanity, historical and contemporary societies, an understanding of growth and the transmission of personal and societal values, customs and traditions as well as an understanding of Canada and her role in the world.

Skills. Some of the skills students are expected to learn include focusing, organizing, locating, recording, evaluating, synthesizing, concluding, applying and communicating.

Attitudes. Students develop attitudes that will enable them to participate and contribute as members of their families and citizens of their community. They include a respect for the environment and a commitment to the wise use of resources, esteem for the customs, culture and beliefs of a wide variety of societal groups, a feeling of self-worth and values related to personal, ethical or religious beliefs and to the common welfare of society.

School Practices

According to the *School Act,* every school's opening or closing exercises are to include *O Canada* and may include *God Save the Queen.* Every school is to fly the national flag of Canada and the provincial flag of Ontario on such occasions as the local school boards direct. However, it is mandatory for all schools to display the Canadian and Ontario flags within the school building.

Primary and Junior Divisions (k-6)

The goals for the development of citizenship in younger students are outlined in the goals for values and Canadian studies. During these years, students are expected to become aware of the values that Canadians regard as essential to the well-being and continuing development of their society, to begin to develop a personal set of values, and to identify and analyze public value issues. They are expected to acquire a reasoned knowledge of and pride in Canada, by becoming familiar with the geography and culture of the community, province and country, by developing an awareness of law and government and of the rights and duties of Canadian citizens, by knowing its history, by developing and retaining a personal identity through a knowledge of the historical roots of the community and their own cultural origin, and by beginning to understand and appreciate the points of view of ethnic and cultural groups other than their own.

Intermediate Division (7-10)

All Ontario students must take the history course "Contemporary Canada: Life in the Twentieth Century," which includes a section on citizenship. The contemporary studies aspect is introduced by a study of the local community and of social themes within the history area. Provision is made at the grade 9/10 levels for the development of courses at the basic, general and advanced levels. Some of the topics relating to citizenship include the effects of living in a community with other people, the rights and duties of citizenship for members of a community, why individuals should vote, processes that women went through to get the right to vote and hold office, and the ways in which an individual can particpate in the political system.

Senior Division (11-13)

The emphasis in the senior division is on history including the parts of the world beyond Canada and contemporary studies in social sciences and law. Provision is made for the development of courses at basic, general and advanced levels. Students can choose from courses in law, politics, economics, man in society, world religions and native studies and from various language courses.

Methods

The learning strategies used include a wide variety of activities such as group discussions, role playing, interactive situations, visual presentations, field trips, specialized research projects, art work, simulations, seminars, team projects, brainstorming, puzzles, game shows and play writing.

Regional Emphasis

When developing the history and contemporary issues program, the Ontario Ministry of Education took into consideration the following: the official multiculturalism policy of the Government of Ontario, which advocates the preparation of all students to live harmoniously in a multicultural society; sex equity which provides for the development of courses that apply and appeal equally to male and female students; opportunities to develop proficiencies in oral and written language; adoption and modification of program content for exceptional students; opportunities for the development of co-operative education experiences; opportunities to assist students with information about careers related to the subject area; an understanding of the arts as they relate to a nation or civilization's development; new technologies; life skills; continuing education and independent study.

Quebec

Goals

The goals of the history programs at both primary and secondary levels are concerned with the values and objectives defined in the ministry's philosophy of education in Quebec. The main objective is to develop responsible Canadian citizens who are knowledgeable about and ready to become involved in the affairs of the nation.

In elementary schools, the objectives are in keeping with civic education and focus on the development and function of democracy in our society. At this level the pupil should be able to describe the functions and mechanics of democratic government at the municipal, provincial and national levels. When studying the national level, the students become aware of individual rights and freedoms in a democratic society.

At the secondary level, history courses follow and complement those in the primary system. Civic education is integrated into the objectives of the subject choices followed by the student. The courses at secondary school help to establish principles of culture, politics and democracy and are oriented toward the knowledge and development of attitudes to encourage the establishment of positive and responsible citizenship. The secondary program also encourages students to develop the capacity to analyze their personal values and those of the surrounding social environment, to develop an attitude of openness and a respect toward values other than their own, and to be conscious of their roles as responsible citizens for the future of the collectivity to which they belong.

In elementary schools the program is called human sciences and includes information on history, geography as well as economic and cultural lifestyles. In the first cycle the goal for citizenship education indicates that the student should begin to realize the culture and economic structure of life in society and in the second cycle, the student becomes aware of ethnic and cultural differences and similarities in Quebec and Canadian society as well as the development and function of democracy in Canadian society.

Knowledge, Skills and Attitudes

Knowledge. In he elementary schools, emphasis is put on learning about the concepts of space, time and the realities of cultural and economic life in society. Some of the knowledge areas are distances on maps, compass directions, days of week, seasons, human needs, geography of Canada, function of government, democratic rights and freedoms of citizens and Quebec and Canadian history.

Skills. Some of the skills required by students to fulfil the objectives of human sciences are map reading, researching, analyzing, decision-making and problem-solving.

Attitudes. The student of human sciences develops a positive attitude toward comprehension and learning in geography, history, culture and economy and a responsible attitude toward the environment and society as well as attitudes of understanding and respect for the diverse cultural values prevalent in his or her own society and others.

Vandra L. Masemann

Methods

A wide variety of presentation methods are used in the human sciences program which emphasize the hierarchy of learning processes through which the student passes such as the familiar to the unknown, the easy to the difficult, the particular to the general and the simple to the complex, in keeping with the gradual development of the intellectual habits and techniques of the child.

In secondary schools the material for citizenship development is covered in a program called "Moral Formation" in the first cycle and "Moral Education" in the second cycle. "Moral Formation" is a course for students who are exempt from religious education in grades 7 and 8. Some of the main objectives in the first cycle are to develop the capacity to analyze their motives, the circumstances and the consequences of their actions on others, to develop the capacity to evaluate their actions according to their moral dimensions and to develop a progressive attitude which enables students to participate responsibly in their environment. In the second cycle, the emphasis is on encouraging the student to take charge and responsibility for his or her action in responding to the demands of fundamental human existence.

Knowledge, Skills and Attitudes

Knowledge. In the first cycle, the students are required to become familiar with their surroundings, the people in authority and the rules and rights of the child as well as knowledge of self-development concepts. In the second cycle, the student is introduced to four stages: exploration, identifying the problem, moral evaluation and choice of action, on which the development of moral education is based.

Skills. Some skills the students are required to learn are group dynamics, decision-making, conflict resolution, confidence-building, communication, and interpreting.

Attitudes. Some of the attitudes the students are expected to acquire are acceptance of the rights of others, respect for personal differences, tolerance, awareness of the consequences of choice, responsibility for actions as a result of making choices, and respect for the quality of life.

Methods

A variety of methods enable the student to progress through the four stages of moral development. The educator encourages the student to draw on personal experience, consider the points of view of others, identify the problems, make moral evaluations based on pertinent information and then define an action according to his or her personal code of ethics.

Regional Emphasis

Citizenship education is also studied in the history of Quebec and Canada in grade 10. The goals include the development of the capacity to analyze personal values, develop respect for the values of others and become conscious of the role of a responsible citizen of society.

The student examines the French government and the Canadian society under the French government system, the British government and the beginnings of parliament, and contemporary Quebec. The course material emphasizes the development of the French Canadian society through conflict, revolution, analysis of the political history and awareness of the difficulties of co-existence of two systems in the same society. In the contemporary Quebec module, the resistance movement is traced from 1917 to present day society, pointing out the transformations and developments of the cultural diverseness of Quebec and its people.

Nova Scotia

Goals
The main aim of the civics program (7-8) in Nova Scotia is to develop students who are aware of and understand their roles as actively participating citizens in the three main levels of goverment. A secondary aim is to give students an understanding of relevant contemporary issues as they affect citizens.

Knowledge, Skills and Attitudes
Knowledge. In the early grades, students acquire knowledge about their families, neighbourhoods, communities and country. Concepts used throughout the elementary social studies program are identity, socialization, environment, change, resources, human needs, institutions, interdependence, values and decision-making. In later grades, students are taught specifically about democratic government and about individual and group roles in government as well as about law and electoral processes.

Skills. Skills considered important are problem-solving, working with others, interpreting pictures and charts and understanding time and chronology. At the higher levels, decision-making, differentiating between rules and regulations, group dynamics, critical thinking, distinguishing fact from fiction, and understanding concepts of cause and effect are encouraged.

Attitudes. Self-awareness, respect for others, awareness and acceptance of uncertainty, and respect for the natural environment are attitudes encouraged in the elementary grades. Tolerance, empathy, examining self-concept, respect for others and respect toward laws are considered important in the grade 7-9 curriculum.

School Practices
There is a great variety of school practices in Nova Scotia which are the specific reponsibility of the individual school. Routine usage of a citizenship program is encouraged and supported by the department of education but is not compulsory.

Grades K-6
The elementary school social studies program combines local, national and global components in a series of spirals and provides for studies of those elements both closely familiar to the children (home, school, neighbourhood and community) and those more removed from their immediate experience (in other regions of Canada and elsewhere).

Vandra L. Masemann

Grades 7-9

The main focus of citizenship education in Nova Scotia is at this level. In grade 7, students learn about the individual and local government, in grade 8 about provincial government, and in grade 9 about federal government. A new component of the grade 9 course is being developed in maritime studies.

Grades 10-12

Students choose from a variety of courses in history, economics, modern world problems, geography, political science, sociology and law. Various concepts of citizenship education are incorporated into each course of study. In particular, the political science course concentrates on the basic institutions and practices of politics, particularly of Canada.

Methods

At the elementary level (K-6) there are various methods used such as bulletin board displays, cooking food, current event displays, dramatics, field/study trips, inteviews, open-ended and problem stories, recording and reporting, resource people, research skills and surveys.

For the intermediate level, methods used include simulation, role-playing, speakers and visits, charts and graphs, involvement in community events, model elections, parliament debates, audio-visual materials, lectures, news, maps, scrapbooks and murals.

The high school courses are more research-oriented and foster the development of intelligent discussion on current world problems and active participation in local community and sociological projects.

Regional Emphasis

As a component of the grade 9 civics curriculum, a new program called maritime studies is being developed. It will focus on political issues facing the region and will deal with social change. In addition, the role of the Nova Scotia fisheries in the context of international affairs is emphasized.

New Brunswick

Goals

New Brunswick's anglophone sector of education has not seen a need to develop a specific definition or philosophy of citizenship education although they are piloting in several areas an elementary curriculum package on human rights developed by the Canadian Human Rights Foundation.

The francophone sector, for several years, has been revising the fundamental objectives of education, with particular emphasis on secondary education. Within the new philosophy the minister of education has defined the role of the education of youth as a citizen. The acquisition of values as well as the roles and responsibilities of citizenship are stressed in the human sciences program which was initiated in grade 9 September 1988, and grade 11 in history of Canada prepared in the 1987-88 school year. Before the new guidelines, citizenship education was integrated into human sciences courses at both elementary and secondary levels.

At the end of the new program, the student will be conscious of his or her role as a responsible citizen and be ready to participate in a constructive and positive way in society in Canada and Acadia, as well as know and practise the elements that determine a responsible interaction between the individual and society. Society today dictates the requirements for informed citizens who respect their cultural heritage and who are capable of reacting in a responsible manner to problems and changes in the real world.

Knowledge, Skills and Attitudes

Knowledge. Students are taught specific knowledge areas such as the structures and functions of government and economy and the judiciary system with regard to the Constitution, protection and evolution of the family in New Brunswick. The history 11 course also enables the student to observe, think and act, not merely accumulate facts, as well as recognize concepts of geography, politics, economy and society.

Skills. Some of the skills that students are expected to acquire are analyzing, synthesizing, applying and using history to explain and interpret the present and future.

Attitudes. Important are respect for the values of the individual and society, development of pride in their culture, consciousness of the diversity of the conditions that influence social change, a willingness to acknowledge the values of other cultures and an awareness of the ways of life of different eras.

School Practices

Particular school routines that symbolize citizenship are left to the discretion of local education officials. The national anthem is taught in grade 6.

Manitoba

Goals

The social students curriculum from k-12 focuses on citizenshp as one of its main goals; greater emphasis comes in grades 5, 0, 9, 11. The major purpose is to develop knowledge, skills understanding and character traits that are essential for effective participation in and responsible contribution to the citizenship of Canada and the world. In presenting an ever broadening understanding of the individual, social studies courses encourage a comparison of contemporary life against a wide range of alternative possibilities and possible courses of citizen action.

Knowledge, Skills and Attitutdes

Knowledge. Students explore such areas of citizen development as political decison-making, groups and their roles, political divisions, Canadian identity, the political process, the legal and economic processes, rights and responsiblities of citizens as well as the concept of federalism.

Skills. The objectives of the social studies curriculum are prepared to assist students in acquiring such skills as critical thinking, gathering data, interpreting data, drawing conclusions, communciating, interpreting symbols and maps, understanding time and chronology and social participation.

Attitude. Students, through the social studies curriculum, develop tolerance, criteria for judging and discriminating, appreciation for procedural values such as respect for truth, freedom, tolerance, fairness and understanding, empathy and respect for those who are different.

School Practices

Students sing the national anthem in most schools and the Canadian flag is flown daily. Pamphlets such as Manitoba Election Simulation, Canadian Charter of Rights and Freedoms, Rights and Responsibilities, as well as multicultural activities have been made available at certain grade levels to complement the social studies program in its goal toward furthering citizenship.

Grades K-4

The curriciulum focuses on the needs and interdependence of individual students, their families and their communities A comparison is made between life within the students' own community, another Manitoba community, a Canadian community and several world communities.

Grades 5-9

The emphasis is on the way people live in Canada today and in the past. The students gain understanding of their own areas, how it is related to other areas in Canada and how it is governed. They also examine the political, legal and economic processes.

Grades 10-12

Emphasis is placed on national and world concerns. Courses at this level give a geographical perspective on the social and political history of Canada with a world issues orientation from the Canadian viewpoint. "'Government, Federalism and Politics" in grade 11 examines the Canadian government and the roles of federalism, political parties and the individual.

Methods

Methods and strategies used in Manitoba social studies programs are consistent with the development level of the student and include open-ended questioning, discovery and inquiry methods, resource persons, research, source materials such as films, pictures, paintings, slides and active involvement/participation in projects of interest.

Regional Emphasis

A new grade 9 social studies curriculum guide being finalized at present will highlight the process of an immigrant becoming a citizen and will examine concepts of citizenship.

The Current Status of Teaching about Citizenship

British Columbia

Goals

The goals of the social studies program are to develop in individuals an understanding of their relationship to the world, the role of the family in society, and their responsibilities and rights as citizens. The aim is to develop in individuals a sense of social responsibility, a tolerance and a respect for the ideas and beliefs of others, and an ability to live and work with other people. Developing an appreciation for the fine arts and an awareness of the cultural heritage and values of Canadian society and a broader world are also emphasized. The specific goals related to citizenship in the social sciences curriculum state that students should know and understand the roles, rights and responsibilities of an individual as a member of society and that they should develop a willingness and ability to use knowledge and understanding as a member of society.

Knowledge, Skills and Attitudes

Knowledge. Students in British Columbia schools are taught specific knowledge such as roles, rights and responsibilities of citizens; roles and function of government, and legal systems at the municipal, provincial and national level, as well as general knowledge concepts of values and morals, disciplines and cultural heritage.

Skills. Some of the skills that students are expected to acquire are decision-making, critical thinking, imparting and acquiring information, creative expression, and interpersonal skills. Specific citizenship skills include acquiring a sense of self-worth, interpersonal relations, group and discussion skills and leadership qualities.

Attitudes. The development of the following attitudes are considered important: interest in learning, appreciation of creative expression, self-motivation, self-worth, pursuit of excellence, physical health, satisfaction through achievement, moral values, respect for others and flexibility.

School Practices

According to Section 92 of the *School Act* in British Columbia, school assemblies are conducted regularly (at least three times a year) and should promote loyalty to the Queen, respect for Canadian traditions, laws, institutions, and human values. They should include observation of occasions of historic or current importance to Canada and the Commonwealth, as well as appropriate references to the Canadian flag.

Grades 1-7

In the elementary system, students study the economy, government and legal system under the headings of families, communities, Canada (including a section on native peoples) and the world.

Grades 8-11

More time is spent focusing on specifics such as the development of democratic concepts and Canada and world affairs including government, law and social issues as well as contemporary Canada and Canada in the global environment.

Vandra L. Masemann

Regional Emphasis

A number of learning resources have been developed for grades 1-7 by British Columbia authors. They highlight specific British Columbia settings where appropriate. In all grades, there is an emphasis on Canada's relations with the Pacific Rim. In the grade 10 social studies course, there is a section specifically devoted to the Pacific Rim.

Prince Edward Island

Goals

The social studies curriculum in Prince Edward Island is organized toward educating students in the issues that face all mankind. The modern world poses many dramatic issues relating to population changes, technological development, economic disparity, the place of the individual in society, the role of culture in the shaping of the modern world, and the increasing confusion over traditonal values. It is the intent of the program to prepare students as tomorrow's decision-makers.

The "Modern World Issues" course at secondary school allows students to examine problems and develop a tolerance and understanding of people and the problems with which they are confronted, regardless of where they live. An awareness of situations will affect the students' attitudes and values and perhaps make them more aware of the reasons for their opinions.

Knowledge, Skills and Attitudes

Knowledge. Some of the specific areas of knowledge taught in Prince Edward Island are privileges and responsibilities of citizenship, development of laws, the government and its purpose, the judiciary system, municipal government and Canadian laws.

Skills. Some of the skills the students are expected to learn are mapping, interpreting, predicting, observing, ranking, graphing, analyzing, collecting, correlating, discriminating, hypothesizing and valuing.

Attitudes. Attitudes that are considered important are understanding the way a group of people think and act, tolerance, and appreciation for the customs of people of other nationalities, and an appreciation of the similarities and differences of cultural lifestyles.

Grades 1-6

In grades 1-6, the social studies program is entitled "Social and Environmental Studies." It was written by Canadians, is metric and the author team includes classroom teachers, a principal and two board office consultants. "The World of Me" (grades 1-2) and "Beaver Hill" (grade 3) make up the primary school social studies program.

Grades 7-8

The grade 8 geography program provides the geographic and historical background to the study of North America.

Grades 9-12
A new geography curriculum was initiated in 1976 using the theme "development" as the main focus from grades 9 to 12, replacing the regional approach of the previous program. The four-year study moves toward educating students in the issues that face all people. Grade 9 and 10 students concentrate on human geography, grade 11 focuses on physical geography and grade 12 students study economic geography. In grade 10, at the general level, a practical social studies course focuses on civics and citizenship, law, geography, consumer education and Canadian personalities.

Methods
A wide variety of learning experiences are used in the program in Prince Edward Island; included are field studies, simulation, role playing, games, lectures, research, debating, audio-visual aids and materials, speakers and curriculum resource aids. Students also participate in mock parliaments and electoral simulations. There is a civics course at the junior high school level, and all students participate in activities related to Canada Day. Students also study peace education. At the elementary school level, students learn community responsibilty through cross-walk programs in co-operation with local police.

Saskatchewan

Goals
The entire social studies program is under redevelopment. Its broad intent is to develop in students the attributes of responsible citizenship which will increase the students' abilities to understand concepts of social change and social differences and to be at ease in a world where the future is not easily predicted.

Knowledge, Skills and Attitudes
Knowledge. The knowledge objectives guiding the development of the social studies program are as follows: (a) know facts about people, places, events in time and space; (b) understand social, political and economic organizations and systems; (c) form generalizations, concepts and principles; (d) interpret situations in the historical past and apply them to the future; and (e) analyze, synthesize and evaluate to predict and theorize.

Skills. Some of the skills that students are expected to acquire are critical thinking, research skills, good work habits, problem-solving, communication, social interaction skills, study skills, and decision-making.

Attitudes. The following attitudes are considered important: appreciation of the past and present, value of diversity, uniqueness of peoples and cultures, acceptance of value of social participation as a responsibility of citizenship, dignity of man, empathy, love, loyalty, justice, equality, freedom.

Vandra L. Masemann

School Practices
Most schools regularly observe routines that symbolize Canadian citizenship. The department of education does not prescribe specific activities, but might occasionally suggest a program for a special day.

The generally observed practice in elementary schools is to start with *O Canada* or *God Save the Queen* on formal occasions. There may be some instances of the Pledge of Allegiance, although it is not formally a part of the *Education Act*. There are also assemblies, patriotic observances, civic visits and special days.

Division I - Grades 1-3 (Year 1, 2, 3)
Emphasis progresses from the actual experiences of the child to the development of a "world view" through the basic concepts and generalizations from history and the social sciences. Units include learning about families, communities and cities and how individuals deal with roles, rules, responsibility and recreation.

Division II - Grades 4-6 (Year 1, 2, 3)
Through the concepts of anthropology, sociology, history and political science, students become familiar with Saskatchewan, Canada and the Americas. The pupils learn about the people of the province, country and continent as well as the functions and differences of government in the three areas.

Division III - 7-9
The student concentrates on such topics as the regional geography of the eastern hemisphere, Canada's heritage and the ancient and medieval worlds.

Division IV - 10-12
In the senior divisions the topics covered include "Man: a Study of the Individual," cross-cultural comparisons, and Canadian studies.

Methods
Some of the methods used to achieve the goals of the social studies program include field trips, assemblies, patriotic observances, civic visits and special day programs, audio-visual materials, government books and pamphlets, use of government information services and use of research facilities.

Regional Emphasis
The Official Minority Language Office (Fransaskois) played a large part in the development of citizenship understanding. The Indian-Métis group have also participated in various projects.

Alberta

Goals
The social studies curriculum in Alberta helps students to acquire the basic knowledge, skills and positive attitudes needed to be responsible citizens and contributing members of society. The content and skills of social studies draw upon history, geography, economics and other social sciences, behavioural sciences and humanities. Responsible citizenship is the ultimate goal of social studies. The responsible citizen is one who is knowledgeable, purposeful and makes responsible choices and understands the role, rights and responsibilities of a citizen in a democratic society, participates in the democratic process constructively and respects the dignity and worth of self and others.

Knowledge, Skills and Attitudes
Knowledge. To be a responsible citizen, one needs to be informed about the past and present and be prepared for the future. Knowledge objectives for social studies topics are organized through generalizations, concepts and facts. Some knowledge areas include economic, social and political aspects of a culture, the political development of Canada, the structure and function of government in Canada and the citizen's role in the political process.

Skills. Objectives for social studies are process skills to gain access to information, communication skills to help the student express ideas, and participation skills to help the student interact with others.

Attitudes. The attitude objectives identify a way of thinking, acting or feeling and are developed through a variety of learning experiences. Some attitudes students should develop are respect for the rights of others, a willingness to exercise behaviour appropriate to democratic citizenship, fairness, dignity, and a willingness to accept responsibility for their own views and actions.

School Practices
The *School Act* of 1980 states that a board may prescribe patriotic exercises and instructions and that a board shall display the Canadian flag at each school. Students can be excluded from religious or patriotic exercises on parental request without discrimination.

E.C.S. (Early Childhood Services) - Grade 3
The following topics provide opportunities for children to become aware of how they are like others, as well as some ways in which they are unique individuals: families, planning neighbourhoods and local communities, and lifestyles in other times and places.

Grades 4-6
In the later elementary grades, students investigate issues pertaining to the use of Alberta's natural resources, historically and today. Topics include "Alberta, Our Province;" "Canada, Our Country," and "Meeting Human Needs."

Vandra L. Masemann

Grades 7-9
In these grades, students develop a framework within which to examine the relationship among various aspects of culture including economic, social and political aspects.

Grades 10-12
In senior high school programs, students examine Canadian issues involving competing values of individual freedom and social control. Citizenship in Canada is explored thoroughly at the grade 10 level through such topics as freedom of speech, Human Rights and the *Canadian Bill of Rights*, language rights, and the role of government at various levels in relation to human rights issues. Grade 11 and 12 continue with Canada in the contemporary world and global issues of concern.

Methods
A wide variety of methods are used, and support materials are available to complement the social studies curriculum in Alberta. These include social studies teaching units, monographs and Alberta Heritage Learning Resources. The focus is moving away from exploration and resolution of social issues to individual responsibility where students acquire the basic knowledge, skills and positive attitudes needed to become responsible citizens and contributing members of society. The current social studies program predates the *Charter of Rights and Freedoms* and therefore will be revised in the coming year to include a citizenship component.

Newfoundland and Labrador

Goals
Citizenship education is dealt with in the social studies curriculum from k-12. The emphasis of citizenship development is on the person as a citizen with rights and responsibilities in society. The major purpose of the social studies program is to develop citizenship qualities through personal development and growth in citizenship. Thus, citizenship education permeates the social studies curriculum in all the grades.

Knowledge, Skills and Attitudes
Knowledge. Students in Newfoundland and Labrador are taught specific knowledge areas such as the present day culture of their province; the principles of democracy; the rights, freedoms, and responsibilities of citizenship; the world, national, provincial and local civic problems; and the functioning of social institutions.

Skills. Some of the skills that students are expected to acquire are critical thinking, group participation, information-gathering, decision-making, perception and concept attainment, and creative thinking skills.

Attitudes. The following attitudes are considered important: respect for the worth of each individual, respect for the values and beliefs of others, appreciation of the heritage of the people of Newfoundland and

The Current Status of Teaching about Citizenship

Labrador, of Canada, and of other countries, honesty, truth, justice, empathy, loyalty, co-operation and tolerance.

School Practices

Students sing *Ode to Newfoundland* as well as *O Canada* during the course of the school year. Special days of note are also celebrated.

The curriculum is based on a "modified expanding environment" theme. Thus the child learns about the family, the community, the province, the nation, and the world. The fundamentals of understanding and values that prepare the child to live in to-day's society are laid down in the early elementary grades.

Grades 4-6

The theme in the later elementary grades is "Community Living" with a particular emphasis on cross-cultural comparison. Children explore the basic processes by which people live, work, and play together in Newfoundland, Canada, and other countries of the world.

Grades 7-9

Students take a wide view of the world, and study selected world cultures, Canadian heritage, and the rights and responsibilities of citizens in a democracy.

Grades 10-12

At this level, students can choose among a variety of related courses in geography, history, economics and related subjects. In one course "Democracy," there is an emphasis on understanding and appreciating the role of the citizen in a democratic society.

Methods

In the early grades, there are a variety of methods used such as experience charts, tours, bulletin board displays, puppetry, art, role-playing, and field trips. As students progress, there is a shift toward the development of the ability to think, expression of independent thought, and personal inquiry. At the senior levels, students participate in simulations, parliaments, and elections.

Regional Emphasis

High school students are offered a course in Newfoundland culture. It is an in-depth study of the culture, and the way of life in the past, the present and the future.

Northwest Territories

Goals

Civics education is compulsory for each of grades 4 through 10 as a unit in social studies. The primary goal is to provide for the development of the good citizen in a democratic society. By gaining an understanding of the nature, purposes and practices of government, and an awareness of alternative forms of government, the students develop the skills necessary to guide and check the powers of government. In its full scope, the civics program involves for students a transformation of knowledge into active power which will be of practical value to them in their pursuit of personal fulfilment.

Knowledge, Skills and Attitudes

Knowledge. Students in the Northwest Territories are taught specific knowledge areas such as rights and duties as citizens, functions of social institutions, Confederation, functions of government and parliament, legal procedures, civil rights in Canada, and local government functions as well as meeting procedures.

Skills. Some of the skills students are expected to acquire are analyzing, clarifying, processing, research, critical thinking, communicating, social participation and leadership

Attitudes. The following attitudes are considered important: justice, loyalty, a willingness to examine problems from more than one point of view, an awareness of the limitations of their own present knowledge, an awareness of the existence of many thoughtful viewpoints and several sources of knowledge, a respect for the contributions of others and a willingness to share knowledge with others.

School Practices

Although it is recommended that teachers start their civics lessons by singing the national anthem, it is left to the individual principals to incorporate citizen-related activities into their school day.

The program begins by inculcating a formal awareness of government, moves to a relatively detailed study of the various levels of government in Canada, and concludes in the final year with an analysis of the issues. Level one (grade 4) identifies the need for government and then formally takes note of its presence. Level two (grade 5) investigates simple forms of government and promotes an appreciation of the nature of people's differences and a respect for one another's rights. Level three (grade 6) turns its attention to the kind of government that exists today and puts some emphasis on its historical development. Level four (grade 7) deals with a more detailed study of government structure and purpose, beginning with local government. Level five (grade 8) continues the more detailed study with territorial government. At level six (grade 9) more detailed study continues with focus on the federal government. In level seven (grade 10), the focus is on the evaluation of the social and political nature of Canada, and an attempt is made to deepen the students' understanding of both democracy and of what it means to be a citizen in a democratic society.

Methods

At each level the establishment of a class club is recommended to foster community awareness and well-being and to provide students with opportunities for the practice of group participation and decision-making skills. Several civics kits as well as audio-visual supports are available for teachers to supplement the curriculum guides.

Regional Emphasis
In grade 4, the "Canada In the World" topic examines some of the contributions made to the world community by people in the Northwest Territories and by other Canadians. The topic develops an appreciation of the unique and distinctive features of Canada life and culture.

Yukon

Goals
Citizenship is considered as a concept to permeate the entire curriculum at all levels. Thus, there is no explicit reference to the philosophy of citizenship education in the social studies program. It is left to the teacher to convey the concept of citizenship at every appropriate opportunity within the course of the school program.

Knowledge, Skills and Attitudes
Knowledge. The curriculum in the Yukon is based on the British Columbia curriculum; the knowledge objectives are similar. However, the content of what is taught is oriented toward the local variations in Yukon life. For example, a book called *Discovering Yukon's Past* has been produced locally. In addition, the Yukon Department of Education works closely with the Council for Yukon Indians which produces kits about the Athapaskan-Tlingit peoples suitable for use at the K-2 level.

Skills. The students are expected to acquire a wide variety of skills similar to those outlined for British Columbia. There is also an extensive outdoor education program which teaches students skills in dealing with a northern environment.

Attitudes. There are approximately 25-30% native students in Yukon schools. There are also non-native students from many other parts of Canada who are part of the mobile life of the North related to government and mining. The aim of citizenship education is to give all students an awareness of what it means to be Canadian, and a sense that they belong to a wider community than their own local one.

At the elementary school level, the social studies program of British Columbia is followed, adapted for use in the Yukon. Native languages are used in the early grades, and students gradually acquire an awareness of their family, their community, the territory itself and Canada.

At high school, there are courses in history, geography, and government which lead the student to an understanding of the workings of the federal system, the history of Canada, and Canada's place in the world.

Methods
The methods used are similar to those in the southern provinces. As well as common classroom practice, outdoor education is used. Moreover, students are taken on field trips to other parts of Canada such as Ottawa and Montreal. Student exchanges are also held with Quebec. The classrooms are well-equipped with excellent resources. The schools differ from those in the south in that in some small settlements, there are some very small schools.

Vandra L. Masemann

There is one high school, in Whitehorse, and students who are not able to handle a regular high school program can enrol in an alternative education program with grade 10 equivalence. In this program, a life skills course is taught in which students learn many of the responsibilities and skills of adult life. Students may also apply to be pages in the Legislative Assembly, and individual classes are taken by their teachers to see the Assembly in action.

Regional Emphasis

As well as local curriculum content for both native and non-native students, there is an effort to have Yukon students understand that they are part of a much broader Canadian society. There is an effort to equip students with the knowledge, skills and attitudes to become responsible citizens of Canada as a whole.

Innovative Models of Citizenship Education from Across Canada

Student Leadership Program - Ontario

In order to train students in leadership qualities, the Ontario Ministry of Education works with the province-wide Ontario Secondary School Students' Association. It is composed of all student councils in some 762 high schools and has both an English and a French version. They send 144 student delegates on a regional and first-come first-served basis to the Ontario Student Leadership Centre at Lake Couchiching every September for an intensive five-day course. Students are given workshops in such areas of leadership as time management, establishing committees, running a meeting, running a conference, fund-raising and school spirit. Students from an increasingly diverse ethnic and racial mix come together to learn skills which they are expected to use with their own student councils. The students are expected to improve the quality of life in their own schools, and to co-operate with others to work as a team.

For the twelve cabinet members in the OSSS Association, the tasks involve a great deal of responsibility. They have to organize a regional council in their own region and a regional leadership conference in their area. Moreover, they attend five weekend meetings of the association in Toronto during the school year. The various cabinet members learn their roles and are responsible for producing a newsletter.

Students have a great deal of work to do as well as ensuring that their school marks do not suffer. They also organize and send delegates to the Canadian National Student Leadership Conference. In 1984, the year of Ontario's bicentennial, they held a mock parliament in the Ontario Legislature itself.

Harold T. Barrett Junior High School, Beaverbank - Nova Scotia

The activities at Harold T. Barrett Junior High School in Nova Scotia exemplify what one school can do to encourage education in the basic qualities of citizenship. Their program was developed in co-operation with the Canadian Intramural Recreation Association, which is active in some 500 schools across Canada. The family of the school's namesake had established a trust award to reward students for demonstrating leadership while making a contribution to their community.

The school's student council organized a week of Harold T. Barrett Days, in which 90.8% of the school's 293 students volunteered and took an active role. Some students worked with seniors in a local nursing home, while others assisted in a local day care centre. Students made visits to homes of local seniors to give them assistance with housekeeping, shopping, gardening or to keep them company. Another group helped as student aides in a nearby elementary school, and others with a certified babysitting course established a drop-in day care service for parents with young children. Lastly, students participated in a roadside clean-up campaign. The Intramural Council has also organized activities for students to help raise money for the Isaac Walton Killam Hospital for children.

Another activity that is widely encouraged at Harold T. Barrett, with community support, is writing projects. These activities do more than promote writing; they involve a wide representation of students and the community. One project, "Authors' Celebration," displayed the work of the children, and was a day-long event with professional authors, illustrators, and publishers attending. Students led groups in which guests participated. The day and evening were open to the entire community and many parents, school board members, and municipal officials attended and took part. The second project centred on the Drama Club, in which approximately 50 students wrote their own play.

Citizenship Courts in Winnipeg High Schools - Manitoba

Many schools in Winnipeg have multicultural populations, and it was thought that students would benefit from observing a Citizenship Court in action and from seeing real people become Canadian citizens.

At St. John's High School in Winnipeg, Judge Elizabeth Willcock presided over a citizenship ceremony in which people from some 15 or 16 countries took their Oath of Citizenship. The high school choir sang for the cermony and several classes of students were respectful observers. Later in the day a workshop was held with immigrants and other Canadians on the rights and responsibilities of a citizen of Canada.

This ceremony and the workshop were tangible efforts to make citizenship real to students. There are plans to continue with further ceremonies. Moreover, the agenda for the ceremony will be included in the grade 9 curriculum guide.

Guidelines on Student Rights and Responsibilities, Vancouver School Board - British Columbia

The Vancouver Board supports and wishes to encourage co-operation and positive relationships among students and the entire school community in every Vancouver school. With this in mind, the board has developed a number of guidelines that represent its point of view on a number of matters that affect these relationships, particularly between students and teachers. The board's guidelines are based on two principles:

Vandra L. Masemann

(1) Students should gain experience at school in making decisions based on freedom, just as adult citizens must do, (2) Order is necessary to have freedom. This means that in a school everyone must accept certain obligations and restrictions for the good of all.

Guidelines for Students
Consideration for Others. Every student is responsible for his or her personal language, manners, habits, and behaviour, because these affect the feelings and safety of others.
Attendance. To gain maximum value from his or her courses, every student must attend and participate in all classes regularly, unless a different arrangement is worked out with the teacher as part of the learning for that course.
Individual Initiative. To gain practice in being an independent learner, every student should take responsibility for doing assignments that help to make him or her know more about the subject or more skilled in using the process.
Pride in the school's appearance. Every student should do his or her share in keeping the school buildings and grounds clean, tidy, and safe, and in preventing damage to school equipment and property.
Private Property and Personal Dignity. To have the right to private property and personal dignity, every student must recognize that every other student has the same right to private property, and the right not to be abused in any way.

Guidelines for Teachers
The Code of Ethics of the B.C. Teachers' Federation, of which every Vancouver teacher is a member, states: "The teacher speaks and acts toward pupils with respect and dignity, and deals judiciously with them, always mindful of their individual rights and sensibilities."

The Vancouver School Board supports the kind of relationship expressed in the Code of Ethics, specifically as it applies to confidentiality of student records and information; students' rights to dissenting views and conscientious objections to religious and patriotic exercise (see policy IGAC, Teaching About Religion); students' rights to private affairs and personal property; students' freedom to publish and distribute publications, within the limits of laws concerning libel, obscenity, and sedition, and the observance of reasonable sensitivity toward the feelings and values of others (see policy IGDB, student publications).

Interpretation and Authority
If the policy guidelines adopted by the board are to be successful, it must be understood that school officials and teachers have the authority to interpret and apply them in a given situation. Students must obey any such interpretation, subject to an appeal.

Under the *School Act*, the board has the legal authority and duty to set rules of conduct for students, and to see that they are observed. Under the same *School Act*, students are required to observe the rules of the school. Fairness requires that students be told clearly the standards of behaviour that are expected of them, and the consequences of misbehaviour; for that reason, the board directs each school principal to make school codes of conduct available to students and their parents through handbooks distributed annually.

CARE (Courtesy, Appreciation, Responsibility, Enthusiasm or Excellence), Saskatoon - Saskatchewan

In School District No. 13, Saskatoon, there is a citizenship program in effect called CARE - Courtesy, Appreciation, Responsibility, Enthusiasm or Excellence. Students are teamed by classroom (younger with older), to read, write and listen to one another, help with numerous activities and watch out for one another. The students develop more responsible attitudes about working and playing with others. Participation in this program enables students to develop a respect for the worth of other people, a sensitivity to right and wrong, an acceptance of differences in belief and customs of others, and understanding of personal rights and responsibilities as they relate to other individuals. Some of the partner activities include baking together, writing books, organizing and running plays and assembly presentations.

The benefits of this arrangement help to build citizenship in both partners. The younger students learn that they can go for help to the older students, and the older students learn responsibility and caring attitudes. Teachers are able to discuss problems within a framework of the CARE policy and to discuss solutions that build qualities of citizenship. This is a program that benefits every student - from the youngest to oldest.

Alex Taylor Community School, Edmonton - Alberta

This school is in an area which was "traditional" until 17 years ago, but since it was in a depressed area of single parents and many ESL students, a need was identified to focus on education for the total child. The first issue addressed was that of nutrition. Children were provided with breakfast and a mid-morning snack. The curriculum later changed to address social, recreational, cultural and spiritual skills.

A "buddy system" is used to help new students adapt and become part of the community. The school uses a cultural approach, such as celebrating various ethnic festivals, to minimize discrimination and teach understanding and tolerance. Police are very actively involved in the school to overcome negative attitudes about law and the police force. They give talks on drugs, safety and preventive services. The police also get involved in special days and activity programs. The principal holds weekly assemblies which include the national anthem, Lord's Prayer, civic personnel giving messages, mention of students' birthdays and honouring the student of the week. These all help to "humanize" education. The addition of native staff and workers encourages native students to attend school regularly.

Travel is also a major focus of the program and there are trips to various destinations both within and without Canada. Community support is very positive and many groups have sponsored travel opportunities. Seniors are also very important in the program, by providing heritage education and becoming part of student-based activities such as lunch programs and bingo. This school is an example of citizenship and multiculturalism in action.

Vandra L. Masemann

Secondary School Course "Democracy" - Newfoundland

The central purpose of the course "Democracy" is to assist students to understand the basic values and ideals linked with democratic thought and practice. The initial emphasis is on the essential principles that distinguish democracy from other forms of government.

Through the use of specific in-class activities, students are encouraged to analyze the divergence between theory and practice, the ideal and reality. The final goal is to help students become more reflective thinkers - to determine the extent to which practice falls short of democratic ideas and to appreciate the citizen's role in our society. One example of such an activity is the use of simulation games in this course. There are four specially designed simulations or role-playing activities in the student text, custom-made for the province of Newfoundland and Labrador. These are "Choosing a Cabinet" (Chapter 7), "One Day to Decide" (Chapter 8), "Parliament in Action" (Chapter 9), and "The Ottawa Conference" (Chapter 13).

"Choosing a Cabinet" is a single-role simulation where each student plays the role of Prime Minister and selects a cabinet. Evaluation activities in which the group compares lists are important in this simulation. On the other hand "Parliament in Action" is a large, seven-day simulation of the legislation process from decision by cabinet to third reading of a bill. To work well, it requires some organizational effort from the teacher, and commitment from the students.

Canadian Society in the Year 2000

Ronald C. LeBlanc
Groupe d'étude en modélisation économique et analyse de politique,
GEMAP, Université de Moncton, New Brunswick

EDUCATION can be defined as a socialization process, the aim of which is to provide individuals with the knowledge, skills and abilities required to become integrated, well adjusted members of society. In this context, the purpose of education is to prepare an individual for the future. One of the basic roles of all members of society is that of acting as responsible citizens. According to Wright:

> *Citizenship confers a particular status on a person, which entitles that person to certain rights and privileges and in turn, entails particular responsibilities.*[1]

He concludes that citizenship involves decision-making. Thus, citizenship education must not simply transmit knowledge about the concepts of society, its values, institutions, processes and structures; it must provide the individual with the means to deal with them, as they relate to each other, as they interact with each other, as they oppose each other and as they change over time.

What changes will there be in Canadian society as it evolves towards the year 2000? The conceptual model underlying this chapter is quite simple, and fairly traditional. It presumes that people, their culture, and their values form the nucleus of a society, and thus constitute the guiding forces that determine the institutions of the social system, its subsystems and the structures of society. Four subsystems will be examined: the information system, created by society to ensure the socialization process;

M. LeBlanc porte un regard sur l'an 2000 et le XXIe siècle. Il étudie quatre sous-systèmes qui permettent de se construire une image de la société de l'avenir. Selon lui, la société deviendra pluraliste, les citoyens et citoyennes auront un meilleur accès à l'information, les institutions seront plus diversifiées et les gens chercheront à diriger davantage leur vie. Pour vivre au XXIe siécle, il faudra avoir une optique plus globale et mieux informée.

Ronald LeBlanc

the judicial system, set up to circumscribe the freedoms and protect the rights of members; the political system, initiated to provide the mechanisms for collective choices; and the economic system which is for generating the wealth necessary to ensure the material subsistence of the members of society. In the real world, a complex set of relationships appears between the nucleus and the subsystems, as members of society define their values, assume their roles and interact with the institutions of these systems. It is this fact that makes the understanding of social reality a complex and neverending task, for society can be perceived as a dynamic organism in continuous change. Attempting to draw a picture of what Canadian society will look like in the year 2000 is an even more complex exercise than that of understanding what it is today, a task quite substantial in itself. The state of Canadian society a dozen years from now will be the product of processes and transformations that are occurring now and of new trends that may develop in the next decade. Any attempt to draw a broad picture in a relatively brief discourse will necessarily involve a substantial amount of synthesizing and generalization.

Three Macro-Perspectives On the Future

As a starting point, the perspective of three authors provides the basis for a better understanding of the future in general, and of Canadian society in it: Kirkpatrick Sales's book entitled *Human Scale* (1980); Alvin Toffler's *The Third Wave* (1981); and Marilyn Ferguson's *The Aquarian Conspiracy* (1980). I do not argue that they are necessarily the most relevant perceptions, or the only ones to consider. Rather, they have been retained for the relevance of the particular reality they describe.

In *Human Scale*, Sales[2], writes of an increasingly dysfunctioning society and civilization, where dissatisfaction and discontent are growing. In the second chapter, he explores the theme of an industrialized civilization which is facing the type of crises never before encountered, and suggests that their resolve will define the dawn of a new age. However, the magnitude and the scope of these phenomena do not lend themselves to the typical industrial society solutions, and more imaginative ones must be devised. As briefly and accurately as possible, these are the trends that he recognizes:

1. *An imperiled ecology:* Our established way of life is threatened by the forces of unrestrained world population growth, resource depletion, irremediable environmental degradation, and endangered species. In other words, the spaceship earth appears to become less and less livable at a time when more and more people depend on it.

2. *Social disintegration:* Community life is becoming more and more threatened, stressful and difficult to sustain in the face of the breakdown of the traditional family unit, the decline of community involvement, the erosion of religious commitment, inadequate education and schooling and mounting illiteracy, contempt for law and deteriorating and congested cities.

3. *Economic uncertainty:* The basic material well-being of many is being shaken and eroded by the dramatic restructuring of economies with its consequent rise in unemployment and inflation, by widespread inefficiency, waste and mismanagement, by mounting personal, government and international indebtedness, and greater inequality of wealth.

4. *Political discontent:* There is a dramatic rise in the disillusionment

with governments and an undermining of confidence and trust of authority as a result of legislative ineptitude, abuses of power, administrative inefficiencies, bureaucratic rigidity, and judicial inequity at all levels.

5. *International instability.* There is a growing era of international instability associated with rising third world indebtedness, famines and deepening poverty, the continuing arms race and military production, local wars, inadequate international laws and the failure of international institutions to deal with world-scale issues on a planet where societies are becoming more and more interdependent.

Sales believes that "bigness" is the culprit. Many issues have become unmanageable, and the large-scale national institutions cannot deal with them, having themselves become unwieldy. He suggests that civilization is at a turning point and believes that "downsizing" institutions and systems to humanly manageable proportions, and addressing problems at a more local or decentralized level, based on more humanistic values is the best way of dealing with the issues. Although many may dispute the extent of the crises which Sales identifies, it appears evident that the Canadian citizen of the future will be faced with making choices on these broad issues, all of which are inherited from industrial society.

A second vision is the one presented by Toffler. He writes:
A powerful tide is surging across much of the world today, creating a new, often bizarre, environment in which to work, play, marry, raise children, or retire....Value systems splinter and crash, while the lifeboats of family, church and state are hurled madly about. [3]

Toffler describes civilization as having previously gone through two major revolutions. The first was the agricultural revolution which transformed societies from a nomadic-tribal to an agrarian extended family organization. Production units were largely independent and autonomous. Wealth resided in the ownership of land and the tilling of the soil. The second was the industrial revolution, characterized by the machine, with the factory and the office as its manifestations. It transformed societies from agrarian to urban; the nuclear family replaced the extended family. Production units became specialized, integrated and interdependent. Massification, standardization and uniformity characterized life. Ownership of capital became the source of wealth.

A third wave is now transforming the basic structures of our civilization and societies. It has taken on a variety of labels, the most popular of which may be the information revolution. The basic technology underlining it is the computer-communication technology, and the basic source of new wealth is knowledge. The electronic technology of computers and communication has dramatically increased the production, processing, storage and transfer of information, thus substantially adding to the stock of knowledge, as well as the opportunities to adapt it to all aspects of society. The shape of the new society is still being defined. Many of the traditional institutions are being transformed as people adapt and change their values, beliefs and attitudes to face the onslaught. What most characterizes this new society is diversity, pluralism and customization.

The new generation of Canadians will confront the need to adapt and adjust to the changes being imposed by this new information society.

Although humanity has always been faced with the prospect of changing its social environment in the face of new technologies the major difference with this wave of change is the speed with which adjustments are required.

The third perspective that can provide some insight into the nature of the future of Canadian society is provided by Ferguson.[4] She stresses that people are changing the way they perceive reality, and they are changing their values, beliefs and attitudes as they desire to take greater control over their lives. This manifests itself in terms of a more holistic rather than reductionist view of things, a more humanistic and less materialistic approach to life, a belief in one's ability through a greater degree of self reliance. People seek a more meaningful existence, and are more and more willing to make choices that reflect their personal beliefs and correspond to their personal development and gratification. It reflects a more liberal philosophy, stressing individualism and self-fulfilment rather than commitment to community. Ferguson, however, notes that there is also a co-operative, self-help spirit which permeates this trend, as individuals become more suspicious and less confident with formally structured and hierarchical organizations.

All three authors write of major transformations which are changing the very nature of the way we function in society. The thrust for change comes from events, scientific technological progress and from within individuals. The social landscape will necessarily evolve to meet the needs expressed by individuals as they cope with these transformations.

Canadian Society in the Year 2000

These three perspectives serve as a background for a preview of Canadian society in the year 2000. A good understanding of this future society requires that we at least pass briefly under review the more relevant changes in the nucleus of our society. Then it is possible to explore how the institutions may adapt and the systems change.

A thorough demographic analysis of Canada from now to the year 2000 is beyond the scope of this presentation. It would involve a look at its growth and its composition, the geographical distribution, household and family formation, labour force activity, internal and external migration and more. A far more modest presentation will be made here. What we conclude from the demography is that the Canadian population is expected to reach approximately 31 million by the year 2000, given the forecasted low birth rate. The rate of family and household formation will also slacken substantially as the "baby boomers" move on in years; household and family size will be smaller. Undoubtedly the most important demographic phenomenon will be the maturing of the boomers, and the consequent gradual aging of the Canadian population. These trends are quite predictable.

The boomers are the single most important generational group of our society. By analogy, they have been compared to a "pig in a python," changing the nature of society as they grow older.[5] Their values are those most likely to be adopted by society, and their needs are those more likely to be served by the social institutions. Born between 1946 and 1966 they were in their youth, a bonus as consumers. In their productive years, they have become a burden for an economic system unable to accommodate all them in their material expectations. They carry with them a set of values which is different from their predecessors. As one author states it, it is primarily an urban generation raised on permissiveness, child-centred, shaded from pain and in an era of economic abundance and rising expectations. The self is their primary commitment. Often referred to as the "Me" generation, they were raised to believe in entitlement, self actualization, lived experiences and immediate gratification, such that the older values of reward, prudence, self denial, dedication to community and sacrifice are less cherished.[6]

Part of the instability in the social institutions results from the rejection of these institutions by this generation when they fail to meet their personal needs. A family, a church, a school or a job that does not meet their expectations is readily discarded. It is also the first generation that was raised primarily on images, practically from birth. To many, the impression rather than the content is more important. Symbols and style play an important role in their life, and possessions serve as the measure of their success. How Canadian society will look in the year 2000 largely depends on how this generation of boomers react. Haaland writes:

The way this generation votes, dresses, consumes, cohabits, thinks, plays and works has altered, and will continue to alter the Canadian social and economic landscape.[7]

However, for many, the material expectations raised have been too high, given the current trends in economic activity. They are also the generation that will experience the full force of the dramatic changes and adjustments of the new age of information. They will not likely experience the stability and security that their predecessors found in such institutions as the family, the church, the school, the work place, a fate also to be experienced by their progeny.

They also leave behind a new generation in search of values and direction, a generation with reduced expectations and centred on itself. Some authors have attached the label of the "Us" generation to this group of young people.

Another demographic element that requires some mention is immigration. Up to 1960, immigration was largely limited to people of European heritage, thus incurring minimal adjustments to the new arrivals. This trend has now dramatically been altered, replaced by a more diverse mix of people from all corners of the world. These new Canadians bring with them a whole new social set which differs from the traditional mode. Integration without assimilation is the desired goal. With this greater diversity of cultures, Canada is becoming a more pluralist society. Value sets and cultural traits are more diverse and require more understanding, flexibility, adjustment and tolerance than in the past.

The most fundamental changes that will determine the nature of Canadian society in the year 2000 relate to our culture and values. Culture can be perceived as the set of accumulated knowledge, attainments and learned behaviour patterns. It is that which gives Canadians their distinctiveness. It covers language, shared experiences, thoughts, attitudes and beliefs, and the art and literature which expresses and records all of this. One can refer to values as the standards and norms with which Canadians guide their actions and judge those of others. The thrust for the changes come both from within the person, namely the changing values, beliefs, attitudes and interests of Canadians, and from the outside. The more universal trends are the globalization phenomenon and the new information society. An exploration of the thrust of these two major trends can provide further insight into the other sources of change, and how Canadian society will likely be affected.

Our world has been shrinking faster and faster as a result of the major improvements in the transportation and communication technologies and the rapid integration of the economies of the world since 1945. Multilateral freer trade and multinational corporations have fueled the latter trend. The opening of economies has given rise to a new phenomenon - that of cross-border integrated production processes. The development of newly industrialized economies has added a new element of international competitiveness, such that a world-wide restructuring of production has been occurring. This has been described as the globalization of economies. A phenomenon of de-industrialization has occurred in the mature industrial economies such as the Canadian economy, as traditional manufacturing activities are being shifted elsewhere. Canada is one country which has substantially suffered from this process, given the industrial structure which it had developed, namely resource-based industries and traditional manufacturing activities. Since the material base of our society is largely founded on a source of wealth of declining importance, namely resources and processing of resources, our society and its institutions must change to meet the new economic challenges which are found in the information economy.

This globalization phenomenon is not exclusively economic in scope. The communication and transportation technologies have narrowed the distances between societies in general. Wars, famines, natural disasters, terrorism, and other similar events become instantaneously part of the daily life of Canadians, as do the cross-border proliferation of culture and ideas. The Canadian way of life is no longer sheltered by territorial or cultural sovereignty.

What some have called the New Economy, or the Next Economy, has been characterized as an information economy. The transition is one of shifting from mass (that is, resources, labour and energy) to information, (that is, knowledge intensive design, utility, craft, durability, newness, etc.) in goods and services, as well as in the production processess by which they are obtained.[8] It also involves the use of more sophisticated machines to replace labour, based on the computer-communication technologies linked to machines in production processes. It is exerting strong influences on all the social institutions. The most dramatically affected institution is work. Not only is the nature of work being redefined, but also the work place. Some have even gone as far as to speak of the end of the labour society as we know it, that is, a society in which institutions and lifestyles are structured around work, a society which believes that personal worth is primarily related to marketable activities, and a society that relies primarily on the market to distribute income.[9]

What is of interest is how such trends will affect Canadian society, and thus what can be expected by the year 2000. Canadian society is an interrelated set of systems and institutions, largely organized around production. Under industrial society, the production unit was centralized, the production process mechanized and broken up into specialized integrated tasks, and the product standardized. Work was defined accordingly, and social institutions and values reflected this model. Toffler provides a clear picture of it when he writes of industrial societies in this fashion:

> These are societies based on mass production, mass distribution, mass education, mass media, mass entertainment, and mass political movements - not to mention weapons of mass destruction. They are societies based on the blue-collar way of life. In blue-collar societies, millions of people arise more of less at the same hour, commute to work in unison, tend the machines in sync with one another, return home, watch the same TV programs as their neighbors, and turn off the lights - all in a kind of mass rhythm. People tend to dress alike, live in a cookie cutter apartments, and share the values of their next door neighbors.[10]

He describes society in terms of a high degree of uniformity and homogenization, imposed by the mechanistic technology. The new revolution is one which is breaking up these mass structures and processes, and adding heterogeneity to our lives. Society is demassifying, and its values and institutions will reflect diversity. The information technology allows us to have a greater degree of choice. Furthermore, as we increase the diversity and distinctiveness, the need for information and the technology to use it intensifies. The impacts of these trends on the four social subsystems will retain our attention. Of interest is how the institutions of these systems are being affected and how they will change from now to the year 2000.

The Economic System

Possibly the one system which may be the easiest to explore is the economic system. Much has been written about the transformations occurring here. The fundamental force behind the changes is the thrust towards the recognition that knowledge is a separate factor in production, and that it is the prime creator of new wealth.[11] Of even greater importance is the fact that this factor of production is not subjected to the law of scarcity, as are the other factors. Production is shifting from high energy and material content to knowledge in terms of newness, design, quality, and customization, in goods and services. The computer and communication technologies are also dramatically changing the production processes, and consequently substantially changing the nature of business and household operation, markets and work itself.

The process of demassification is generating a whole new set of productive activities centred on small and medium-sized businesses; as the chain of production subdivides, goods and services become more customized, markets are fragmented, and services gain importance. However, this same information technology is providing big business with the opportunity to increase its control through the centralization of information-related activities such as management, accounting, finance, research and development and supervision. Many intermediaries are disappearing, especially in the activities related to the collection, storage, treatment and transmission of information as computers replace people in offices, one of the basic economic institutions of the industrialized economy. In the factory, the computerization of machines, or robotization, is doing the same thing to production workers. This new economy is creating two types of employment opportunities for displaced workers and new entrants: information-related activities which require higher qualifications, and low-skilled service sector employment.

As suggested earlier, the household will also feel the effect of this transformation. As a consumer, not only will it have more diversity in its choices, but will also see some lifestyle changes as electronic mail, electronic banking and electronic buying enters the home. Much is said about the electronic household, programmed and controlled by computers and video technology.[12] As a provider of labour services, the household will also undergo important transformations as the nature of work changes. Obviously, one important change is the polarization of workers into know and know-not. For the know-not, work will take the form of less meaningful activities, generally low paying, interrupted by periods of unemployment, and more strictly supervised and controlled activities. For the knows, work will take the form of roles, be more dynamic and creative and personally rewarding, with less rigorous control and enhanced social status. The nature of the work place will also change. The demarcation between the home and the place of work will become blurred, as will the demarcation between education, work and leisure time. The home will become an electronic cottage industry for more individuals, where members may choose their hours of work, initiate their own work activities as autonomous workers and co-ordinate work and leisure activities between members of the household. The concepts of electronic highways and telecommuters is now more than mere fiction: they are a part of the lifestyle of a growing number of information workers. This scenario will apply more and more to knowledge workers, whether they be employees or autonomous workers doing subcontracting, free-lancing, and enterprising activities.

The most important socio-economic issue in Canada over the next decade is likely to be that of the growing gap between the haves and the have-nots, as the economy magnifies the polarizing effect.

The Information System

The information system is composed of those institutions which provide the members of society with the principles and guidelines for behaviour in society. It includes such institutions as the family, the school, the church, unions, and the media as the most important. The transformation of society from an industrial to an information one, along with the changes in values, attitudes and perceptions, will have a substantial impact on these institutions.

The family is considered to be the most fundamental institution of this subsystem. Demographic trends predict that the average size of the family will continue to decline. Of even more importance, the institution of the family is taking on a new look. With the rise of individualism, and the growing desire to have more customized forms of personal relationships, the traditional nuclear family, which was the building block of industrial society, will lose importance. In fact, in its true form, it only constitutes a minority of family types which now exist. At present, we can identify several other forms of personal relationships which are accepted in the family category: single parent family, child free couples, common law couples, roommates with long standing relationsips, the aggregate families (or polyparents), solos, homosexual couples, communes, group households, etc.[13]

The wide diversity of relationships is the product of a change in societal values and attitudes and will undoubtedly continue into the 21st century. For one thing, relationships that do not bring the immediate gratification or desired ends are losing their permanency as people assert their independence and autonomy. Also, the general trend to design or determine the type of relationship one desires is changing the nature of this fundamental building block of society. As Toffler argues, the nuclear family was the product of the industrial wave, which sought to standardize and stabilize key aspects of the industrial technology. The information technology is characterized by diversity, and this will be reflected in the family unit. Because of the changing nature of work, it is no longer essential to maintain the homogeneous nuclear model of the family. Furthermore, as the nature of the family changes, so does the definition of the roles and relationships of its members, be they parent-children roles and relationships, sexual roles or economic roles. It is also likely to be a less discriminating economic environment as the information economy searches for qualified knowledge workers.

The school as an institution of society will also undergo a transformation, as the information technology makes its way, and new types of lifestyles and work styles develop. The direction of change will again be towards diversity and more individuality in learning. The factory-style education system is not meeting the diverse needs of individuals and society. More and more, students will have access to stores of knowledge at their fingertips, as well as access to expert services and analysis and instantaneous computational capabilities through the computer and data banks.[14] The teacher, as a store of knowledge and as a purveyor of information, will become more and more obsolete. The information explosion will, however, help create what has been termed information overflow and information pollution. John Naisbitt argues that the emphasis is shifting from the supply of information to the selection of information.[15] The role of the teacher will become more and more one of helping students to learn how to learn. Basically, this implies the ability to search for information, to retain the essential, to sort out the useless or false, and to organize and process it. In summary, they will become knowledge designers rather than information dispensers.

The computer-communication technology which will induce this will also allow students to tailor learning to fit their needs and wishes. The school facilities and regimentation rather reflects an industrial structure of society. Content is defined to bring students to fit a predefined mold. The facilities and the education process is scheduled in factory style, chain-line production mode. The new school will have to reflect the requirements of a more flexible environment.[16] It will be less and less possible to strictly provide learners with absolutes, with rigid programs, with traditional teaching techniques, with the obligation to be present in body regularly at a fixed location. Furthermore the complex issues that Sales describes will require broader based knowledge and abilities to fully understand and deal with them. The dramatically changing nature of work, the growing desire to be distinctive and to design one's life to one's needs will force education to take a more flexible approach.

As we become more and more imbedded in the information society, the need for continuous or lifelong learning will also grow, if individuals do not wish to find themselves in the ranks of the know-not. The traditional scheduling of education services, along with the rigid format and content is relegating a growing number of individuals to the status of know-not and illiteracy as they drop out. The Canadian school of the year 2000 should be more open, more flexible more accessible and provide a more general form of education, thus providing individuals with the knowledge and skills to understand how to deal more effectively with the frequent adjustments that will occur, and to face the large complex problems that are already upon us.[17]

We are already witnessing similar transformations in the church. Two of the important ones are the diversity of religious leanings and the electronic church.

Two opposite trends are evident in church affiliation. One trend regroups those who feel the need to harbour themselves in absolutes, or revealed truths, as they face the growing diversity and instability brought about by the new information society and the more individualistic values. The plurality of thought makes it more and more difficult to find single answers or secure and stable positions. The reaction is one of going back to fundamentals for these individuals. Note that this advocacy of going back to the basics is also evident in education; also, those individuals who deplore the disappearance of the nuclear family and call for its return conform to this pattern. The other reaction is that of abandoning the traditional industrial society church, which is highly structured and whose teachings are more rigid or intransigent, in the face of a population that seeks institutions capable of responding to their needs in the face of a rapidly changing society, and of changing values and attitudes. The new religious forms range from abandonment of organized religion to the multiplication of customized religious associations and practices.

The second transformation is that of the shift to electronic religion. Its present manifestations are the radio and television evangelist and the televised religious services. As more and more computer networks are created, one can even imagine the establishment of religious teaching and guidance conducted and accessed by computer, as it is now available through telephone, television and radio. All these modes provide the variety, flexibility and convenience that people are seeking. These are major reasons for their popularity now and in the future. Another reason for the success of this style of church is the fact that it adopts the modern technology and the imaging process which characterizes life and learning in the information society. The splitting up of churches thus also follows the trend towards demassification.

Unions are another institution that will bear the brunt of change. It is suprising how they are now being attacked and undermined in society, while their cousins, the professional associations, are growing in stature. One obvious reason is the fact that the traditional basis for organizing and functioning of unions is being eroded. It was the concentration of workers in large production units, namely the factory or the office in the industrial economy. In the information economy, this model of production and work is slowly being transformed as smaller units are created, and as autonomous workers are replacing the salaried person, as part-time work multiplies and as decentralized low-wage service employment grows. Fewer and fewer individuals become identified with an organization structured around the place of work. Ogden has gone as far as to predict the total disappearance of unions by the year 2001.[18] Professional associations do not organize their members on this principle. In fact, since they are founded on the basis of professional interest, they are likely to flourish as the demand for professional services increases. Another probable cause of the uninterest in unions is the loss of individuality which is required of members, as it is based on the collective principle "in union there is strength." Without questioning the basis for this fundamental principle, to the extent that it reduces the individual's freedom to assert his individuality, it becomes less and less interesting to individuals.

One last institution of the information system that must be noted is the media. It has been typically labelled the mass media as it conformed to the need of industrial society to spread standardized information to the mass of Canadians from sea to sea. Canadian receive a large proportion of current information about themselves and other societies from the written press, and the electronic media of radio and television. The new information-communication technology has not only increased the quantity of information provided, it has also increased the speed at which it is delivered and has also provided the visual images. A further consequence of the new information society is the multiplication of information sources. Canadians have access to a greater variety of print forms, radio and television channels that ever before. New concepts such as desk top publishing, electronic narrowcasting, netwirks, netwarks, and floworks are suggested to reflect the new style of information flows.[19]

The exact face of the media in the year 2000 remains to be drawn. However, it is possible to present some of its features. First, one can expect a decline in the relative importance and influence of mass and standardized processes of providing information. Second, Canadians will have greater access to international networks of information. Third, there will be a greater diversity of information not only because of the increase in specialized information, but also because of the multiplicity of sources. And fourth, Canadians will have access to interactive information systems, allowing them to select the information they wish. Finally, much of the information will be in image form rather than simple print. Thus, the Canadian citizen of the year 2000 will have access to a wealth of information, and be subjected to numerous and diverse influences. The Canadian identity and the sovereignty of Canadian culture will undoubtedly be influenced by this new environment.

Many believe that it will be impossible to prevent the gradual assimilation to the more powerful cultural influences of those societies which dominate the information content. Canadians will therefore have to develop critical and discriminating skills in order to select and assimilate the information at their disposal, if they are not to become puppets of those who define the content. However, on a more positive note, this new media era will provide Canadians with the opportunity to present their culture, ideas, beliefs, and creativity to others.

There is obviously a great deal more that has been written about these institutions, and how they must change or lose their prominence in the environment that is developing. Their treatment in this text is merely intended to provide a glimpse of these changes.

The Political System:

The political system is yet another component of society that will be affected by these major transformations and the dramatically changing issues that society faces. Many present day problems that cry for solutions are beyond the scope of national governments to deal with. The concentration of power at the national level has followed the general trend of industrialized society. The consequences of industrialization and the new information wave is generating problems and issues which appear insoluable with national political institutions. Globalization and downsizing phenomena are creating issues that can only be adequately addressed at the international scale or at the more disaggregated scale. Bell has argued that the national-state has become too small for the big problems in life and too big for the small problems.[20] On the smaller, more local level, the increased desire of individuals to control their lives and destinies advocates more direct participation in the decision-making process. The large scale of some problems means that they must be simultaneously addressed by smaller scale manageable units in conjunction with world-scale organizations. In all, what is implied is that the general dissatisfaction, especially with political institutions, is due to their inability to meet the specific needs of individuals and minority groups, and also to deal with the world-scale problems that individuals are daily reminded of, in Canada and elsewhere. The manifestations of this trend is reflected in terms of calls for referendums or plebiscites on issues of local concern, special interest single issue groups, self-help organizations, local protest groups and even calls for more direct democracy through the electronic medium.

The new social reality is globalism; national political action is becoming less and less effective in controlling it for national purposes. Issues such as environmental pollution, famines and armed conflicts are of proportions that can only be addressed by international institutions. Socio-culturally, the new information-communication technology is generating an assault on previously sheltered values, attitudes, beliefs, traditions and institutions, as it opens the door to the diverse lifestyles around the world. The global village phenomenon is undermining the specific collective identity of national and subnational units. Another social reality is the growing desire to control one's destiny, and to participate in the political decisions that concern individuals as citizens and members of special interest groups. Whereas the former trends suggests a higher level of political institutions, the latter requires institutions at the more local levels.

Finally, the new information-communication technology is forcing the political systems and their institutions to deal with new processes and practices. For instance, imaging is a new trend in the information society. What it implies is that more and more importance is attached to the image than the content. Politicians that appear to have a better appearance or style succeed while those who may have more depth of perception or abilities are rejected. Public opinion polls have become a major phenomenon in the

Canadian Society in the Year 2000

political arena, be it at election time or otherwise. More and more political decisions are made on the basis of this short-term phenomenon, rather than on addressing the longer term issues. Interactive communication techniques, which allow for immediate feedback, are new and challenging phenomena that will force the political institutions to change. The more pluralist structure of society is still another element of pressure on the political choices. One could go on with the enumeration of such novelties which the information society brings. In summary, political institutions and processes will have to change to meet the challenges society and its members are facing.

The present trend in Canada towards downsizing government, to more privatization and deregulation appear to be attempts to respond to these needs. The search for a reformed constitution, in addition to correcting the problems of the past, may well be subtle strategies to address growing discontent with the present system, especially decentralizing the actions of government and allowing a greater local or regional participation. The growing debate over representation also reflects the desire to be more involved in decision-making, as well as the trend towards task forces, parliamentary committees, the broadcast of debates and committee hearings. The substantially greater number of interest groups constitutes another aspect of the political system of tomorrow.

Canada's political system of the year 2000 will be one that will reflect these trends. It will undoubtedly participate in the creation and operation of new international institutions and also rely on existing ones to solve some of its problems. Nationally, it is fair to assume that a more direct form of democracy could evolve, and that a growing number of issues may be dealt with at sub-levels of government, or simply relegated to private groups, which could better identify and serve the specific needs of citizens. For instance, it may be less and less possible to adhere to national standards, to develop uniform national programs than in the past. Political parties may find it more and more difficult to define uniform policies for a majority, such that political factions or splinter parties may appear to serve the growing diversity of interest groups. Given the volatility of situations, we may find ourselves developing policies and programs with explicit termination clauses or at least defined flexibility to allow for more rapid change to meet the challenges as they arise rather than continue to face the rigidity and decision log jams that plague the present system.

In conclusion, the pressure of the information society, globalization and the trend towards individualization will force our political institutions to develop ways to deal with greater diversity, a more intense desire to participate in the decision-making process, and to address increasingly complex issues. The probable changes now appear to follow the line of the more indirect approaches in terms of closer attention to opinion polls, more opportunities for interest groups to be heard, more diversity in political groups, the use of communication technology to inform and debate issues. One may even see the creation of special mechanisms to mediate between competing interests within the political system, within society or between different societies as Toffler suggests,[21] or even shared governance between government and non-government institutions as Boyer advocates.[22]

65

The Legal System

The new trends in Canadian society will require the legal system to change. Only a few of these changes will be discussed here. One of the major issues that the information society is generating is the question of privacy. Paquet, among others, starts by making the distinction between personal privacy and collective privacy.[23] The information-communication technology is allowing government and private interests to amass and collate, at alarming speed and accuracy, vast stores of information on individuals from the diverse sources. According to Cordell, the Canadian government alone already has 1500 data bases on Canadian citizens, with many exchanges of information among them.[24]

The trend towards the sharing of information, the ease of processing and transmitting it at low cost implies that individual privacy is seriously threatened. Individuals are generally not aware of how much information on them is already available to anyone who wishes to collect and organize it. Such things as directories, mailing lists, school transcripts, health records, financial records and credit ratings, credit card records and similar sources can easily be coded and correlated, once obtained. They allow interested parties to intrude into the private lives of citizens. The use of the telephone and linking it to the computer allows interested groups to invade our privacy at minmal cost, and it is beyond our power to prevent it. Also, such practices as telephone polling and telemarketing constitute invasions of privacy when not solicited. The future citizen will be faced with increased activity of this nature, and will have little power to control it, unless aggressive legislation is imposed on such practices. Cordell even suggests that we may be forced to revise our understanding of what constitutes privacy, when faced with the onslaught of the information-communication technology.[25] He even suggests that Canadians may be forced to adapt to a society with less personal privacy, given the enormous difficulties of legally controlling the diffusion of the information collected. Furthermore, he argues that legislation alone cannot be expected to solve the problem. It will be necessary to promote a sense of responsibility among data base managers and users to prevent abuse.

Collective privacy can be invaded through trans-border communications and can undermine our cultural sovereignty. The communication technology already available can easily induce cultural assimilation. In the recent Canada-United States free trade debate, for instance, Canadians have been made aware of the extent of foreign penetration in the cultural industries of our society. For instance, the Canadian Labour Congress has reported that United States magazines account for 77% of Canadian newsstand sales, that U.S. television programs account for 70% of English Canadians' viewing time, that foreign books account for 75% of all books sold in Canada, that 75% of film revenues go to foreign film distributors, and that foreign recordings make up 85% of Canada's tape market.[26] Another phenomenon which affects our collective independence and objectivity is the use of mass communication to influence and change the course of events. This point is well argued by Brandt when he writes, "We live in a media age. Our view of the world is shaped by the information we receive and the manner in which we receive it."[27] The information can be selected, distorted or biased to direct public opinion in a desired direction.

One other aspect of the information society which involves our collective consciousness is the need for information and the right to know. Some important strides have been made in the direction of right to know legislation with respect to the information that government has amassed, but not on the information gathered by the private sector. Little progress has been made on the issue of the availability of information on public issues as our society progresses towards greater participation in the democratic process. The public's access to such information is essential for effective decision-making by the ordinary citizen. At present, our legal system has not been able to deal adequately with these issues, to the expense of individual security and privacy and collectively to the expense of cultural sovereignty and informed decision-making by citizens.

The information-communication technology is also rendering more and more difficult the protection of personal property that takes the form of intangibles, that is, new information. Access to low-cost, highly accurate duplicating and receiving devices in the home and work place makes it very difficult to protect the property rights of the creators. Although some attempts have been made to resolve this issue they have only had marginal effects, and the unauthorized use of intellectual property is expanding rapidly.

Finally, the legal system has been slow to react to the customizing trend in values of individuals. Laws relating to the family and work are a case in point. They still retain the traits of the industrialized society. On work, for instance, they do not adequately reflect the substantial modifications that are occurring in work: youth employment, part-time work, autonomus activities, cottage industries, increased supervision and control of production workers, etc. Much of the legislation centres on the protection of the worker who falls into the standard industrial mode — the full-time, one career, continuous job with the same employer, not the new more floating type of work experiences of the new economy.

The shape of the judicial system in the year 2000 is unclear. One can believe that more progress will be made in the protection of privacy and intellectual property, but the extent of this is hard to predict, given the nature of the technology which affects it and the generally slow process of adjustment. One could also explore the extent of white collar criminality which is rising as a result of this same technology, and how society will deal with it. There is consensus that it is not regarded as severely as crimes of the blue-collar industrial society, which is on its way out. If not adequately dealt with, Canadian society in the year 2000 may be a less orderly society, as more people find the opportunities to choose this type of activity. Some progress has been made in the area of the security and protection of workers, but there is ample evidence that more needs to be done in the employment of youth, the cottage sweat-shop phenomenon, retirement and pension legislation, and the rights and protection of part-time employees.

The Implications for Citizenship Education

The purpose of citizenship education is to provide future citizens with the knowledge, abilities and attitudes that will be required to exercise their rights and fulfil their responsibilities as active, productive, and committed members of society. Citizenship education curriculum designers

Ronald LeBlanc

and teachers must be aware of the developments that will influence the course of Canadian society if they are to provide students with insight into what they must expect in the future. Furthermore, it is not enough to simply instil the knowledge of society, its institutions and its processes. It must do more than provide the skills, to gather, process and use information in constructive ways, and even more than instil positive attitudes of respect, tolerance, truth, honesty and commitment to a better collective life. It must attempt to provide all of these with a vision of the future. This implies a recognition that one must expect and accept change. Over the next decade, changes will likely occur more often and more rapidly than ever before. It can be of great value if some of these changes can be anticipated or foreseen.

It is possible to provide some insight into what the ordinary citizen should expect to have, or be equipped with, in the year 2000. Obviously, he or she will be dealing with a more diverse, pluralist society. The citizen of tomorrow will have access to, and be subjected to, a substantial volume of information from many sources. Knowledge-related activities will be the most materially and socially rewarding. There will be a greater variety of models of the more basic institutions to deal with. Values, beliefs and attitudes will be more pluralist, and it will require more understanding and tolerance to deal with them. The fact that individuals will seek to gain more control over their lives and to seek to define a more customized lifestyle will divide and fragment social institutions so that they can respond to the specific needs. The broader issues of society and the world will be more complex and require a more holistic and informed approach to resolve them.

There is an entirely different set of issues which have not been developed in this paper. They relate to the ethical and moral aspects of some of the changes which are now occurring and will affect Canadians in the year 2000 - the growing inequality of income and wealth among Canadians and between societies themselves, the progress of science and technology in biogenetics and genetic engineering, and the entire field of medical ethics as science broadens the spectrum in life and death choices.

---

1 I. Wright, *Elementary Social Studies: A Practical Approach to Teaching and Learning*, 2nd ed. (Toronto: Methuen, 1984), p. 166.

2 K. Sales, *Human Scale* (New York: Coward, McCann and Geoghegan, 1980).

3 Alvin Toffler, *The Third Wave* (New York: Bantam Books, 1981), p. 1.

4 M. Ferguson, *The Aquarian Conspiracy: Personal and Social Transformations in the 1980s* (Boston: Houghton, Mifflen, 1980).

5 L. Jones, *Great Expectations* (New York: Ballantine Books, 1981).

6 B. Haaland, "In Pursuit of Self: The Values of the Post-war Baby Boom Generation and the Implications for Continuing Education," *Canadian Journal of University Continuing Education*, Vol. 12, No. 2 (October 1986), pp.57-72.

7 *Ibid.*, p. 58.

8 P. Harken, *The Next Economy* (New York: Ballantine Books, 1983).

9 R. Dahrendorf, "The End of the Labour Society," *World Press Review*, March 1980, pp. 27-29.

10 Alvin Toffler, "Artificial Intelligence," *Omni*, October 1984, p. 42.

11 G. Paquet, "The New Telecommunications: A Socio-cultural Perspective," working paper, Faculty of Administration, University of Ottawa, Fall 1987, p. 3.

12 D. Godfrey and D. Parkhill, *Gutenberg Two*, 2nd ed. (Toronto: Press Porcepic Ltd., 1980).
13 Alvin Toffler, *The Third Wave, op. cit.*, pp. 211-216; and John Naisbitt, *Megatrends* (New York: Warner Books, 1982), p 261.
14 G. Ainsworth-Land, "The Future of Education," *The Journal of Creative Behavior*, Vol. 13, No., 2. (1979), p. 82.
15 John Naisbitt, *op. cit.*, p. 17.
16 D. Godfrey and D. Parkhill, *op. cit.*, p. 159.
17 G. Ainsworth-Land, *op. cit.*, p. 107.
18 F. Ogden, "Canada at 120: Future Shocks," *Maclean's*, 6 July 1987, p. 44.
19 Alvin Toffler, "Artificial Intelligence," *op. cit.*, p. 42; and D. Godfrey and D. Parkhill, *op. cit.*, p. 190.
20 Cf. W. Boyer, "Management of Macrotransition," *Technology Digest*, 2nd quarter, 1986, pp.12-15.
21 Alvin Toffler, *The Third Wave, op. cit.*, pp. 424-428.
22 W. Boyer, *op. cit.*, p. 15.
23 G. Paquet, *op. cit.*, p. 19.
24 A. Cordell, *The Uneasy Eighties: The Transition to an Information Society: Summary of Background Study 53* (Ottawa: Science Council of Canada, Supply and Services Canada, 1985), p. 9.
25 *Ibid.*, p.10.
26 *Our Canada or Theirs?* (Ottawa: Canadian Labour Congress, 1988).
27 D. Brandt, *Is That All There Is?* (New York: Poseidon Press, 1984), p. 111.

Part 2: Citizenship, Schools and Teaching

The Charter and the Teaching of Human Rights and Citizenship

Edwin Webking
*Department of Political Science,
University of Lethbridge*

AS A TEACHER and educator for nearly a quarter of a century, I have become aware that the kinds of attitudes we can expect of adults in the future are determined by a combination of educational events in the present. These events are included in the formal curriculum as well as the informal curriculum. Thus, while the person is being educated by formally prescribed curriculum determined by a department of education and administered by the local school district and classroom teacher, there is also a cognitive development that occurs independently of specific educational instruction. This is the informal curriculum, which is made up of experiences, observations, impressions, observed behaviour and specific occurrences. This transcendental or informal curriculum, together with the formal curriculum, forms the educational process through which we are educating children and youth who will, by their actions and deeds as adult citizens in the last tenth of this century, determine the shape of law, the administration of justice and the social and political institutions.

It is difficult to take a long-range view, but we must, for whether we realize it or not, we are creating our own future through the kind of education now being provided to our young people. A new course here or a new extra-curricular project there will not even approximate the degree of understand-

> *L'auteur s'intéresse à la démarche d'apprentissage et à la conception du rôle particulier de l'éducation dans une société démocratique; selon lui, l'éducation doit promouvoir les valeurs, les connaissances et les aptitudes qu'il faut avoir dans une telle société. M. Webking définit le « civisme » comme le terme générique englobant la liberté, l'égalité, la justice et la souveraineté d'un peuple. Il s'attarde aux problèmes et aux échecs suivants : comment les citoyens deviennent des objets du pouvoir, pourquoi la théorie démocratique ne correspond pas en pratique à l'enseignement, pourquoi le matériel didactique est inadéquat et ce qui a amené l'école à n'accorder qu'une attention secondaire au civisme. M. Webking croit que l'instruction civique doit être un programme d'ensemble qui serve à contrecarrer l'inertie caractéristique du système politique, inertie qui empêche les citoyens d'atteindre l'idéal : la démocratie.*

ing needed for citizenship education unless there is also equally strong attention paid to the political socialization process. While developing courses, resource materials and learning modules, we must be concerned with the unplanned outcome of actions and practices that are encompassed by the socialization process and make up the informal curriculum. The formal curriculum constraints are quite straightforward and consist of the curricula guides laid out by the respective educational bureaucracies all across the country. These include, for example, hours of instruction, course content, recommended or prescribed textbooks, certification of teachers, funding, departmental exams, etc.

The informal curriculum encompasses a more subjective, but perhaps is an even more important aspect of the educational process. This is the transcendent aspect, which includes the processes, the atmosphere or ambiance, attitudes, commitments; in other words, the social and political context in which schooling takes place. There is some overlap between the formal and informal. For example, the imposition of departmental exams (formal curriculum) may cause the teaching process to become directed toward ensuring that students pass the departmentals. This may mean that spontaneity in the classroom is sacrificed, or that the curriculum is reshaped to meet exam objectives at the expense of the intended or designed curriculum objectives. In conversations with both teachers and school district administrators, it has been suggested that student performance on these departmental exams may influence teacher evaluations.

In general, education in a democracy has a special function: to promote the values, the knowledge and the participatory skills necessary for maintaining and improving the politics of the democratic community. At the same time, it must strive to enhance and strengthen the values of freedom, equality, justice and popular sovereignty. In short, we are talking about the concept of "civism":

> *In English, the word civism refers generally to the "citizen principle" as envisioned in the ancient Greek and Roman republics, especially the tradition of self-sacrifice for the public good. It came ..., by extension, to mean the principles of good citizenship. Civism is a useful single shorthand term for the longer phrase "principles of good citizenship" .... It connotes the need for building a sense of cohesion that will bind citizens together into a viable political community."* [1]

Webster's New International Dictionary defines civism as "the principle of civil government" or "devotion, adherence, or conformity, to civic principles or to the duties and rights belonging to civic government."

Political scientists and educators have for some time been concerned about the extent to which we ignore this most important educational aspect of our democratic society. Citizenship education should be the foundation of public education because it is essential for the achievement and maintenance of the democratic ideal which we claim as the philosophical basis for our way of life. Despite this professed belief in the democratic ideal, our approach to citizenship education is casual and almost indifferent. We spend far more time training our students and citizens to be computer programmers, beauticians, dieticians, technologists, and in perfecting other occupational pursuits, than we do in preparing them to perform

The Charter and the Teaching of Human Rights and Citizenship

as responsible citizens. Citizenship responsibilities and educating people about these, surely, is as important as vocational training or education in life skills. That education in a democracy needed to include more than the basics was noted by a team of educational researchers when they wrote:

> ...it is insufficient for citizens in a society to know how to read and write, to perform mathematical operations and to understand physical facts. They should also be capable of understanding social realities and must hold attitudes toward each other and toward social and political institutions which allow society to function. To phrase it in another way, citizens should be capable of exercising the fundamental freedoms which are guaranteed to them, willing to grant these rights to others, and prepared to cope with future social and political events whose character cannot be predicted.[2]

It is for this reason that civism education, or education for citizenship, is so fundamentally important to any society. The quality and nature of this type of education has a direct bearing on the quality and extent of political participation and the valuing of human rights in a society.[3]

Another team of researchers some years later noted:
> Civic education is a topic of concern to a variety of members of society. The political socialization process, as it creates and influences these orientations at both the adult and pre-adult level is important for predicting the future course of citizen political action and opinion.[4]

Although this process is carried out in many different ways, both formal and informal, probably one of the most important institutions formally involved is the school. The importance of civic education and the role of the school in this function was recognized as far back as Plato and Aristotle, who both supported the notion of a common public education. Despite the importance attributed to schools in the civic education process, it is not clear they are meeting or fulfilling these expectations. Edgar Friedenberg has written a scathing indictment of Canadian society for its lack of adherence to the principles of the democratic ideals embodied in the concept of "civisim." Friedenberg not only faults the schools but the political, economic and social order for the cultivation and perpetuation of a numbing docility that results in a chronic deference to authority when he notes that "Canadian Society is deficient not in respect for law but in respect for liberty."[5]

A currently used high school social studies textbook would seem to support Friedenberg's assertion. In a section entitled "The Individual and Politics" the following is found:

> Confronted by important and articulate leaders who are charged with the responsibility of creating public policy, individuals often feel like shrugging their shoulders and saying: "What can I as a concerned citizen do to make things better?" The honest answer is that most people can do very little alone. Unless you are very rich, very powerful or very dedicated, it is unlikely that you can change anything by yourself.
>
> However, . . . the individual has many rights and responsi-

bilities. The first responsibility is . . . to obey the law of the land.[6]

What is the informal, yet nevertheless real message of something like this?

Erich Fromm was concerned about this tendency in our mass society to denigrate the ability of the individual to function within the framework of the ideal of the democratic citizen when he wrote his book Escape From Freedom in 1941. Fromm observed:

One kind of smokescreen is the assertion that the problems are too complicated for the average individual to grasp . . . to let them appear to be so enormously complicated that only a 'specialist' can understand them . . . tends to discourage people from trusting their own capacity to think about those problems that really matter. The individual feels helplessly caught in a chaotic mass of data and with pathetic patience waits until the specialists have found out what to do and where to go.[7]

A recent example of this tendency to denigrate the ability of the so-called non-expert is the reaction by some to the document entitled Ethical Reflections on the Economic Crisis from the Episcopal Commission for Social Affairs, Canadian Conference of Catholic Bishops, issued in January of 1985. One person observed:

So while making asses of themselves in areas they know nothing about, the senior clergy neglect and ignore responsibilities indisputably conferred upon them. Instead of preaching the faith, the preach half-baked Marxian economics.[8]

Each of us can probably recall dozens of other examples that tend to show how the intelligence of the average citizen is denigrated daily. The upshot of this is that people are discouraged from trusting their own ability to think about any problem of real significance. The individual is led to believe that only a specialist can sort out the data and explain it to him or her and can then tell him or her what to do. The consequence of this syndrome, which stresses the hopeless complexity of all things and the need of an expert to interpret it for us, is twofold. First, it encourages skepticism and cynicism towards everything that is said or printed while, encouraging the development of a deference to almost anything that a person is told by anyone with any semblance of authority.

This, unfortunately, has come to be very typical of the contemporary individual in our society and the effect is to discourage each from doing his or her own thinking and decision-making. We have become subject to a new kind of authority, one that is to some extent self-imposed, yet no less dangerous to the ideal of democracy than authority that is overtly imposed from without. "The conventional citizenship virtues - the product of political socialization in North America, including high school civics courses - are essentially passive: what mainly matters is loyalty, obeying the law and voting."[9]

Although the problem, or challenge, can be identified, the remedy is not so easily applied. We do know that passivity and acquiescence are not determined by biology - there is no gene for political apathy. People learn to be politically passive from discovering that political change is difficult to achieve and sometimes costly to attempt. People learn that there are those

The Charter and the Teaching of Human Rights and Citizenship

who stand ready to block any efforts to secure gains when these go beyond simple voting or other passive forms of participation. Citizens learn to be ignorant and misinformed. As a result, people become uninterested in politics, inexpert in public affairs and preoccupied with the pursuit of private interests. Rather than shaping the political system, the citizen is moulded by the system. Political passivity is the citizen's response to the non-participatory manner in which the system is operated.[10]

If passivity and acquiescence are learned, then activism and participation can also be learned, through an effective civics education program. The prime purpose and highest priority for education in a democracy is to empower the people to exercise their rights and to cope with the responsibilities of a genuinely democratic citizenship. This need not be the sole responsibility of the formal education system, but the school, nevertheless, is a proper place to begin.[11]

There is a serious discrepancy between what is professed and what is practised in our schools. Many Canadian schools espouse the concepts of democracy, but too many are operated as autocratic communities where students have little or no voice in decisions that affect them. On the one hand, the contrast between the "hidden curriculum" of the schools, which is sensed through teacher and administration behaviour and attitudes and the subsequent methods by which school affairs are conducted, and the democratic concepts and ideals taught in the social studies curriculum on the other, does not go unnoticed by the students. For example, although the female student may be attending classes where the notion of equality of the sexes is taught, she notices that men far outnumber women in administrative positions within the school and the school system. Or a given practice (for example, a school policy limiting the discussion of controversial issues) may have a series of desired outcomes, such as less conflict in the classroom, but also unintended ones (a belief by students that freedom to express one's opinion is not a universal or important principle). Thus, the organization of the schools, together with the formal curriculum in civics and government, combine to create a situation where democratic theory has been so divorced from practice that students are skeptical of both and are unable to develop an understanding or appreciation of the skills necessary for meaningful participation in the practical life of the democratic society.

There are also shortcomings with the textbook curriculum materials that deal with civics and government. Much of this material conveys a naive and unrealistic image of political life that confuses the ideals of democracy and the realities of politics. It fails to convey sufficient knowledge about political behaviour and processes and ignores or poorly treats such traditionally important political concepts as responsibility, freedom, sovereignty, consensus, authority, class, compromise, rights and power. The same is true for some newer concepts such as roles, socialization, culture, system, decision-making, etc.[12] The curriculum material is deficient in developing within students a capacity to think about political phenomena in conceptually sophisticated ways, or to acquaint them with the process of social science scientific inquiry, or to provide them with a capacity to analyze political decision and values. And finally, the material fails to develop within students an understanding of the capacities and skills needed to participate effectively and democratically in politics. We seem to be a long way from the

principle endorsed by one educator that states:
> *Educators agree that the overarching goal of education is to develop informed thinking citizens capable of participating in both domestic and world affairs. The development of such citizens depends not only upon education for citizenship but also upon other essentials of education shared by all subjects.*[13]

Although being deeply concerned about the formal education of the individual, we have, somehow, excluded from that concern the importance of the development of citizens. Citizenship preparation has come to be viewed as a peripheral aspect of curriculum development rather than as an integral part that transcends the education process. Civics education should focus on the meaning of citizenship as well as the specific roles public citizens (as distinct from private persons) are not expected to perform in the social and political life of the democracy. It is not clear that this is being done. There is much moralizing about democracy and human rights, but less concern about the person-as-citizen and his or her preparation for the responsibilities of being a citizen in a democracy.

In order to correct this, the essential ideas and values of democratic citizenship should become the core of knowledge, thinking, and participation that constitute the curriculum design for the educated person. The emphasis should be on instilling rather than imposing. It is not being suggested that we develop long lists of goals and purposes, or behavioural objectives, or subject competencies, learning modules, or any of the other typical accessories of the education profession. All that we need to do is to look seriously at the fundamental, democratic ideals and values upon which our political order is said to be built. These should become the core of sustained and specific study. In turn, this study should constitute realistic, scholarly knowledge and critical analysis which should be a part of the education process from kindergarten through high school, college and into what are now called "lifelong-learning" education programs. There may not be agreement as to what these ideals and values are, but it is more likely the disputes will be over implementation rather than the actual ideals. What is suggested, to paraphrase Ernest Becker, is education for the ideals of society as it might be, rather than education for society as it is.[14]

It is no accident that the term civic learning is used. The term encompasses the several meanings that the word "learning" has come to suggest over the years.
> *Learning in this sense is a corpus of knowledge and scholarship that informs and challenges the highest reaches of the intellectual moral, and creative talents of humankind. Thus a revival of civic learning must be based upon the major disciplines of knowledge and research.*[15]

Learning also includes the way in which people develop knowledge, values, and skills at all of the different phases of development in a lifetime. Civic learning encompasses the skills and experiences that relate to the political process and the ideals or mores that form the basis of the system. In summary:
> *Civic learning embraces the fundamental values of the political community, a realistic and scholarly knowledge of the working*

The Charter and the Teaching of Human Rights and Citizenship

of political institutions and processor, and the skills of political behavior required for effective participation in a democracy.[16]

Civic education is education about the political system and should include more than the descriptive accounts of how legislation is passed in the House of Commons. The goal of civic education in Canada should include more than what might be called the "picture postcard" approach that reduces the political process to a simple, sanitized description of structures and institutions. The goal should be to deal with people, beginning at the student level in schools, in such a manner so as to motivate them and to prepare them to perform as informed, responsible, committed and effective members of a political system based on the ideals of democracy which itself embraces the primacy of human rights.

If a citizenship education program in the schools is to be truly effective, it cannot be limited only to curriculum or subject matter content. If the program is to be a comprehensive learning program it will encompass the whole school system - organization, administration, governance, its "hidden curriculum," and its relationship to all the other agencies concerned with civic education. The formal curriculum as well as the informal curriculum must be structured so as to instil the value of democracy and human rights rather than imposing these upon the students. A civic education program should not only be committed to imparting the best scholarly knowledge, but, also it ought to exemplify the very same democratic values it professes by functioning throughout the whole system in a way that will encourage students to learn and acquire the skills of political participation. Many teachers will need special preparation for these new roles which will help them to utilize not only available materials, which are now not often used, but also possibilities for meaningful interaction among students and between student and teacher. The practice of patriotic rituals and the imparting of factual material will need to be supplemented by more dynamic discussion.

It is not being suggested that the schools alone can undertake the process of citizenship education in a society influenced by mass media, peer culture, powerful single issue interest groups, the power of advertising and wealth, and deference to authority. "The recognition of the interdependence of these systems of socialization is critical to our understanding of the process."[17] Nevertheless, schools by definition have several roles that cannot be performed as well by other agencies or institutions.

The first is to provide a continuing study of and commitment to the values of democracy claimed by the society. The values are asserted and debated regularly and so casually that it is doubted most people give them a second thought, let alone question them. These values are normative concepts, long debated and disputed, and include such things as justice, equality, freedom, diversity, due process, individualism, public welfare, community and human rights.[18] However these values might be stated or ordered, they are the components of democracy and require nothing less than a life time of consideration if they are to be more than debased currency in the market-place of patriotism. These values should be confronted and debated regularly in the classroom in a manner that is appropriate to the age and ability of the students.

A second role for the schools in a civic/citizenship education program is the transmission of knowledge and the training of students in the most rigorous, critical, analytical and realistic methods available to scholarship. Schools should be the best instruments for making the efforts of general scholarship relevant to the civic and political matters and then accessible by the younger generation. History, the social and behavioural sciences, languages, literature, philosophy and other humanities should be studied not simply as separate, peripheral subject areas, but as topics that document and speculate about the human quest and concern for the ideals and truth that are the foundations of democracy and should form the basis for a civics program.

A third role for the schools is to instruct the students in the skills of political participation. These should be learned through the involvement of students in the public affairs of the community as well as the school itself. This ought to include more than just voting in school elections, which for many has become a meaningless obligation. Students should learn the skills of research, writing, speaking, conducting meetings, negotiating, leadership and decision-making. Freedom is meaningless if it cannot be exercised. Freedom from external authority is hollow if we are prisoners of our own powerlessness.[19] The idea of participation is central to the whole concept of democracy and it should be debated, studied and practised by students. If these three roles are combined in a civics/citizenship education program in the schools, we then will be well on the way to resolving the concerns many have about both the quantity and the quality of the participation by the citizen in the democratic political process.

The effort will not be easy for we have to overcome decades of inertia that has gradually crept into the political process and have crippled the citizen's ability to fulfil the promise and the ideal of democracy. In the process, the individual has become a political automaton performing his or her citizenship duties in a non-thinking and non-critical manner and doing so under the illusion of being an independent and self-willed individual. The inertia that has overtaken the political process and prevents us from realizing the ideals associated with democracy is also evident in the educational process, which seems less and less capable of creating independent and fully enlightened individuals. Instead, one could make the claim that education has become ". . . a mass technique for brainwashing the child into automatic obedience to social conventions."[20] This aspect of the educational process is merely a reflection of what occurs in our contemporary society where we have also perverted the concept of democracy.

Democracy has become equated with a particular commercial-industrial process in which the end is the facilitation of business and commercial transactions and people become the means for achieving this. We have, in effect, perverted the concept of democracy so that equality is defined as equal rights to consumer goods and the unfettered pursuit of self-interest. This focus on individual behaviour or "rugged individualism" is most often associated with the moralizing slogans of those who promote the more bizarre notions of free enterprise, most of which are detrimental to the sense of community which is basic to a civism program designed to program the ideals of democracy.

We cannot hope to reform our present civics program until and unless we reconsider our current approach to the concept of democracy. Because of the cause and effect relationship that links civics education and the ideal of democracy, it is critical that we have the appropriate definition. Ernest Becker asserted that we do not have a proper definition when he wrote:

> We have made a wholly false definition of democracy as the freedom to buy and sell goods and to perpetuate the ideology of commerece. We understand democracy as just another ideology. Instead, we should have seen that democracy is an ideal. As an ideology, democracy differed little from Stalinism - it treated the individual as a means and not as an end. As an ideal, democracy would treat the individual as an end ... The word "democracy" simply cannot stand for any social system which treats individuals as means.[21]

Becker's admonition implies that we have to abandon the prevalent, false concept which defines democracy as a commercial ideology and return to the original definition of democracy which embraced the idea of the maximum realization of individual capacities.

Not only is democracy a system and process it is also a frame of reference, or state of mind. Therefore, one of the more important purposes of education, it would seem, is to develop and nurture this state of mind, no matter how dear the effort or the cost. The promise, the hope, and the basic elements inherent in undertaking this endeavour was stated by Alexander Meiklejohn, who wrote:

> Together free speech and democratically distributed liberal learning would provide the country with a sort of grand interative process - replacing the invisible hand either left or right with the human mind - in which everyone participates to attack and solve national and international problems. Give a person, any person a little coaching, access to books and data, and time to think and eventually he or she will be able to tackle with other citizens whatever social or political questions need to be addressed. A democracy only works if its people are educated and education only works if the expression of ideas is absoutely unrestrained.[22]

The alternative to not making the attempt to reassert the quest for the realization of the democratic ideal through a revived civisim is too frightening to contemplate.

James Thurber tells the story of an incorrigible young moth, who, in adolescent revolt, refused to fly around ordinary street lamps. Despite parental scolding, he persisted in what became a lifelong crusade to reach a particularly enticing star. While brothers and sisters burned their lives away one by one, dashing against scorchingly hot light bulbs nearby, he lived to a ripe old age, endlessly reaching for the unreachable star hundreds of light years away. Like Thurber's intrepid moth, we have to continuously strive to reach that goal of realizing the democratic ideal.

---

1 R. Freeman Butts, *The Revival of Civic Learning*, a publication of the Phi Delta Kappa Education Foundation, 1980, p. 10.

Edwin Webking

2 Judith V. Torney, A.N. Oppenheim, and Russell F. Farnen, *Civic Education in Ten Countries* (New York: John Wiley, 1975), p. 23.

3 Gabriel A. Almond and Sydney Verba, *The Civic Culture* (Boston: Little, Brown and Co., 1967).

4 Judith V. Torney *et al.*, *op. cit.*, p.330.

5 Edgar S. Friedenberg, *Deference to Authority* (White Plains, N.Y.: M.E. Sharpe, Inc., 1980), p. 54.

6 Daniel J. McDevitt, Angus L. Scully, and Carl F. Smith, *Canada Today* (Scarborough, Ont.: Prentice-Hall, 1979), p. 211.

7. Erich Fromm, *Escape from Freedom* (New York: Avon Books, 1941), pp.275-276.

8 *Alberta Report*, 17 January 1983.

9 Christian Bay, "Self Respect as a Human Right," *Human Rights Quarterly*, Vol. 4, No. 1 (Spring 1982), p. 71.

10 John Gaventa, *Power and Powerlessness: Quiescence and Rebellion in an Appalachian Valley* (Urbana: University of Illinois Press, 1980).

11 Judith V. Torney, *et al.*, *op. cit.*, p.322.

12 Patrick Babin and Robert Knoop, *Bias in Textbooks Regarding the Aged, Labour Unions and Political Minorities* (Toronto: Ontario Ministry of Education, 1975).

13 R. Freeman Butts, *op. cit.*, p. 84.

14 Ernest Becker, *Beyond Alienation — A Philosophy of Education for the Crisis of Democracy* (New York: George Braziller, 1967), p. 18.

15 R. Freeman Butts, *op. cit.*, p. 121.

16 *Ibid.*, p. 122.

17 Judith V. Torney, *et al.*, *op. cit.*, p. 336.

18 R. Freeman Butts, *op. cit.*, pp. 124-130.

19 Erich Fromm, *op. cit.*, pp. 266-281.

20 Ernest Becker, *The Structure of Evil: An Essay on the Unification of the Science of Man* (New York: George Braziller, 1968), p. 291.

21 *Ibid.*

22 Howard Schneider, "Alexander Meiklejohn: Teacher of Freedom," *Human Rights Quarterly*, Vol. 4, No. 2 (Spring 1982), pp. 305-306.

The Charter of Rights and Freedoms and Legal Literacy

Michael E. Manley-Casimir, Wanda M. Cassidy, and Suzanne de Castell
Faculty of Education,
Simon Fraser University, Burnaby

OVER THE PAST fifteen years the need for Canadians to know about the law has increased.[1] Law is now considered, proverbially, too important to be left to lawyers. The reach of the law is both pervasive and extensive; it regulates almost everything in life - birth, schooling, relationships, employment, movement and even death. Kindred comments that law
> *operates at moments at the most exalted level of state, at the same time it affects the most humdrum aspects of individual life.... In fact, law is the major overt and organised means of regulating social life.*[2]

The recent patriation of the constitution from Britain and the adoption of the Charter of Rights and Freedoms has placed the rights and freedoms afforded Canadians in the public eye. But "legal rights are meaningless unless they are known and can be exercised... and our legal system is premised upon an informed public."[3] Understanding law is a prerequisite to effective citizenship. Law is the "cornerstone of society"[4] reflecting its values,[5] giving it structure and order[6], and offering a mechanism for resolving its disputes.[7] "Canada is founded upon principles that recognize...the rule of law." This rule of law stands in oposition to the "changing whims of policy" and applies to all members of the community; it is "the legitimate base and anchor of the society by which conduct may be

Les auteurs de cet article croient que les bons citoyens doivent d'abord posséder des connaissances de base en droit. Pour acquérir ces connaissances, ils doivent connaître et comprendre les caractères propres à la tradition, aux institutions et aux coutumes socio-juridiques du Canada. Les auteurs décrivent brièvement certains modèles de valeurs des États-Unis et du Canada (le respect de l'autorité et les droits de la personne), ils présentent une définition pratique des connaissances de base en droit et discutent de ses conséquences sur l'instruction civique.

judged, affairs regulated, rights and obligations performed..."[8]

In a multicultural society it is particularly important that all citizens have access to knowledge about how Canadian society works. A recent study reports that many new Canadians do not know that courts are open to the public or understand the difference between civil and criminal law. Many expressed fear about the justice system.[9]

"A principal duty of citizens in a democratic society is participation in the legal system."[10] If Canadians are going to be informed citizens, to develop the capacity to have an impact on law-making and become involved in changing and improving society, then knowledge of the law and its processes is essential.

> *Knowledge of the institutions that control the society is a prerequisite to intelligent democratic action. Since it is the law that organises and supports these institutions, legal education is the obvious way...to learn of them. In addition, it is important...to know not only...civic responsibilities, but also...freedom of action within the Canadian system of government. The measure of good citizenship is not inculcated conformity, but a healthy respect for the rights of others as well as one's own and an allegiance to orderly process, even in diversity.*[11]

The argument in this paper, then, flows from these concerns. It is, in short, that the development of legal literacy is prerequisite to effective citizenship for Canadian citizens. In turn, legal literacy is a contextual notion requiring knowledge and understanding of the distinctive features of the Canadian socio-legal tradition, institutions and practices. Accordingly, this paper proceeds by sketching in broad brush strokes the distinctive features of the legal and constitutional context, then moves to a working definition of legal literacy and thence to a discussion of the implications for citizenship education.

Changing Legal and Constitutional Context

The idea of a person being "literate" is grounded in the social, cultural and political context within which that person is to function. Literacy is essentially a contextual notion. The addition of "legal" to "literacy" thus focuses our attention directly on the legal properties of the context in which literacy is to be developed, acquired and used. So, in Canada, "legal literacy" takes on the distinctive character of Canadian legal and constitutional traditions. One approach to characterizing the distinctiveness of the Canadian legal and constitutional traditions is to contrast, in broad brush strokes, the differences between the U.S. and Canadian political and historical experiences, the role of law in the two countries, the attitudes of the public towards the law, and at the same time to note the changes that are taking place in the structure of Canadian law and legal institutions.

Value Patterns in Canada and the United States:
A Contrast in Pre-Charter Terms*

Seymour Martin Lipset's 1968 analysis *Revolution and Counterrevo-*

---

* A major portion of the ensuing discussion first appeared in the *Canadian School Executive*, November 1982, pp. 18-21.

lution: Change and Persistence in Social Structures[12] provides a useful contrast of the dominant value-orientations of Canada and the United States. Comparing Canada and the United States, Lipset observes that commentators and social analysts classify the United States as more achievement-oriented, universalistic, egalitarian and self-oriented than Canada. He goes on to argue that the respective historical experiences and particularly their different political and national origins, religious traditions and frontier experiences help to account for the substantial differences between the values of the United States and Canada.

The United States, conceived in the womb of political and religious dissent, grew with democratic forms and practices of self-government, and was born as a nation in the revolutionary fervour of an avowedly egalitarian social ideal. Canada, by contrast, lay quiescent under imperial rule for a century, endorsed a more elitist society, worshipped in established churches and left the business of government in the hands of those supposedly qualified by birth and training.

As Lipset observes:
> *The success of the Revolutionary ideology, the defeat of the Tories and the emigration of many of them north to Canada or across the ocean to Britain — all served to enhance the strength of the forces favoring egalitarian democratic principles in the new nation and to weaken conservative tendencies. On the other hand, the failure of Canada to have a revolution of its own, the immigration of conservative elements, and the emigration of radical ones — all contributed to making a more conservative and rigidly stratified society.*[13]

Robert Presthus extends this line of analysis by arguing that the evolution of Canadian political culture has insured the persistence of traditional values which, interacting with the unique character of Canadian national development, has created a style of governance that he terms "elite accommodation."[14] This means that
> *...policy-making and political leadership are delegated to elites representing the major subcultural groups in society. They reconcile divisive issues and determine major policies in context, isolated from their various subcultural constituencies.*[15]

One of the noteworthy effects of elite accommodation is that such a style of governance requires "...deferential constituencies who will delegate considerable autonomy to their leaders."[16] Such deference permeates Canadian political and economic life. The net result is a greater acceptance of traditional forms of governance, of authority and civic obligations. This acceptance creates a built-in resistance to change. Indeed, change in Canada is typically ordered and gradual. Incrementalism and traditionalism have characterized the evolution of Canadian political structures and institutions. The development of educational systems also reflect these tendencies.

Conversely, the nature of the revolutionary experience in the United States encouraged experimentation and modernity.[17] As Crevecoeur wrote in his *Letters from an American Farmer*, published in 1782 at the time of the War of Independence, "The American is a new man, who acts upon new principles; he must therefore entertain new ideas, and form new opinions."[18] Central to this 'new American man' is a strong egalitarian ethos that contrasts strongly with the traditional elitism found in Canada. So, concern for equality is a persistent theme in U.S. history and has become particularly evident in what Kurland called "...the egalitarian revolution in judicial doctrine...."[19]

Partly as a function of the frontier experience in which settlers etched their own law, the law in the U.S. is regarded as the bastion of individual redress for violation of rights. Our Canadian experience was basically different because the extension of governmental control over the empty prairies was seen as a necessary act to prevent land hungry settlers from the American west pre-empting land in Canada. Hence the frontier experience was sanctioned and supported by the national government and the claim to the continent was staked not by frontiersmen but by the Canadian Pacific Railroad and the North West Mounted Police, acting as the agents of the duly constituted government. The N.W.M.P. preceded the mass infusion of settlers and effectively established control over the lands in question.

In one sense, therefore, the Canadian experience has been quintessentially legal. Apart from several unsuccessful rebellions, social and political change (or the lack thereof) has occurred under the rubric of legitimate authority. Duly constituted governments and social institutions have initiated and maintained the direction and pace of societal development. In contrast, the United States' experience has either been extra-legal or been characterized by the development of a spontaneous and situationally specific law. Thus, with the frontier settlement occurring ahead of institutionalized law enforcement procedures, a spontaneous "rule of thumb" law emerged.

Legal Traditions, Respect for Authority, and Individual Rights

Although the legal systems in English Canada and the United States have common origin in the English Common Law, their divergence began with the 1776 War of Independence. By throwing off the yoke of imperial rule the youthful United States broke dramatically with European traditions. The American Revolution created both the need and the opportunity to forge new law — law that would reflect the aspirations and ideology of the new nation. Following the Declaration of Independence, the statesmen of the United States framed a written Constitution embodying the principles of the Revolution, defining the form of government and the rights of citizens. Not only does the Constitution entrench basic civil liberties, it also provides the ultimate recourse for infringement of political rights and interests.

The prominence of the Constitution as a vehicle for redressing individual grievances or class action claims is reflected in the crucial role of the U.S. Supreme Court, its judicial function in interpreting the Constitution and its propensity for handing down precedent-setting decisions affecting the entire federal system. Canada, by contrast, lacked such a document until 1982; the historic absence of an entrenched Bill of Rights meant that no tradition of interpreting civil rights in constitutional terms developed in Canada. The British North America Act, for so long the Canadian "Constitution," reflected the extension of British law over imperial dominions but did not entrench basic civil rights in the same way as the Constitution did in the United States. The link to Britain and the English Common Law tradition is much stronger in Canada than in the United States and has had a continuing impact on Canadian jurisprudence.[20]

Respect for Authority

Related to the distinctive historical experiences, charter values, and legal traditions of the two countries is the general question of respect for authority, particularly traditional authority. The fact of the "revolutionary" origin of the United States, the affirmation of an avowedly egalitarian ethic in that revolution and the institutions of government, the commitment of popular sovereignty as the basis of the state together with the experience of frontier expansion seems to explain, at least in part, the greater willingness in the United States to challenge traditional authority, to use litigation to achieve redress of grievance.

Whereas in the United States the dominant emphasis seems to be the preservation of individual freedom in a society of equal citizens, in Canada the dominant emphasis seems to be the preservation of social order in a more elitist and traditional society. There is greater respect in Canada for traditional authority, greater acceptance of elitism, of hierarchical differentiation, of administrative authority. Greater respect for authority in Canada may be due to the historical experience of living under monarchical authority, of accepting a hierarchical social structure and established religion, and of becoming accustomed to the lesser concern for equality noted by Naegele:

To be more specific: there is less emphasis in Canada on equality than there is in the United States. At least this claim is worth disproving. In Canada, there seems to be a greater acceptance of limitation, of hierarchical patterns. There seems to be less optimism, less faith in the future, less willingness to risk capital or reputation. In contrast to America, Canada is a country of greater caution, reserve, and restraint.[21]

Consequently, the socio-legal context of Canadian life has historically been relatively quiescent when contrasted with the United States. Canadians typically have not used litigation as a means of redressing grievances to the extent the courts are used in the United States.

Individual Rights

This difference is particularly evident in the arena of individual rights. The historic tradition of civil rights in Canada is much weaker than in the United States. Until the proclamation of the Constitution Act, there was nothing to prevent Parliament from overriding civil rights if it wished to do so; the constitutional support for civil rights in the United States simply did not exist in Canada. The net effect, however, has been that judicial cases involving civil rights claims in Canada are rare when compared to the United States. Even now, with the Charter of Rights and Freedoms entrenched in the Constitution, individual provincial legislatures may opt out of particular provisions through the "notwithstanding" clause.

Indeed, the whole development of human rights legislation in Canada differs markedly from the U.S. experience in large part due to the fundamental structural differences in the legal traditions of the two countries. Without constitutional entrenchment, the protection of human rights in Canada has depended on the passage of provincial legislation. But it is only since 1962 that all ten provinces and the two territories have enacted anti-discrimination legislation. Canadians, consequently, have not experienced a long-established human rights tradition; furthermore, as Macdonald & Humphrey point out,

> ...there have been fewer remedies available in Canada for the protection of human rights.... Canadian lawyers have perceived the law and their own role as defenders of human rights in ways that differ radically from corresponding professional attitudes in the United States. These attitudes are important not only because of the preponderant role that lawyers play in the life of a nation, including their role in most branches of government, but also because of their role as formers of public opinion.[22]

The Canadian legal tradition has been one of social order and preservation:

> ...lower priority is given to personal freedom and the traditional civil and political rights than to collective rights and the egalitarian economic and social rights, which often come into conflict with individual rights and freedoms.[23]

At root, then, there is a basic difference between Canadians and U.S. citizens in their perception of their respective rights. U.S. citizens are convinced that they are legally entitled to rights and that these rights should not be violated. This attitude is not nearly as potent in Canada. Indeed, Edgar Friedenberg points out that the B.N.A. Act was designed to secure "peace, order, and good government," but the U.S. Constitution was designed to secure "life, liberty, and the pursuit of happiness." Herein lies a basic difference which helps to explain the evolution of contrasting attitudes towards freedom and judicial sanctions. Furthermore, Friedenberg observes, "what is clearly absent from Canadian political consciousness, though salient in the American, is the conviction that the state and its apparatus are the natural enemies of freedom."[24]

Radical Changes in the Constitutional and Legal Context

Law is, of course, one of our social institutions that changes. Often law changes slowly, even imperceptibly; sometimes the law changes dramatically, as happened recently in Canada with the patriation of Canada's constitutional authority and the entrenching of the Charter of Rights and Freedoms. As Smith and Weisstub note in their excellent book *The Western Idea of Law*:

> Cultures have critical moments in history when their values are constitutionally structured according to a legal design. The Magna Carta and the American Constitution are both examples of such an historical birth. These constitutional statements embody the most fundamental values that the society commits itself to at the time. When this is accomplished in law it means that the society undertakes to harness its energies to ensure that these values are protected and that the future of the society is shaped by them. The constitutional

document then serves as a monitor of the society's conduct.[25]
The Canadian *Charter of Rights and Freedoms* represents the culmination of such a process. It is the expression of a constitutional restructuring according to a legal design. It embodies values agreed upon by the constitutional architects and negotiators. Subject to "notwithstanding" provisions, replete with an amending formula, the Charter nevertheless has become the measure of social definition in Canada. Furthermore, the Charter re-affirms traditional rights and values while also enshrining new values: values like freedom of religion and conscience, full gender equality, equal protection and equal benefit of the law, affirmative action, the principle of multiculturalism *inter alia*.

So the Charter has dramatically changed not just the literal provisions of Canada's Constitution, not just the ground of Canadian jurisprudence — both evident and latent — but more importantly, the Charter has radically altered the constitutional context of and for the legally literate person - the Canadian citizen. It is now not enough to be familiar with the British North America Act. The "legally literate" citizen must now know, understand and be able to think critically about the Charter and its potential applications.

While the Charter is the obvious example of fundamental change in the legal institutions of the culture, there are other examples: the Young Offenders Act (1984) is an example of a radically new federal statute that has had and is continuing to have important effects on the treatment of young offenders in Canada. Like the Charter, new statutes — federal and provincial — clearly alter the socio-legal context of the Canadian citizen thereby also altering what it means to be "legally literate" in Canada. In addition, agreements like Meech Lake, if ultimately implemented, reflect on-going modification to the original Charter. The ground of legal literacy is therefore the distinctive socio-legal context of the polity, the culture, the society. Literacy, to reiterate, is intrinsically contextual. So for us to talk seriously about legal literacy in Canada, or about citizenship education, implies not only knowledge, understanding and perspective on the historic role of law in the evolution of Canadian society; it requires also knowledge, understanding and a critical perspective on the new constitutional and emerging legal features of Canada's social context. The problem of citizenship education is one of public legal education.

Public Legal Education

Education refers to the intentional cultivation of the kind of human being conceived by a society to embody the finest and furthest attainments — intellectual, emotional, aesthetic, and moral — the culture has thus far been able to realize. As Plato long ago realized, the health of a state depends upon the education of its citizens. And for such education information is not enough. Facts and even skills barely scratch the surface of the concept. As educational philosopher R.S. Peters put it, education consists in the initiation into forms of knowledge and understanding thought to be of most worth, including the development of abilities and dispositions most highly valued for the fullest realization of human beings. Peters speaks of this process as the development of a "cognitive perspective" requiring both depth of knowledge, and breadth of knowledge. This criterion of cognitive perspective excludes the "jack of all trades" as much as the narrow specialist. Human beings inhabit a world which is at once subjective, social and material, and being educated means being educated in all three aspects of human experience — thus "cognitive perspective" entails breadth of knowledge. Peters describes depth of knowledge thus:

> To be educated also requires some understanding of principles, of the 'reason why' of things....Failure to grasp underlying principles leads to unintelligent rule of thumb application of rules, to the inability to make exceptions on relevant grounds and to bewilderment when confronted with novel situations.[26]

The educated person is described in the same terms by Barrow as having "understanding of principles or the reason why of things...some breadth of understanding and not a narrow specialization".[27] More specifically, Barrow says this person should: (a) have an understanding of his or her own society and of the world community, both from a present-day perspective and with an awareness of major historical developments — the focus here is on general principles as opposed to random facts; (b) be cognizant of the significant role that individuals have played and can play in shaping the world around them; (c) be able to think logically in terms of relationships between ideas and "have the ability to distinguish logically distinct kinds of questions...empirical questions...moral questions...aesthetic questions..."[28]; (d) possess the ability to think (and thus communicate) in terms (and thus language) that are clear and specific.

Knowledge of the law was once considered an essential ingredient in the education of the person.[29] This view is once again being recognized. "Education in law" however, means this notion described above — an understanding of law in breadth and depth, an understanding of law's role and function in society, the ability to think critically, and the cultivation of active citizen participation. Arons characterized the study of law from the standpoint of the liberal arts, as well as general literacy. He writes:

> The last decade has seen a resurgence of interest in legal studies, attempts at the repossession of law by the public, and a broadening of the meaning of law study to re-establish its age-old connections with general education....It is consistent with history that studying the law's relationship to social issues and ethics — the formation of consensus and legitimacy, the resolution of human conflict, and the use of reason to temper the exercise of power — is once again being recognized as central to social life and personal development.[30]

A "legally educated" person, then in this context, should understand that:

1. Law is an integral and pervasive presence in society. Law has a significant role to play in the way society functions. Abraham Lincoln once said that "a nation may be said to consist of its territory, its people and its law."[31] In Canada the rule of law is granted paramountcy through the Constitution Act. Although law is sometimes viewed as the "glue" that holds society together, it is not necessarily a negative or repressive force. Rather, the law can serve a positive role in resolving conflict and balancing competing rights.

2. Law cannot be understood by the Oxford Dictionary definition alone: "a body of rules, whether formally passed as statutes, or customary

law which a state or community recognizes as binding on its members, a code or system of rules." Law is far more than statutes, case law and enforced unwritten customs. People may have different perspectives on what law is depending upon their status in society or their philosophical perspective. For example, a religious person might view law as a reflection of God's commandments for an orderly and peaceful society; someone else might see law as the expression of the wishes of a sovereign or people's attempt to establish justice; a capitalist might conceive of law as a set of procedures to enable and legitimate the accumulation of private profit, wheras a Marxist might view law as an instrument of exploitation and oppression.

3. As a means of dispute resolution law has limitations. Often it is seen as the only way to resolve a problem instead of the vehicle of last resort, following personal encounters, community and family alternatives, peer solutions. Law may bring about a solution but it may not necessarily resolve the problem. A court, for example, may determine that a landlord may not discriminate on the basis of race but this ruling does not eliminate racial conflict in the community nor does it prevent landlords from renting only to Caucasians. The law may be able to resolve an immediate difficulty, but cannot be seen as the solution to all of society's problems.

Indeed, the rule of law itself is frail and subject to many challenges; often the greatest challenge coming from those elected to make and uphold our law. For example, in Quebec in the 1950s this operating principle was challenged by the Premier and Attorney General of the province (Roncarelli v. Duplessis, 1959, SCR 121). The rule of law "partakes of an inner fragility which it shares with human nature"[32]; it is up to people to maintain and support this principle.

4. Law is a "people system." Law is not a static body of rules and principles, inflexible, applied consistently and with rigidity. It is a system formulated, administered, enforced, and altered by people. Problems cannot merely be tapped into a computer listing all Canadian laws in the hope that the "right answers" will emerge. Elected government representatives make the law, judges interpret the law, police officers and administrative bodies enforce the law, citizens are called upon to participate in the legal process as jurors or witnesses and may choose to become involved in efforts to improve and change the law. People make a difference in the development of law and the way it is applied. This involvement requires a public that is willing to become involved and is sufficiently knowledgeable about what to do and possesses the necessary skills to make a significant contribution. The law is "our law," it can change and should reflect society's needs as determined by the people within that society.

5. Law may reflect society's values, but law and morality are not the same. Unlike law, morality cannot be created by fiat. Law may embody many values of a society (e.g., as in concepts of "guilt," "innocence," "intention," "neighbourliness," "duty of care") but whether the values of the majority in society should be entrenched in the law is a matter of dispute. The debate between Hart[33] and Devlin[34] clearly outlines the two positions. Hart postulates that law should concern itself with the protection of citizens rather than reiterating social morality whereas Devlin argues that moral principles need to be in law to ensure their continuance.

These differing perceptions of law's role need to be acknowledged if they are to be understood, as they must be if procedures for democratic, noncoercive, rational negotiation of consensus are to be possible. For while most Canadians would agree with former Minister of Justice, Mark MacGuigan, that law -- le droit -- means "not only law but also right or justice...law (must be) directed towards justice,"[35] justice and law are different words and legal rulings are not always "just" in some people's eyes.

When one talks about being "educated in the law," then, it means having a broader understanding about these and other related aspects of law — not only what law is, but what it is for.[36] This perspective might be labelled "conceptual" or "jurisprudential"; law is studied in terms of its role in society, the expectations of the individual, and from a perspective requiring critical thinking. This perspective on learning about law differs greatly from an approach that emphasizes the acquisition of "facts and details" about law. This approach to teaching/learning law dwells on acquiring information, such as the penalty options under the Young Offenders Act, the terms of a valid contract, trial procedures from arraignment to sentencing; minimum wages under each province's labour law, steps needed to bring about an appeal under the Unemployment Insurance Act, legal obligations of a common-law spouse, change of name stipulations, or the consequences of an estate intestate. A myriad of details about law are learned here; one's knowledge could be tested in a game of Trivial Pursuit.

The "how to do it approach" falls into this category. This approach, unfortunately results in an incomplete and fragmented view of law. Only the pieces are presented, and these pieces are never put together into a whole. Moreover legal knowledge of this sort quickly goes out of date or is forgotten as memory fades. And as Peters pointed out, without a grasp of underlying principles, disjointed items of information, however useful in the short term and for specific purposes, do nothing for one's ability to perceive relevant exceptions or relevant similarities between knowledge when it is of this fragmented kind, or to perceive novel situations with which one may be confronted in the future.

This "literal" or "black letter law" approach to law likely fulfils an immediate need on the part of selected members of the public for legal information, therefore, it can not be construed as "education" nor should it remain the ultimate objective of public legal education programs. The preferred "conceptual" approach does not exclude the latter "literal" approach but rather incorporates it — builds on it to help cultivate in people those broader understandings necessary for intelligent citizenship.

Public legal education programs that work in the school setting should, in particular, make this conceptual orientation their focus. As educational institutions, schools are designed to give all people a common ground of knowledge, understanding, ability and disposition intended not merely to cultivate the mind, but as will lay firm foundations for adulthood as fully participating citizens. The primary aim in this context is "preventative" rather than "curative." In a legal context, all school children should have equal opportunities to know, understand, and critically evaluate the basic concepts, that is, the 'organizing principles', of the law while at the same time they should have the opportunity to examine some specific legal topics that impinge upon their rights and responsibilities as young people.

For, as Peters reminds us,
> *The grasp of principles is inseparable from the acquisition of knowledge of a more mundane sort ... .Critical thought is a rationalistic abstraction without a body of knowledge to be critical about.*[37]

It is important to point out here that this educational perspective to learning about law is not being adopted on a consistent basis in schools across Canada.[38] Curriculum guides in law generally stress factual topics, to be memorized. The Nova Scotia guide to the law elective is one refreshing exception; the intention here is to examine law's functions and uses in society and issues of law and "to know the major principles, standards and distinctions of law" (p. 4, 1978).

School textbooks also emphasize detail about different legal topics while failing to substantially address broader notions about law - placing all bits and pieces together into a conceptual framework. Only one of the seven major textbooks used in the schools adopts a conceptual orientation. It is described by the author as a book about law, a book to explore searching, fundamental questions, to problem solve, to examine judicial decisions — all for the purpose of understanding the world and society.[39] Most other school-based materials, as well, are geared to provide the student and teacher with factual information about such topics as labour law, criminal procedure, family law, torts. This perspective is also predominant in materials produced for the general public.

Teachers cannot, therefore, expect that students will be "educated" in law through reading the materials available or by following admonitions in existing curriculum guides. Instead, teachers must use their own initiative to design curriculum that moves students beyond the limited detailed examination of law to a discussion of these broader notions that require critical thinking.

In the non-school context of the community the "education approach," or understanding those broader notions about law, may not be as important, at least not for each and every program. The constituents differ and the *raison d'être* is not necessarily to provide common educational foundations. It is in the out-of-school public legal educational contexts that differences in need and provision, rather than similarities, are the focus. Specific groups are demanding specialized knowledge about very particular areas and aspects of law. Their needs are often immediate. For example, an unemployed person may need to know how to obtain a review of his unemployment insurance claim; a native woman may need to know how to have her Indian status reinstated. The aim of programs working in these areas will very likely be more "curative" than "preventive," and perhaps more the provision of surrogate legal competence than the development of the client's "legal literacy." To the extent that such programs claim to be educational as well as simply informative, however, the demand is that public legal education programs will do more than simply meet ad hoc and short-term needs.

Literacy viewed in such contexts may have a narrower focus; however, the call for all people to have a broader and deeper "conceptual" understanding of law should not be ignored. This requirement, which constitutes the essential conceptual core of "education," needs to be considered in the formation of goals for public legal education, not perhaps for each and every program, but certainly for the field as a whole. Immediate needs may demand attention first, but the further-reaching interests, both of individuals and of the nation as a whole, must be incorporated into long-term objectives of the field of public legal education.

Defining Legal Literacy:
A Definition in a Conceptual Framework

In a recent paper entitled "Literacy in Three Metaphors," psychologist Sylvia Scribner discusses the multiple meanings of literacy, expressing skepticism over what she calls "the 'one best answer' approach." An alternative strategy, she suggests, is to "disaggregate" various levels and kinds of literacy.

> *If the search for an essence is futile, it might appropriately be replaced by serious attention to varieties of literacy and their place in social and educational programs. In this disentangling process, I would place priority on the need to extricate matters of value and policy from their hidden position in the definitional enterprise, and address them head on.*[40]

This suggestion is one we have used to guide our approach to the central concern of this inquiry: the construction of a definition of "legal literacy."

Etymologically, the word "definition" comes from the Latin *definitio* (de=from+finis=boundary), meaning "to limit" and referring to the presence of boundary conditions. A few remarks are in order at this point on the purpose of definition, forms of definitions possible, and the kinds of boundaries a good definition must set.

Most often, people expect definitions to come packaged in a phrase or a sentence. We provided this kind of definition when we stated that "literacy generally refers to mastery over the processes by means of which culturally significant information is coded." This kind of definition, all too familiar from our school-days, we may call "archival definition." It is the kind of definition found by looking words up in a dictionary. It is simple and short, it is easily memorized and recited. Archival definitions are statements of word-meaning which are intended to be formal, not substantive, and context-independent, so that they can be inserted into any context in which the word defined can be inserted — in this way, a word and its "archival" definition are more or less interchangeable, more or less synonymous.

A second approach to definition consists in a working out of meaning, an explication and elaboration of meaning which isn't just a synonym for the term, but a semantic expansion of it, which tells us more than the defined work itself did. It is this kind of definition which is needed when we seek to do something — to answer questions or solve problems — in relation to a term, as in the present project we seek to do in relation to "legal literacy." For this kind of task, literal "archival" definitions won't take us very far. What we need is a set of boundaries which are conceptual, not literal, and this requires, in turn, the specification of a definitional context.

Recall here the agrument that failures to respond effectively to questions or problems most often stem from a failure to define, or, in Watzlawick's words, to "frame" that question or problem properly. And so it happens that "a phenomenon remains unexplainable as long as the range of observation is not wide enough to include the context in which the phenomenon occurs."[41]

The definition we propose — because we see definition as a "framing" problem — takes the form of a framework. In order to understand the concepts which make up, that is, which define its boundaries, we have discussed in the full report the three contexts in which the concept of "legal literacy" is situated: (1) the context of education; (2) the legal context, and (3) the context of literacy. The Canadian legal context was considered with particular reference to the historic juncture at which we find ourselves, not merely with a new constitution, but, in an important sense, with a constitution for the first time in this country. Reliance on cultural tradition can no longer suffice — if indeed it ever really did so — to acquaint Canadians with the fundamentals of their legal rights and responsibilities. More than at any other time in our history, we have suggested, there needs to be the conscious, intelligent and systematic cultivation of legal literacy for the populace as a whole.

And our efforts to this end require, as we argued when discussing what is entailed by the intention to educate the public, far more than the mere provision of information for the ad hoc management of current legal problems. Education is a formative enterprise, which, in relation to the legal context, calls for active engagement in legal reform just as much as it requires the intentional cultivation of knowledge about and obedience to, the laws as they currently exist.

In the preceding discussion in this inquiry we identified important properties of legal literacy. We established

i) that the phrase "legal competence" implies a constraining, minimalist notion of legal education; it is, in effect, a baseline on which full legal literacy may be built;

ii) that legal literacy is a broader, contextually defined idea, one that involves knowledge, understanding and the development of critical judgement;

iii) that the body of law-related knowledge required to function effectively includes the substance, the process and the resources available to individuals or groups.

With these notions in mind it is possible to create a map — a definitional construct — of the elements comprising legal literacy. The accompanying chart, "A Continuum for Legal Education" maps the boundaries of legal literacy. (See page 96.)

This chart juxtaposes the notions of legal substance, legal process, and legal resources along the horizontal axis conceived as a continuum from *information* to concrete *action*. The stages and properties in the development of full legal literacy are plotted along the vertical axis. Note that in this latter case the progression to full legal literacy starts from "basic legal competence," moves through the acquisition of knowledge, to the development of understanding, thence to the capacity of critical judgement, and full legal literacy. When juxtaposed with the properties of the legal system, this continuum yields a 3 x 3 matrix that implies essential capacities of the "legally literate" person.

So we may say first that becoming fully literate in a legal context is a cumulative process. It builds upon a foundation of basic legal competence

A CONTINUUM FOR LEGAL EDUCATION: THE INTERSECTION OF THEORY AND PRACTICE

	Substance	Process	Resources
Full Legal Literacy / **Critical Judgement**	Comparing the intent of the legal system with its effect in practice (e.g., critically judging the moral rightness of a given law or legal process) and its entitlement to command obedience by the citizen; determining the desirability of preserving, modifying or abandoning a given law or legal process, from the standpoint of one's duties as a citizen.	Acting to promote, in practice, recognition and acceptance of one's view of legal (individual & collective) "best interests." How to use democratic process for legal reform (e.g., voting, lobbying, organized protests, boycotts). How new agencies can be constituted (e.g., citizen's action groups; media watch; environmental protection groups).	Being able to identify and access power-holding individuals and groups (e.g., M.L.A.s, community action groups, consumer-protection agencies, civil liberties associations, etc. for information guidance in decision-making and action aimed at legal reform).
Understanding	Understanding intent of law(s) in terms of principles of justice. (concepts of guilt, innocence, liability, negligence, rights, evidence, proof, as intended purpose and justification for legal domain substantive laws, legal processes, legal institutions, legal roles and legal relations as these affect the citizen).	Understanding the effect of law(s) in practice, in relation to basic principles of justice. Perceiving and being able to explain how and why actual effects of legal system operate differentially across social sub-groups, e.g., race, class, gender divisions. Understanding how law as social institution, is susceptible to same structural weaknesses as other social institutions.	Understanding the purpose of existing legal resources, services, agencies and agents. Understanding the functions and uses of public records; understanding the functions and uses of legal representatives; understanding code of ethics governing legal professionals.
Knowledge	1) Constitutional rights as statement of fundamental principles basic to all substantive laws (e.g., right to council; of free association; right to legal representation). 2) Knowledge that laws exist actualizing these basic principles in relation to the various roles citizen assumes (e.g., consumer; tax; marriage and family; employer-employee; home ownership vs. rental; motor vehicle; wills, criminal law).	Knowledge of legal process in practice as it affects the citizen in contact with agencies and agents of the law, (e.g., what the ordinary person in contact with police needs to know about exercising rights to remain silent, to have legal representation, to refuse police entry to one's property, proper procedures for detention, proper procedures for search and seizure).	Knowledge of resources which enable the citizen to interact with the legal system by means of relevantly skilled and knowledgeable agents and agencies (e.g., when to consult a lawyer, a notary, general or legal library; knowledge of legal services and conditions of access to these public records, e.g., deeds, titles, births, deaths, etc.).

Basic Legal   i n f o r m a t i o n   a c t i o n

Charter of Rights and Freedoms

and enriches this basic competence through the acquisition of knowledge, understanding and critical judgement to full literacy. At the same time it entails familiarity with the substance of the law, legal process and resources, and implies that the legally literate person has more than knowledge and understanding, that the legally literate person has the capacity and motivation to follow thought with action, to move from "theory" to "practice." In brief, then, the working definition of literacy would read as follows:

Full legal literacy goes beyond the development of a basic legal competence and implies the acquisition of knowledge, understanding and critical judgement about the substance of law, legal process and legal resources, enabling and encouraging the use of these capacities in practice.

The chart, "A Continuum for Legal Education" reflects this definition of legal literacy and describes the kinds of properties in each cell of the matrix. The next step in the process of rendering the definition operational is to identify more precisely and in concrete terms examples of the various properties of the contents of each cell.

Application of the Working Definition to Citizenship Education

The further elaboration and specification of the framework definition of "legal literacy" will enable programs and agencies concerned with public legal education and citizenship education to map what they currently do, what they do not do either by intent or oversight, and make decisions about what they want to do. Such elaboration and specification would further enable the development of corresponding items suitable for use in a program assessment evaluation questionnaire. An assessment questionnaire like this would, assuming the correctness of fit of the framework definition, permit programs and agencies to assess the impact of their programming.

This framework is intended to make possible development in three areas (1) curriculum, (2) instruction, and (3) evaluation. Such extrapolation from the framework is beyond the scope of this paper. These three dimensions of educational provision are, however, closely related to one another, such that they need to be developed together. Furthermore, if the results of research into the *retention* of literacy in the general sense applies with equal force to the retention of legal literacy as a specialized form, then citizenship programs, whatever their theoretical virtues and however effective they might appear on the basis of short term evaluations, will *not* be retained. So programs will *not* have significant impact with respect to public legal *education* in the long term unless the kind of legal literacy skills and knowledge they provide correspond with the actual functions and uses of legal literacy for the Canadian citizens in their concrete and particular social contexts. Ascertaining the functions and uses of legal literacy in the actual context of various individuals' and groups' day to day functioning thus appears, on the basis of plausible parallels between legal literacy and linguistic literacy, to be a research *priority*. For, without intending to anticipate the findings of what is clearly an empirical research project, it could well turn out that *extending* the functions and uses of legal literacy for the lay public might rank high on the agenda of public legal education as a whole. Given the tradition in Canada of relative lack of participation in the legal system by "lay" citizenry, it could transpire that for any substantial degree of effective citizenship education, public legal education programs and agencies will need to play a leading role. Indeed, with appropriate federal and provincial funding these agencies are uniquely well placed to carry the flag, so to speak.[42]

---

    1 W. Cassidy, "Teaching Law in the Secondary School Curriculum: The Case for a Concept Approach," unpublished master's thesis, Simon Fraser University, Burnaby, B.C., 1986.

    2 H. Kindred. "Legal Education in Canadian Schools?", *Dalhousie Law Journal* 5:2 (May 1979), p. 538.

    3 J. Finley, "Public Lacking Legal Education," *The National*, 1981.

    4 The Hon. Mr. Justise W. McIntyre, "The Rule of Law in Public Legal Education," in E. Myers (ed.), *Legal Education for Canadian Youth: Proceedings of a Conference*, Regina, University of Saskatchewan College of Law, May 1980 (Ottawa: Canadian Law Information Council, 1981), pp. 1-6.

    5 S.M. Waddams, *Introduction to the Study of Law* (Toronto: Carswell, 1983).

    6 N. Gross, "Law and the Humanities in Elementary and Secondary Schools," article prepared for the American Bar Association Fund for Public Education, A.B.A. Special Committee on Youth Education for Citizenship, 1980.

    7 P. Lader, "The Need for Undergraduate Law Study," *American Bar Association Journal* 59 (1973), pp.266-269.

    8 The Hon Mr. Justice W. McIntyre, *op. cit.*

    9 R. Craig, *Kingsway Legal Literacy Project* (Vancouver: The Law Courts Public Education Program, 1985).

    10 M. MacGuigan, remarks to the closing session of the People's Law Conference, Ottawa, Ontario, May 23, 1983.

    11 H. Kindred, *op. cit.*, p. 538.

    12 S.M. Lipset, *Revolution and Counterrevolution: Change and Persistence in Social Structures* (New York: Basic Books, 1968).

    13 *Ibid.*, p. 51.

    14 R. Presthus, "Evolution and Canadian Political Culture: The Politics of Accommodation," in Richard Preston (ed.), *Perspectives on Revolution and Evolution* (Durham, N.C.: Duke University Press, 1979), p. 103.

    15 *Ibid.*, p. 126.

    16 *Ibid.*, p. 127.

    17 *Ibid.*, p. 105.

    18 J.H. St.J. Crevecoeur, *Letters from an American Farmer* (New York: Doubleday) Reprint of the original edition of 1782, p. 50.

    19 P. B. Kurland, "The Supreme Court, 1963 Term Foreword: Equal in Origin and Equal in Title to the Legislative and Executive Branches of the Government," *Harvard Law Review* 78 (November 1964), p. 144.

    20 B. Laskin, *The British Tradition in Canadian Law* (London: Stevens, 1969), p. 7.

    21 K.D. Naegele, "Canadian Society: Some Reflections." in B.R. Blishen et al., (eds.), *Canadian Society* (Toronto: Macmillan, 1961), p.27.

    22 R. St. J. MacDonald and J.P. Humphrey, *The Practice of Freedom* (Toronto: Butterworths, 1979), p. xv.

    23 *Ibid.*, p. xvii.

    24 E.Z. Friedenberg, *Deference to Authority: The Case of Canada* (White Plains, N.Y.: Sharpe, 1980), p. 17.

    25 Smith and Weisstub, *The Western Idea of Law* (1983), pp. vii-viii.

26 R.S. Peters, "What Is an Educational Process?", in R.S. Peters (ed.), *The Concept of Education* (London: Routledge & Kegan Paul, 1967), p. 6.

27 R. Barrow, *Educational and Curriculum Theory* (Vancouver: Centre for the Study of Curriculum and Instruction, University of British Columbia, 1981), p. 23.

28 *Ibid.*, p. 14.

29 S. Arons and J. Cole, "Importance of the Study of Law and Legal Institutions to General Education," unpublished report to the Ad Hoc Education Committee, University of Massachussets, Amherst, Mass., 1981.

30 *Ibid.*, p. 3.

31 Cited in P. Fitzgerald and K. McShane, *Looking at Law: Canada's Legal System* (Ottawa: Bybooks, 1979), p. 1.

32 Chief Justice J. Deschenes, *The Sword and the Scales* (Toronto: Butterworths, 1979), p. 191.

33 H.L.A. Hart, *Law, Liberty and Morality* (London: Oxford University Press, 1963).

34 P. Devlin, *The Enforcement of Morals* (London: Oxford University Press, 1965).

35 M. MacGuigan, *op. cit.*, p. 18.

36 Cited in L.C. Falkenstein, "Internationalizing Law-related Education," in E. Myers (ed.), *Legal Education for Canadian Youth: Proceedings of a Conference*, held in Regina, University of Saskatchewan College of Law, May 1980 (Ottawa: Canadian Law Information Council, 1981), pp.32-37.

37 R.S. Peters, *op. cit.*, pp. 18-19.

38 H. Kindred, *op. cit.*; W. Cassidy, *op. cit.*; and R.W. Ianni, "Reflections on the State of Public Legal Education in Canada," *Canadian Community Law Journal* 3 (1979), pp. 3-11.

39 P. Fitzgerald, *This Law of Ours* (Englewood Cliffs, N.J.: Prentice-Hall, 1977), preface.

40 Sylvia Scribner, "Literacy in Three Metaphors," *American Journal of Education* 93:1 (1984), pp. 6-21.

41 P. Watzlawick, J.H. Beavin and D.D. Jackson, *Pragmatics of Human Communication: A Study of Interactional Patterns, Anthologies and Paradoxes* (New York: Norton, 1967), p.21.

42 This article is edited and exerpted from a longer research report "Legal Literacy: Towards a Working Definition," commissioned by the Canadian Law Information Council, Toronto, Ontario, 1987. Sections are reprinted here with permission.

Literacy for Citizenship: The Literacy Role of the Secretary of State Department

Brad Munro
National Literacy Secretariat,
Department of the Secretary of State, Ottawa

IN VANDRA MASEMANN'S study we find the following definition of active citizenship:

> ...active citizenship may be defined as a process in which citizens participate in Canadian life at the individual, community or societal level, by acquiring and acting on the knowledge, skills and attitudes (or values) which will enable them to exercise their rights and responsibilities as Canadian citizens.[1]

She states further:

> When citizenship is conceived of in this manner, then the promotion of citizenship and citizenship education, are processes which touch all Canadians in terms of developing the knowledge, skills and attitudes to equip them to realize their full participation and involvement in the affairs of our country.[2]

Obviously, in our highly developed technological society someone who is completely illiterate or functionally illiterate is lacking in certain skills necessary for their full participation in Canadian society. Literacy is a citizenship participation issue. Literacy is a necessary prerequisite for adequate participation in Canadian society - let alone for full participation.

L'auteur rappelle les événements qui ont entrainé la création du nouveau Secrétariat national à l'alphabétisation par le Secrétariat d'État. Puisque l'alphabétisation est essentielle pour être un citoyen actif au Canada, les projets d'alphabétisation du gouvernement sont du ressort du Secrétariat d'État et de sa Direction de l'enregistrement de la citoyenneté. M. Munro se reporte à l'enquête effectuée par la Southam Press en 1987 dont les résultats pour le moins surprenants indiquent que 24 pour cent de la population adulte au pays est totalement ou partiellement analphabète. Afin d'améliorer la situation, le gouvernement accordera de l'argent aux provinces et aux groupes qui s'occupent de l'analphabétisme.

The importance of literacy to full citizenship participation is the reason why the Secretary of State was made lead federal minister for literacy.

Literacy was placed on the national agenda in the Speech from the Throne read in parliament on October 1, 1986. The Governor-General read the following:

> My government will work with the provinces, the private sector, and voluntary organizations to develop measures to ensure that Canadians have access to the _literacy skills_ that are the prerequisites for participation in an advanced economy.

Since the citizenship responsibility rests with the Secretary of State it was natural that he would be charged with developing measures in partnership with the provinces, the private sector and voluntary organizations to make sure that Canadians have the necessary literacy skills to participate fully in Canadian society.

In September 1987 Southam Press published a series on literacy in Canada based on a national survey that they did at a cost of approximately $300,000.[3] The headlines on the articles placed the illiteracy level for Canada at an "astonishing" 24% of the adult population. A shocking figure but not a new statistic.

For many years various literacy advocacy groups (such as the Movement for Canadian Literacy; the Canadian Business Task Force on Literacy, and the Canadian Association for Adult Education) have argued that there are roughly one million adults in Canada who cannot read or write and three to four million adults who are functionally illiterate. These figures were generally determined by using scholarity as a measure. The 1981 census reference data for educational attainment show that, among the adult out-of-school population, about 4.7% or 776,000 Canadians were basic illiterates or lacking in the most elementary skills of reading and writing (which requires the equivalent of an education beyond grade 4). Adult functional literacy, which is having the reading and writing skills needed for effective functioning in the community, is defined as requiring the equivalent of schooling beyond grade 8. Using this definition, then 23% or the 3.7 million Canadians with less than grade 9 are considered to be functional illiterates.

For years people have been skeptical about these statistics. We all know someone who has less than grade 9 education who is a voracious reader and capable of writing difficult prose. We also know of people who have graduated from university and are not capable fo writing a single letter home. (We all have difficulty with some government forms, especially the tax form).

The statistics from the 1986 census are not yet available but I suspect that the picture will be very much the same. The labour force survey shows that in 1985 there were 3.75 million Canadians aged 15 and over or 19.3% of the total adult population with less than grade 9 education. In 1986, there were 3.66 million in the same category (18.5% of the adult population).

The Southam Press survey, using reading assessment tasks to measure literacy performance (based on the U.S. study entitled National Assessment of Educational Progress [NAEP]), showed that 8% of adult

Literacy for Citizenship

Canadians are basic illiterates, and a further 16% are functionally illiterate for a total illiteracy rate of 24% or the equivalent of 4.5 million adult Canadians.[4]

Whichever way one determines it, the total figures come out about the same (although the statistical profiles are slightly different). The figures are somewhat alarming if true.

The federal government has decided that a national effort is required to deal with the problem. On November 22, 1986, soon after being assigned as lead minister, the then Secretary of State, the Honourable David Crombie, held a consultation with the key literacy organizations. The following organizations were represented: World Literacy of Canada, Laubach Literacy of Canada, the Movement for Canadian Literacy, le Regroupement des groupes populaires en alphabetisation, the CLC, and the Business Task Force on Literacy, among others. Written submissions were requested from these key organizations. Those submissions combined with the Cedar Glen Declaration of February 1987, which was drafted by a coalition of the key literacy organizations in Canada, formed the basis for the strategic work developed by a departmental task force on literacy. This departmental task force drafted a discussion paper on the community's submissions. This paper was distributed before the Minister's second consultation with the major literacy organizations on May 8, 1987. This discussion paper also served as the basis on which the Secretary of State went to Cabinet for start-up funds for the federal government's new literacy initiative.

On World Literacy Day, September 8, 1987 the Secretary of State released a statement which outlined the various initiatives which are to give effect to the commitment made in the Throne Speech. In that statement the Minister re-emphasized the partnership approach to be taken with the provinces and with groups in the public and private sector which are working to combat illiteracy.

David Crombie announced the establishment of a National Literacy Secretariat in the Department of the Secretary of State to develop the partnerships with the provinces, volunteer and community groups, labour, and the private sector - as well as to administer the literacy program. He announced that a National Literacy Council will be appointed to advise the government on the major issues in this area. It is expected that this council will be made up of representatives from the key players in literacy. A small amount of developmental money was made available to be provided to major community groups - chiefly to help them develop their infrastructures and networks. For example $50,000 was provided to the Movement for Canadian Literacy to hold a national conference in September 1987, following the international conference on "Literacy in the Industrialized Countries: A Focus on Practice." The National conference was entitled "Literacy in Canada - the Next Decade."

The Minister's announcement also provided moneys for research to enable us to begin to understand more the nature and extent of illiteracy in Canada so that future funds can be accurately assigned to deal with the issue.

Further discussions have been held with several provinces and, before the end of November 1987, every province will have been visited. Joint project proposals have been received from six provinces and a proposal is on its way from one of the territories. The first of these joint projects was announced in Saskatoon during the Post-Secondary Forum (on October 23, 1987). This involves joint funding of the activities of the new Saskatchewan Literacy Council. Other joint federal-provincial projects were announced each week in the fall of 1987.

The last item in the Minister's announcement pertained to the sponsorship in 1988 of a National Symposium on Literacy. This conference brought together the interested parties from governments, the voluntary organizations, labour and the private sector.

One of the things that we expect to give a boost to the literacy issue is the designation of 1990 as International Literacy Year. The National Literacy Secretariat will be co-ordinating the plan of action for Literacy Year.

We believe that literacy is an essential prerequisite for full and active participation in Canadian society. This is why the literacy issue has been placed with the Citizenship Branch of the Secretary of State. Currently we are following the direction set out in the May 8, 1987 discussion paper that was based on the needs and expectations based on the Minister's consultations with representatives of the literacy community in Canada.

We are supporting projects that promote public awareness and national commitment. A good awareness campaign is essential to raise public consciousness of the problem and to encourage greater involvement in finding solutions and reduce the stigma attached to illiteracy. We have been asked by the community to move carefully in this in order not to generate a large demand for literacy training in advance of adequate programming being available. As you know, the majority of non-literate or semi-literate persons tend to conceal this aspect of their life because of the social stigma attached to it. So the community did not want us to encourage them "to come out of the closet" and seek training - only to have them have to "stand in line" for an opening (they would never be seen again and would never seek training again).

Another aspect of our current activities is to provide sustained support to organizations which advocate on behalf of community-based literacy. It is hoped that this will allow for the development of responsive programming.

Another key need expressed by the literacy community was for support for co-ordination, information-sharing and networking. In this respect we will be developing partnerships with provincial governments, the private and labour sectors to develop resource centres that can provide access to information and resources for those involved in literacy across Canada. We will be helping in the development of more Canadian-developed learning materials (print, audio-visual, and computer) specially designed for adult learners. In doing this we will be considering the development of resources for specific target groups, women, natives, and visible minorities in particular.

We will be looking at innovative projects that deal with carefully designed outreach programs with features that are necessary to draw learners to literacy programs (features such as childcare, transportation support systems combined with flexible delivery models).

Finally we are supporting Canadian research on literacy aimed at the needs of literacy practitioners in Canada. For example, we need to know more about the comparative effectiveness of particular teaching techniques and about the practicality of various types of delivery strategies. Of course, it is important in all of this to come to terms more precisely with what illiteracy actually is in order to be able to construct strategies for reducing illiteracy in Canadian society.

---

1 Vandra Masemann, "Citizenship Education in Canada," background paper prepared for the Canadian Education Association's Forum on Citizenship and Citizenship Education in Schools and Communities, "Challenges for the Present and Future," Edmonton, Alberta, November 9-11, 1987, p. 2.

2 *Ibid.*, p.2.

3 The series appeared in Southam papers for one or two weeks beginning 12 September 1987. The series has been republished in book form: *Broken Words: Why Five Million Canadians are Illiterate* (Toronto: Southam Press 1987). Available at a cost of $2 from Literacy, Southam Newspaper Group, Suite 900, 1500 Bloor Street West, Toronto, Ontario M5S 2Y8.

4 *Broken Words*, p. 9.

Ways of Teaching Values: An Outline of Six Values Approaches

Ian Kupchenko
McNally Composite High School, Edmonton
and
Jim Parsons
Department of Secondary Education,
Faculty of Education,
University of Alberta, Edmonton

THERE ARE a variety of ways to teach values in the classroom, some formal and some informal. Some approaches are highly structured; some are not structured at all. Some are based on democratic principles; some are not. In this chapter six different formal approaches are reviewed; each has distinguishing characteristics. For example, each is based on a distinct view of human nature and the nature of person-environment interaction. Each reflects a definite conception of the nature of the process of valuing.

In most cases, approaches embody an agreement by their proponents on the nature and source of values. Also, each seems to imply certain fundamental or ultimate aims. Each approach uses different teaching and

> *Les auteurs de cet article décrivent six façons d'enseigner les valeurs en classe, certaines sont bien définies, d'autres n'ont pas de règles fixes, d'autres encore sont bien structurées et d'autres pas. Dans chaque cas, les auteurs présentent le fondement de la méthode, l'objectif, le modèle d'enseignement, le rôle de l'élève et celui de l'enseignante ou de l'enseignant et les principales caractéristiques du matériel utilisé. Ces méthodes sont les suivantes : 1) l'inculcation, qui tâche d'inculquer aux élèves des valeurs choisies et souhaitables afin que certaines valeurs sociales, politiques, morales ou culturelles en viennent à faire partie d'eux; la société est perçue comme un système dont les buts et les besoins l'emportent sur les buts et les besoins des individus et finissent même par définir les buts et les besoins des personnes; 2) le développement de la moralité; 3) l'analyse; 4) la clarification; 5) l'apprentissage actif; et 6) la méthode affective-rationnelle qui aide les élèves à apprécier un style de vie fondé sur l'attention à leur prochain tout comme à eux-mêmes et à l'adopter.*

learning methods, dictates specific roles which the student and the teacher must adopt, and uses particular characteristic teaching and learning materials.

These six approaches are inculcation, moral development, analysis, clarification, action learning, and emotional-rational. The rationale of the approach will be identified and the nature of the human being will be explained. The process of valuing will be explained. The nature, source, and fundamental or ultimate values which the approach implies will be highlighted. The teaching methods used to achieve the specific purpose to the approach will be identified and explained. An instructional model(s), a system(s) of procedures used by teachers will be delineated. The roles of the student and the teacher will be identified and explained.

Characteristics of the teaching and learning materials will be identified.

Approach No. 1: Inculcation

Rationale and Purpose. The rationale of the values *inculcation* approach is to instil certain desirable and chosen values to students. Regardless of the particular values being instilled, proponents of inculcation see that humans react to their environment. Society, a rule-making superstructure, is seen as more important than each individual. As Superka noted, "extreme advocates of inculcation tend to perceive society as a system whose needs and goals transcend and even define the needs and goals of individuals." [1]

According to Krathwohl [2] the central purpose of inculcation is to socialize students so that certain social, political, moral, or cultural values are interiorized. Students are not encouraged to make free choices, but to act according to pre-specified values.

A secondary purpose of the inculcation approach may involve meeting the individual's needs of insecurity and competence, or the need to dominate. For example, inculcated values may set bounds of behaviour for students. By acting within these set bounds, the student's feelings of insecurity and inadequacy may be decreased. By inculcating students with their values, teachers could meet their need to dominate and might relieve feelings of inadequacy or insecurity.

Valuing and Values. From the point of view taken by the values inculcation approach, valuing is considered to be a process of identification and socialization. An individual, sometimes unconsciously, is inculcated with the standards or norms of another person, group, or society. These values are, one hopes, incorporated into the individual's own value system.

Values, from this perspective, are usually conceived to be standards or rules of behaviour which stem from the society or culture. A wide range of values can and have been transmitted through the socialization / identification process. In the political arena, autocratic values, ranging from absolute state control to individualism have been socialized. In the social sphere, a fundamental commitment to whatever values best maintain and develop the health and stability of society and foster the adjustment of individuals to that society might be central. In the moral realm, standards of behaviour such as honesty or charity can be internalized through the socialization process.

Although values may change, some are considered universal and absolute. The traditional Western churches' concept of values having their source in God would be one example of this orientation. Some social studies educators, such as Oliver and Shaver, have expressed a similar position.

For us the most basic values of the (American) Creed, as they relate to the function of the school in society, are to be treated as more than psychological facts. They describe certain potentially universal characteristics of man, which, at least from our particular cultural frame of reference, make him "human" - such as quest for self-respect, a sense of sympathy and love, a concern for fairness and justice in his dealings with others.[3]

Teaching Methods. Joyce and Weil, and Superka[4] have identified a variety of teaching methods that can be used to inculcate values. Examples include explanation, manipulation, positive and negative reinforcement, and modelling. These methods can be used separately or in combination with one another to inculcate specific values or to modify a behaviour. Perhaps the most common method used for inculcation is explanation. Teachers often simply tell students what they should believe and how they should behave. Explanations or threats are given to promote and justify why certain values or behaviours are appropriate. The teacher may also manipulate the environment or the experiences to which the students are exposed. Often techniques such as role playing or games and simulations are used.

One of the most widely used and, according to Superka, the most effective, methods for inculcation is positive and negative reinforcement. Positive reinforcement includes such actions as a teacher praising a student for behaving in accordance with a particular value. Negative reinforcement includes actions such as the teacher punishing a student for behaving contrary to a certain desirable value. Such reinforcement assumes that when students are punished for infractions of rules and praised for obedience they will take on the values associated with the desired behaviour. It is very difficult, if not impossible, for a teacher to avoid some form of reinforcement. Often merely a gesture, smile, or frown will reinforce certain values. Reinforcement, however, can be applied in a conscious and systematic fashion, as it is in behaviour modification. Behavioural modification requires that the teacher analyze a given situation to determine the goals and purposes of activities and the appropriate methods needed to produce a desired behavioural change. Various techniques are used to achieve desired value outcomes. The most widely used technique involves the use of "tokens." Students are provided with "tokens," such as play money, time off from class, or grade points for doing desirable tasks such as helping other students, remaining quiet in class, or completing an assignment.

Modelling is another effective method of inculcating values in students. Students are given examples of exemplary behaviour and desirable values and encouraged to duplicate the models. Instances of modelling behaviour may be drawn from history, literature, legends, or more directly from examples set by teachers and students. The teacher is a model, in many cases, simply by personifying values like punctuality, enthusiasm for learning, or caring for others. Students often assume modelling roles, setting both positive and negative examples. When a teacher asks a student to read his or her essay to the class, the student is assuming a positive modelling role. The student's work is being singled out as an example to be followed by other students. The praise and recognition the student receives can instill the desire to produce similar essays and may inculcate the values of learning and hard work in other students.

Students can be negative models as well, such as when a teacher asks a poorer student to read his or her essay to the class. The student's work is being singled out as an example not to be followed by other students.

The criticism and embarrassment the student receives instil in other students the desire to or fear to produce better essays and may inculcate the values of learning and hard work.

Instructional Model. A systematic approach to the inculcation of values is possible. Superka, Johnson, and Ahrens[5] developed a rigorous and detailed instructional model for teaching values using the inculcation approach. The authors combined the taxonomy of educational objectives in the affective domain developed by Krathwohl[6] with a system of behaviour modification adapted for Sulzer and Mayer.[7] The resulting synthesis is outlined below.

1. Determine the value to be inculcated—choose the value to be instilled (perhaps in co-operation with students and parents).

2. Identify the level of internalization desired—select the degree of internalization that will be sought:

(a) *Receiving*
  (1) Awareness—learner takes into account that a phenomenon exists.
  (2) Willingness to receive—learner is willing to listen to stimulus.
  (3) Controlled or selected attention—learner selects and responds to favoured stimuli.

(b) *Responding*
  (1) Acquiescence in responding—learner complies with requirements.
  (2) Willingness to respond—learner volunteers to exhibit an expected behaviour.
  (3) Satisfaction in response—learner's reaction is associated with enjoyment.

(c) *Valuing*
  (1) Acceptance of a value—learner's response shows consistent identification with a class or phenomena.
  (2) Preference for a value—learner seeks out a particular value because of a commitment to it.
  (3) Commitment—learner displays conviction or loyalty to a cause.

(d) *Organization*
  (1) Conceptualization of a value—learner begins to relate one value to other values by means of analysis and synthesis.
  (2) Organization of a value system—learner begins to integrate a complex of values into an ordered relationship.

Ways of Teaching Values

(e) *Characterization by a Value or a Value Complex*
  (1) Generalized set—learner orders the world with a consistent and stable frame of reference.
  (2) Characterization—learner formulates a code of conduct and a value system which is completely internalized.

3. Specify the behavioural goal—specify the behaviour and the level of performance required to indicate attainment of the value at the particular level of internalization: this behaviour could be in the form of an overt action (such as working for a political candidate) or a certain response to an item on a value or attitude questionnaire.

4. Select an appropriate method—choose a procedure appropriate to the type of behavioural change desired:
  (a) Increase a behaviour—positive reinforcement, provision of a model, removal of interfering conditions, games and simulation, role playing.
  (b) Teach a new behaviour—shaping, chaining, response differentiation, games and simulation, role playing.
  (c) Maintain a behaviour—one or more of several schedules of intermittent reinforcement.
  (d) Reduce or eliminate undersirable behaviour—withdrawal of reinforcement, punishment, stimulus change.

5. Implement the method
  (a) Determine the baseline by measuring the dependent behaviour (the behaviour that is to be changed) before applying the inculcation method.
  (b) Apply the method and measure and record the change.
  (c) Conduct a probe to determine what factor was responsible for the behavioural change by not applying the behavioural procedures for several days.
  (d) Reapply the behavioural procedures.
  (e) Maintain the behavioural change.

6. Graph and communicate the results—collate the recorded data, graph the data, make inferences concerning internalization of values, and communicate the results to appropriate persons.[8]

Roles of Student and Teacher. The inculcation approach assumes that students will take a passive learning role. Students are to follow the teacher's instructions, answer the questions, and modify their behaviour. They are to act in accordance with pre-specified values. Students rarely, if ever, are allowed to make free value choices or to initiate learning activities.

The teacher's role is to lead and initiate learning experiences, structure and manage classroom activities, and act as questioner and clarifier of student's values. Specific values to be inculcated, however, are not always established by the teacher. Developers of instructional materials using the inculcation approach frequently have made value decisions. Simpson, for example, in his textbook *Becoming Aware of Values: A Resource Guide in the Use of Value Games*[9] outlines the role that the teacher must take.

Ian Kupchenko and Jim Parsons

Value Category	Role of Teacher
Affection	Provide a climate supporting acceptance, trust, emotional security, love, congeniality, friendship, and intimacy.
Respect	Provide an atmosphere in which each individual may achieve identity, a recognized social role, and self-esteem without fear of undeserved deprvation or penalties from others.
Skill	Provide opportunities for awareness and openness and encourage students to find their own truth in every issue without losing sight of their social norms and the significant events of human achievement.
Enlightenment	Provide experiences for awareness and openness and encourage students to find their own truth in every issue without losing sight of their social norms and the significant events of human achievement.
Power	Provide situations in which the student will have opportunities to participate in making important decisions and to exert informal influence according to his/her talents and responsibilities.
Wealth	Provide facilities, materials, and services to promote excellent learning while guiding the student to produce wealth in the form of materials and services to himself/herself.
Well-being	Provide resource and interpersonal relationships which nurture the physical and mental health of each student.
Rectitude	Provide experiences enabling the student to develop a sense of responsibility for his/her own behaviour, consideration for others, and a high sense of integrity.

Characteristic of Materials. Materials using the inculcation approach usually contain a combination of both modeling and reinforcement. Texts usually draw examples of exemplary behaviour and desirable values from sources such as the Bible, literature, legends, or history. Combined with modelling, reinforcement is usually provided within the text of the story or article. Characters who behave in an exemplary fashion are usually rewarded for their actions, thus providing positive reinforcement. Characters who adopt negative behaviours are always punished, thus providing negative reinforcement.

Questions and discussion sessions related to the story or article usually re-emphasize the positive modelling behaviour and give explanations as to why such behaviour should be followed. Activities such as role-playing, games, and simulations are often used as alternative methods of re-emphasizing the positive values and behaviour.

Approach No. 2: The Moral Development Approach

Rationale and Purpose. The rationale of the moral development approach is primarily to stimulate students to advance their powers of moral reasoning through a series of increasingly advanced and complex stages.

Ways of Teaching Values

Kohlberg, perhaps the leading proponent of this approach, sees the purpose of moral development not as the increasing of students' knowledge of cultural values nor as the instilling of an external value in students, but rather as the encouraging of value patterns towards which the students are already tending.[10]

Proponents of the moral development approach see humans as active initiators. An individual cannot fully change the environment, but neither can the environment fully mold the individual. "Genetics structures already inside the person are primarily responsible for the way in which a person internalizes that content, and organizes and transforms it into personally meaningful data."[11]

The foundation for the moral development approach was laid by Piaget[12] and refined and extended by Kohlberg. Within the moral development approach, Kohlberg sees moral reasoning as a developmental process over a period of time. He identifies three levels and six stages of development. The concept of stages of moral development refers to the structure of one's reasoning and implies the following set of characteristics:

1. Stages are "structured wholes", or organized systems of thought. This means individuals are consistent in level of moral judgement.

2. Stages form an invariant sequence. Under all conditions except extreme trauma, movement is always forward, never backward. Individuals never skip stages; movement is always to the next stage up. This is true in all cultures.

3. Stages are "hierarchical integrations". Thinking at a higher stage includes or comprehends within it lower-stage thinking. There is a tendency to function at or prefer the highest stage available.[13]

A main assumption of the moral development approach is that students are attracted to high levels of reasoning. When a student is presented with arguments both for and against a course of action, the level of the argument determines its effect. Although students at higher levels can influence the reasoning of those at lower stages, the reverse is not true. Research findings[14] indicate that students will reject judgements below their own level as inadequate ways of thinking, but will understand and prefer judgements made from the point of view of one level of development higher than their own. The specific purpose of the moral development approach is to create situations in which students are confronted with and interact with instructional materials and other students at a higher stage. The hope is that they will be lifted into that higher stage of "moral development".

Valuing and Values. The moral development approach, in contrast to the other approaches, does not conceptualize a specific process of valuing. It is more concerned with how rather than why value judgements are made, or which judgements should be made. How persons develop values would depend upon their level or stage of moral development. The common valuing activity centres around the process of developing more complex moral reasoning patterns through the series of successive stages.

In examining the moral development approach, Superka[15] was unable to find a specific definition for the term "values." He concludes that proponents of the approach seem less concerned with values per se than with the level of moral reasoning involved in attaining those values. Stages or levels of values are crucial. When one examines a value or moral concept, the value seems to become quantitatively different from stage to stage. For example, in Kohlberg's six-stage interpretation of the "value of human life," persons may hold this value for different moral reasons at each stage.

Kohlberg has often affirmed that justice, fairness, equality, and a sense of human rights are at the core of moral development. The highest stages of reasoning involve the ability and disposition to make value judgements on the basis of universal principles of justice. Justice is defined as those "universal modes of choosing which we wish all men to apply to all situations which represent morally, self-justifying reasons for action."[16]

Teaching Methods. The most characteristic method used to stimulate moral development has been the use of moral dilemmas which are situations in which values conflict, where claims can be made for several choices, and where each choice is made at the price of another. Students are asked to think about how dilemmas should be resolved, to identify the moral issues involved, and to offer reasons justifying their positions.

Although moral dilemmas might be presented through role-playing, skits, or simulations, the technique most often used has been the classroom discussion. The teacher encourages students to comment on and challenge each other's reasoning. The main focus is on the students' reasoning rather than on the particular choice to be made. Kohlberg has identified several conditions that appear to be important in conducting discussions on moral dilemmas in the classroom. They are:

1. Knowledge of the stage of functioning. (Understanding the meaning of the moral judgements made by the child.)
2. Exposing students to reasoning one stage above their own thoughts.
3. Exposing students to problems which pose genuine moral conflicts and disagreement. (Posing problems and contradictions for the student's current moral structure will lead the student to be dissatisfied with his other current level.)
4. Creating an atmosphere of interchange and dialogue in which conflicting moral views are compared in an open manner. (The teacher's task here is to help the student see inconsistencies and inadequacies in his or her way of thinking and find ways to resolve such inconsistencies and inadequacies.)[17]

Some additional methods have been suggested by Frank Simon and Robert Craig.[18] Simon states that the elementary teacher who instructs children at Kohlberg's pre-conventional level should employ motivational activities which appeal to and develop the child's desire for social approval and acceptance. He suggests that children be rewarded (non-materially) for behaviour that indicates assuming responsibility, working well with others, and respecting the rights of others. Punishment is discouraged since it appeals to the lowest stages of development.

Craig urges that students be given as much freedom as possible in making decisions. To enable students to develop a sense of justice and reciprocity, he advocates that students help make decisions about classroom procedures and regulations. Craig emphasizes that students must recognize the distinction between procedural rules and moral rules. Finally, he claims that there must be a general consistency in the administration of school and classroom regulations.

Instructional Model. While working with the Carnagie-Mellon/Harvard Values Education Project, Jones and Galbraith created an instructional model for teaching moral development using moral dilemmas. The following instructional model was adapted by Superka, Johnson, and Ahrens from Jones and Galbraith's work:

1. Confronting a moral dilemma : (a) introduce the dilemma; (b) help students to define the terms used in the dilemma; (c) state the nature of the dilemma.

2. Stating a position on the original or alternative dilemma; (a) help students establish their individual positions on the action; (b) establish the class response to the position on the action (if there is not enough conflict, introduce an alternative dilemma); (c) help students establish the reasons for their individual positions.

3. Testing the reasoning for a position on the moral dilemma; (a) select an appropriate strategy for grouping the students (small groups of students who agree on the action but for different reasons or small groups of students who do not agree on the action); (b) help students examine individual reasons with the group or class; (c) ask probe questions to elicit additional reasoning about the moral problem or a similar one or that focus on a particular issue involved in the dilemma; (d) examine reasons as they relate to the probe questions.

4. Reflecting on the reasoning: (a) ask students to summarize the different reasons they have heard; (b) encourage the students to choose the reason which they feel represents the best response to the moral dilemma; (c) ask students if they believe there is a best answer for this problem; (d) add any additional reasoning which did not occur from student discussions; these should be added not as the "best" reasons but as additional reasons to ponder.[19]

Roles of Student and Teacher. In the model just described, students are to be active learners. They are actively involved in the classroom environment, making decisions and expressing their opinions. Students are required, however, to go beyond the mere sharing of opinions and information. They must reveal thoughts concerning their basic beliefs.

Self-reflection is a prime requisite of the moral development approach. This self-reflection is stimulated by three types of student dialogue: (1) student dialogue with teacher, (2) student dialogue with other students, and (3) student dialogue with self. A student's dialogue with him/herself stimulates reflection upon the student's own thinking process. Reflection leads to a re-evaluation of the student's thinking and, thereby, to the development of higher stages of moral reasoning.

Beyer and Barry examined the teacher's role in moral development dialogues and suggested that the teacher:

1. Establish a supportive, non-judgemental atmosphere. (It is important to recognize the students' right to hold and express views without sanctioning those views as right or justifiable).
2. Seat students so that they can see and hear each other.
3. Listen carefully to what students say.
4. Ask questions which do not threaten students.
5. Encourage student-to-s`tudent interaction.
6. Develop discussion skills in students.

7. Keep the class working constructively by using probe questions, alternative dilemmas, or dilemmas which have been used previously.
8. Plan carefully but remain flexible to cope with substantive diversions.[20]

The teacher's role in the moral development approach is to initiate activities which would develop teacher-student, student-student, and student-self dialogues. This does not imply that the teacher is the centre and controlling force of the classroom. Rather, the teacher enters the classroom with planned activities and encourages dialogues that might lead to greater moral development.

Characteristics of Materials. Materials are usually based on moral issues or dilemmas. A moral dilemma has five general characteristics: 1. It builds upon work in the course. (Dilemmas may be derived from a real-life situation in contemporary society, life experiences of students, or should be as simple as possible, having a central character or primary group or characters. 2. It should be as simple as possible, having a central character or primary group of characters. 3. It should be open-minded. (There should be no single, obvious, or culturally approved right answer). 4. It should involve two or more issues that have moral implications. 5. It should offer a choice of actions and pose the question, "What should the central character do?" (This should help the students to engage in moral reasoning about the conflict presented in the dilemma.)[21]

Dilemmas can be presented in a variety of ways. These ways include written or oral forms, films, recordings, sound-film-strips, or stories and historical documents. Kohlberg has suggested that moral dilemma topics should be centred on the following ten universal moral issues: 1. punishment, 2. property, 3. roles and concerns of affection, 4. roles and concerns of authority, 5. law, 6. life, 7. liberty, 8. distributive justice, 9. truth, 10. sex.

Approach No. 3: Analysis Approach

Rationale and Purpose. The rationale of the analysis approach to values education rests on helping students develop logical thinking and using scientific inquiry procedures in solving value issues. In addition, value analysis attempts to help students develop their own values in response to value conflicts within society.

According to Superka, the analysis approach views humans as rational beings who can attain the highest good by subordinating feelings and passions to logic and scientific method. Only by suppressing personal feelings can people resolve value issues according to logic and science. "The philosophical basis for the analysis approach.... seems to be a fusion of the rationalist and empiricist view of human nature."[22]

From the perspective in the analysis approach, our society is seen as free, democratic, and plural. Many active groups exist and act. Oliver and Shaver have postulated that this plurality is necessary because

> ...it is the only natural mechanism that can insure some freedom of choice. Pluralism, as we are using the term, implies the existence of not only difference or political partisan groups within the society, but of various sub-cultures that claim the mutual respect of one another, at least to the extent that there is free communication among them.[23]

Ways of Teaching Values

In other words, Oliver and Shaver envision that a democratic society requires a multiplicity of positions on the important issues in society. Groups which support these various positions must be able to negotiate with, rather than confront, one another.

The rationale of the analysis approach involves the development of logical thinking and the use of the scientific method so that students can participate and resolve open conflicts between various groups in society. Such resolutions are seen as essential to the continued existence of a free and democratic society. More specific purposes of the analysis approach have been outlined by Coombs: 1. Teaching students to rate a value object in a particular way. 2. Helping students make the most rational judgement they can about the value object in question. 3. Teaching students to make rational value judgements. 4. Teaching students how to operate as members of a group attempting to come to a common value judgement about some value object.[24]

Valuing and Values. The analysis approach conceives of valuing primarily as cognitive, intellectual inquiry into the goodness or worth of phenomena. Bond notes that proponents stress that valuing is "guided not by the dictates of heart and conscience, but by rules and procedures of logic."[25] The valuing process involves the rigorous application of logical thought and scientific procedure to any issue.

Since values are based on facts, they are verifiable. Valuing and value judgements are subject to tests of logic and truth as much as any other aspect of the real world. Coombs specified the following as standards which a value judgement must meet to qualify as being rational and defensible.

1. The purported facts supporting the judgement must be true or well confirmed.

2. The facts must be genuinely relevant, i.e., they must actually have relevance for the person making the judgement.

3. Other things being equal, the greater the range of relevant facts taken into account in making the judgement, the more adequate the judgement is likely to be.

4. The value principle implied by the judgement must be acceptable to the person making the judgement.[26]

Most authors who support the analysis approach point to survival as the ultimate value, and to constant, rigorous use of reason in the world as the best means to achieve it. Other proponents such as Oliver and Shaver hold that human dignity is the fundamental value of our society against which all other social values must be measured. Although human dignity is considered to be the most fundamental, Oliver and Shaver prescribe other basic values, called "creed values", that should be respected and applied as standards when making value judgements. These values include the quest for self-respect, a sense of sympathy and love, a concern for fairness and justice, majority rule, and due process. "Creed values" help to define and suggest means of achieving the more basic value of human dignity.

> *The analysis approach is usually applied to issues involving public policy or social values rather than issues involving personal values. The approach does not focus explicitly on moral issues; however, statements are presumed to be factual statements and thus subject to empirical study.*[27]

117

Teaching Methods. The teaching methods most frequently used in this approach are individual study and group study of social value problems and issues, library and field research, recitation, and Socratic and seminar class discussions. These methods make use of common teaching techniques in analyzing various social issues like stating or clarifying the issue, questioning or substantiating the relevance of statements, applying analogous cases to qualify and refine value positions, pointing out logical and empirical inconsistencies in arguments, weighing counter arguments, and seeking and testing evidence.[28]

Instructional Models. There appears to be no single sanctioned instructional model used in teaching value analysis. Rather, several prominent models are frequently used. Most notable are the Reflective-Value analysis model of Hunt and Metcalf,[29] the Columbia Associates model of Massialas and Cox,[30] the Jurisprudential model of Oliver and Shaver[31] and Shaver and Larkins,[32] and the Value Inquiry model of Banks and Clegg.[33]

The curriculum model of Hilda Taba[34] could be included as it does have an analysis component. However, its rationale and purpose do not fit easily into the analysis approach. Its major emphasis lies in helping students use categories and improve their ability to categorize. In addition, Taba wished to inculcate specific values such as "the capacity to identify with people in different cultures," "self-security," "open-mindedness," "acceptance of changes", "tolerance for uncertainty and ambiguity," and "responsiveness to democratic and human values."[35]

The reflective-value analysis model of Hunt and Metcalf emphasizes the analysis of value concepts and the consideration of consequences of value alternatives. Students must define value concepts, predict consequences, appraise them using set criteria, and attempt to justify the criteria used.

Reflective-Value Analysis Model

I. What is the nature of the object, event, or policy to be evaluated?

This question plainly poses a task in concept analysis. If the students are trying to evaluate the welfare state, they should define this object as precisely and clearly as possible.

A. How is the welfare state to be defined intentionally and extensively? By what criteria is it to be defined intentionally?

B. If students disgree over criteria, and therefore in their definition of welfare state, how is this disagreement to be treated? Must they agree? Can they agree to disagree? Are there criteria by which welfare state ought to be defined? On what basis can we select among different sets of criteria?

II. The consequences problem

A. What consequences can be expected or anticipated from the policy in question? Is it true, as some have claimed, that the growth of the welfare state destroys individual incentive? How does one get evidence for answering this kind of question?

B. If students disagree in their projection of consequences, how is this difference to be treated? Can evidence produce agreement? What is the difference between a disagreement over criteria and a disagreement over evidence?

Ways of Teaching Values

III *Appraisal of consequences*
    A. Are the projected consequences desirable or not?
    B. By what criteria are the consequences to be appraised? How do different criteria affect one's appraisal of consequences?

IV *Justification of criteria*
    A. Can criteria for appraising consequences be justified? How?
    B. If students disagree on criteria, and therefore in their appraisal of consequences, how can this difference be treated? What relationship ought to exist between one's criteria and one's basic philosophy of life?
    C. Are students consistent in their use of criteria?[36]

The Columbia Associates model of Massialas and Cox assumes that social issues can be resolved only when a dissenting group of students can identify the basic value involved. When students have reached agreement on a high-level value, the issue in conflict can be considered in terms of whether it leads to consequences consistent with that value. A scientific method of inquiry can be used to determine which course of action will most likely result in the realization of the higher-level value accepted by the students. [37] Banks and Clegg have summarized their decision-making model by using an example:

Columbia Associates Model
    1. What value judgement is made regarding the occupation of persons in the United States? Given value judgement: White persons, particularly white Christians, should be given the more skilled jobs, the positions of executive authority in most businesses, high government offices, and professional positions.
    2. What opposing value judgement is also made by many persons in the United States which is clearly contradictory to the value judgement given above?
    3. If the given judgement were acted upon in the United States, what consequences are predicted in terms of the practices and policies which would be put into effect? What factual consequences would be expected to result if the given value judgement were acted upon?
    4. Can you offer any proof that any of the above predictions for the given value judgement would actually take place?
    5. If the opposing value judgement were acted upon in the United States, what consequences are predicted in terms of the practices and policies which would be put into effect? What factual consequences would be expected to result if the opposing value judgement were acted upon?
    6. Can you offer any proof that any of the above predictions for the opposing value judgement would actually take place?
    7. What third value would you propose as being relatively noncontroversial and logically appropriate to use for judging between the given and opposing values?
    8. Which of the value judgements, the given or opposing, appears to be more clearly instrumental in achieving the third, relatively noncontroversial value?
    9. Concisely support your choice of either the given or opposing value by giving the reasons for choosing the one and for rejecting the other.

10. In summary, assuming you have proved your case, state the relationship between the given or opposing value judgement and the third, noncontroversial value in the following formula: "If either the given value judgement OR the opposing value judgement - NOT BOTH, then (the third, noncontroversial value) will be achieved."[38]

Oliver, Shaver and Larkins have based their jurisprudential model on the assumption that public controversy can be resolved through rational discussion. The authors suggest that public controversial issues involve three components: (1) a moral value issue, (2) a definitional issue, and (3) a fact-explanation issue. Strategies which can resolve value issues include illuminating the relationship between specific and higher order values, determining value conflicts resulting from inconsistencies in personal positions, and dealing with incompatable frameworks.[39]

The authors have noted the difficulty of conceptualizing their method in terms of an instructional model. However, they have summarized the major intellectual operations as follows:
1. Abstracting general values from concrete situations
2. Using general value concepts as dimensional constructs
3. Identifying conflicts between value constructs
4. Identifying a class of value conflict situations
5. Discovering or creating value conflict situations which are analagous to the problem under consideration
6. Working toward a general qualified position
7. Testing the factual assumptions behind a qualified value position
8. Testing the relevance of statements.[40]

The value-inquiry model proposed by Banks and Clegg emphasizes the analysis of problems in decision-making situations in society. Using this model, students must identify the key concepts of the dispute, recognize values, identify relevant facts, identify and order alternatives, and predict consequences.[41] A summary of this model is presneted below.

Value-Inquiry Model
1. Defining and recognizing value problems: Observation - discrimination.
2. Describing value-relevant behaviour: Description - discrimination.
3. Naming values exemplified by behaviour described: Identification - description.
4. Determining conflicting values in behaviour described: Identification - analysis.
5. Hypothesizing about sources of values analyzed: Hypothesizing (citing data to support hypothesis).
6. Naming alternative values to those exemplified by behaviour described: Recall.
7. Hypothesizing about the possible consequences of the values analyzed: Predicting, comparing, contrasting.
8. Declaring value preferences: Choosing.
9. Stating reasons, sources, and possible consequences of value choices: Justifying, hypothesizing, predicting.[42]

Although the models proposed by these authors differ, each emphasizes the rational analysis of value statements and judgements as well as the resolution of value conflicts. In each model students are asked to follow specific steps to analyze public or social issues, to come to a decision, and to justify that decision.

Roles of Student and Teacher. The analysis approach requires that students take an active learning role that centres on solving problems of public controversy. This role necessitates that students identify types of issues, ask and gather evidence and information, identify inconsistencies in data and in arguments, and use and recognize analogies.

Classroom discussions (student-teacher and student-student dialogues) are essential components of this approach. As a result, students are encouraged to listen and respond to different points of view, identify relevant questions, and summarize different value positions. They must make decisions and express their opinions. The teacher's role is the creation of the proper conditions for the solving of public issues within the classroom. The teacher's major responsibility is to choose appropriate public issues, to provide enough relevant data to begin the discussion process, and to construct model analogies from which students may begin to develop their own.

Creating analogies and guiding discussion are complex tasks for the teacher. Oliver and Shaver have characterized the teacher's position in the following way:

> The role of the teacher in such a dialogue is complex, requiring that he think on two levels at the same time. He must first know how to handle himself as he challenges the student's position and as his own position is challenged by the student. This is the Socratic role. Second, he must be sensitive to and aware of the general process of clarification or obscuration that takes place as the dialogue unfolds. He must, that is, be able to identify and analyze the complicated strategies being employed by various protagonists to persuade others that a stand is 'reasonable' or 'correct'. Nor is it sufficient for the teacher simply to teach a process of questioning evidence, questioning assumptions or pointing out 'loaded words'. In matter of public policy, factual issues are generally handmaids to ethical or legal stands which cannot be sloughed off as "only matters of opinion'." Clarification of evaluative and legal issues, then, becomes a central concern.[43]

For vigorous analysis of public issues to take place, the teacher must create a classroom environment which is open and sometimes abrasive. The teacher's actions must, however, be tempered with kindness, tolerance, and fairness. Individual student's views and opinions are to be equally respected and subjected to scrutiny.

Characteristics of Materials. As with the moral development approach, materials embodying the analysis approach are usually based on moral issues or dilemmas. Issues have the same five general characteristics as those used for moral development. However, differences exist: (1) the issues are always based on social value issues or community problems rather than personal dilemmas and (2) the issues usually embody not only moral or ethical disputes but also factual and definitional (language) disputes.

Textbooks based on the analysis approach present issues in the form of short articles and/or stories. Usually a number of readings are grouped around current topics of public controversy.

Approach No. 4: Clarification Approach

Rationale and Purpose. The rationale of the clarification approach is to help students clarify and actualize personal values. Additionally this approach attempts to help students develop both rational thinking and emotional awareness to explain their own personal behaviour patterns. The major goal is to achieve consistency between one's personal behaviour and the values that one holds.

Raths, Harmin and Simon[44] believe that any approach that attempts to impose values is both unethical and unsound. They recommend that students be allowed to create their own value system. The emphasis should be on individual freedom, healthy spontaneous growth, and respect for the values of other people, societies, and cultures.

According to Superka, the clarification approach views humans as initiators of interaction within society and their environment. Internal rather than external factors are seen as the prime determinants of human behaviour. The individual is free to change the environment to meet his or her needs. In order to achieve this, however, a person must use all of his or her resources - including rational and emotional processes, conscious and unconscious feelings and mind and body functions.[45]

Simons outlined the more specific purposes of the clarification approach:

1. Values clarification helps students "become more purposeful." Students who know what they want will not fritter away time on pursuits that don't seem beneficial.[46]

2. Values clarification helps students "become more productive." When students know what they want, they channel all energy to achieve those goals.[47]

3. Values clarification helps students "sharpen their critical thinking." Students who have clarified their values can be seen through other peoples' foolishness. They seem to get the larger picture of what is good, beautiful, and right, and to know what is wrong.[48]

4. Values clarification helps students "have better relations with each other." When students know what they want, believe strongly, and follow up on commitments, they can be counted on by other students. When conflicts do arise, they know how to work them through.[49]

Valuing and Values. This approach sees valuing as complex, changing, integrated, and centred on the individual. The most explicit statement of the valuing process from this point of view is that of Raths, Harmin and Simon. They have formulated the following seven-fold outline of the process of valuing: 1. Choosing from alternatves. 2. Choosing after careful consideration of the consequences of each alternative.3 .Choosing freely. 4. Prizing, being glad of one's choice. 5. Prizing, being willing to affirm publicly one's choice. 6. Acting upon one's choice, incorporating choices into

Ways of Teaching Values

behaviour. 7. Acting upon one's choice repeatedly, over time.[50]

Values, as defined by Raths and his associates, have resulted from the seven sub-processes of valuing. Thus, values have been reflected upon, freely chosen, internally prized, publicly affirmed, and incorporated into behaviour repeatedly over time. According to Raths, values are not needs but are closely associated with basic human needs. They are not merely predispositions to behave but behaviour itself.[51]

The most fundamental goal of the clarification approach is self-actualization. That which enhances self-actualization is good; that which hinders self-actualization is evil. For an examination of Rath's conception of valuing, certain specific process level values stand out. These include thoughtful reflection, free choice, and consistent behaviour and might represent the ultimate, intrinsic values of the clarification approach of valuing. Inevitably they lead one to self-actualization, Rath believes.

Teaching methods. The clarification approach, more than any other value education approach, utilizes a wide range of teaching methods. Some of these, like role-playing, hypothetical, contrived and real value-laden situations, group discussions are used in other approaches. Methods specific to clarification include self-analysis, listening techniques, games, journals, songs, and interviews. As a result of Simon's work, the clarification approach has concentrated on developing these teaching methods into specific valuing strategies which are designed to actualize one or more aspects of the valuing process.

The self-reaction worksheet is a teaching strategy which exemplifies the characteristics common to most of the teaching methods used in values clarification. The worksheet usually consists of short readings, questions, drawings, or activities designed to stimulate students to reflect on their own thought, feelings, actions, and values.

Instructional Model. The instructional model of the clarification approach is based directly on the seven-fold process of valuing developed by Raths, Harmin and Simon. Unlike some analysis approach models, this model is not a rigid set of procedures, but a flexible set of guidelines. The following instructional model was adapted by Superka, Johnson and Ahrens from Raths *et. al.*

1. Choosing from alternatives—help students discover, examine, and choose from among available alternatives.

2. Choosing thoughtfully —help students weigh alternatives thoughtfully by reflecting on the consequences of each alternative.

3. Choosing freely — encourage students to make choices freely and to determine how past choices were made.

4. Prizing one's choice—provide students the opportunities to make public affirmations of their choices.

5. Affirming one's choice—provide students the opportunities to make public affirmations of their choices.

6. Acting upon one's choice—encourage students to act, behave, and live in accordance with their choices.

7. Acting repeatedly, over time—help students to examine and to establish repeated behaviours or patterns of actions based on their choices.[52]

Roles of Student and Teacher. Students are to be active. They both

123

participate in the classroom environment and initiate activities. The approach requires students to clarify their own values and increase their understanding of themselves. To accomplish this task students must participate in the various clarification activities, express their opinions and value stances, listen to other students' opinions and statements, and compare their own perceptions and experiences with those of their classmates.

The teacher's role is that of facilitator and leader. The teacher must create the proper classroom atmosphere and assist students in becoming aware of their own value positions. The teacher process involves several essential elements: 1. The teacher must make efforts to elicit attitudinal and value statements from students. 2. The teacher must accept the thoughts, feelings, beliefs, and ideas of students non-judgementally, without trying to change them or criticize them. 3. The teacher must raise questions with students which help them think about their values. The teacher is permitted to express opinions or views, but only as examples of ways to look at things.[53]

Characteristics of the Materials. Materials embodying the clarification approach usually are characterized by a series of group exercises called "strategies." These "strategies" are designed to help students clarify their own values and contain what Raths, Harmin and Simon call "clarifying responses." "Clarifying responses" may involve either oral or written exercises which focus on the following questions:

Where do you suppose you first got the idea?
What else did you consider before you picked this?
What would be the consequences of each alternative available?
Are you glad you feel that way?
Would you tell the class the way you feel sometimes?
I hear what you are for; now is there anything you can do about it? Can I help?
Have you felt this way for some time?[64]

These questions are linked to the seven-step process of arriving at a value.

Clarification approach "strategies" are designed so that students experience important and personal aspects of conflicting confusing values. Typical areas of value conflict or confusion found in the clarification materials include politics, religion, work, leisure time, school, love, sex, money, aging, death, health, race, war-peace, rules, and authority.

Approach No. 5: Action Learning Approach

Rationale and Purpose. The rationale of the action learning approach is to develop students' abilities to act directly in personal and social situations so that they might cry out their personal values. In addition, this approach attempts to enhance the student's sense of community and to develop their abilities to exert influence in public affairs. Superka claims that the distinguishing characteristic of the action learning approach is that it provides specific opportunities for students to act on their values. Values education is not confined to the classroom or group setting, but extends to individual experiential learning in the community.[55]

Action, from this perspective, is not just the "act of doing." Developers such as Newman have carefully defined action as representing "assertiveness as opposed to passivity, a tendency to exert influence on reality, to take some responsibility for, rather than be controlled by, events."[56] Action is not divorced from thought and reflection. Newman states that, "action presupposes reflection, for in order to act one must have conscious thoughts as to one's aims. Though the quality of reflection may vary, it is impossible to act without reflecting about one's intent."[57]

The action learning approach perceives humans as being interactive. Humans do not totally fashion their environment, nor are they totally fashioned by it. Humans and their environment, from this perspective, are mutual and interactive co-creators. Bigge clarifies this concept:

The basic principle of interaction is that nothing is perceivable or conceivable as a thing-in-itself; no object has meaning apart from its context. Hence, everything is construed in relation to other objects. More specifically, a thing is perceived as a figure against a background, experienced from a given angle or direction of envisionment. Persons in a given culture have a common social matrix, and a person devoid of a society is a rather meaningless concept.[58]

Newman has outlined the more specific purposes of the action learning approach. Students will develop competencies to: 1. communicate effectively in spoken and written language; 2. collect and logically interpret information on problems of public concern; 3. describe a political-legal decision-making processes; 4. rationally justify personal decision on controversial public issues and strategies for action with reference to principles of justice and constitutional democracy; 5. work co-operatively with others; 6 discuss concrete personal experiences of self and others in ways that contribute to resolution of personal dilemmas encountered in civic action and that relate these experiences to more general human issues; 7. use selected technical skills as they are required for exercise of influence of specific issues.[59]

Valuing and Values. Proponents of action learning view valuing in much the same way as those who favour the clarification approach. Valuing is a process of self-actualization in which students consider alternatives, make choices, and prize, affirm, and act upon them. The action learning approach, however, extends the valuing concept in two ways: (1) it places more emphasis on action-taking than is reflected in the clarification approach and (2) it views the process of self-actualization as being tempered by social factors and group pressures. This second concept draws heavily upon Dewey's theory of valuing.

Dewey viewed valuing as the process of constantly reconstructing values as means to ends. New values then become means to other ends. The process emphasizes the "social" and "interactive" aspects of valuing. As Dewey stated; "Valuing is as much a matter of interaction of a person with his social environment as walking is an interaction of legs with a physical environment."[60]

Two characteristics distinguish the action learning approach's concept of the nature of values from those of the other educational value approaches. One is related to the proposed source of values and the other to the instrumental nature of values. The first distinguishing characteristic is that values do not have their source either in the person or in the physical or social environment. Their source lies instead in the "simultaneous and mutual interactive" process (Bigge's phrase) between the person and the environment. "Values do not inhere in objects, activities, persons, or anything else; they arise through intelligent relationships of persons with other persons and with objects around them."[61] According to this approach, the person may be the prime initiator of the process of reconstructing values, but values do not inherently reside inside the person.

The "interactive" source of values leads to the second distinguishing characteristic of values. The action learing approach sees values as experimental and instrumental means rather than absolute ends. Bigge offers this explanation of means becoming ends:

> *Even our most basic ideals and ends should be shaped as hypotheses to provide satisfaction for human needs and desires. Values, then, are relative, not absolute; they are relative to developing human needs and desires, reflectively evaluated within an individual-social context....*[62]
> *Values, then, are instrumental, not final; they are exposed to a continuous test of experience. The appropriateness of an act is dependent, not on some absolute standard, but upon the individual and group purposes and foresights which are involved in it.*[63]

Values, from the action learning perspective, are instrumental criteria for determining goodness and worth in varying situations. The specific values that are most frequently mentioned in this approach are democracy, freedom, equality, justice, peace, happiness, survival, rationality, efficiency, truth, self-determination, and human dignity.[64]

Teaching Methods. The action learning approach utilizes many teaching methods that are applied in the moral development, analysis, and clarification approaches. These methods include individual or group study of social issues, the exploration of moral dilemmas within the issue, value clarification activities related to the social issue, role-playing, sensitivity and listening techniques, simulations and games, and small group or entire class discussion.

Two teaching methods are unique to this approach. The first involves skill development in group organization and interpersonal relations, either with the student body or with the community at large. The second involves activities that strive for social change within the community by having students engage in political or legislative experiences.

Instructional Mode. The action learning instructional model is conceived of as circular rather than linear. That is, one may enter into the model at several points and move backward or forward through the various steps. The following instructional model was taken from Superka, Johnson and Ahrens:

1. Becoming aware of a problem or issue—help student become conscious of a problem troubling others or oneself.

2. Understanding the problem or issue and taking a position—help student gather and analyze information and to take a personal value position on the issue.

3. Deciding whether or not to act—help student to clarify values about taking action and to make a decision about personal involvement.

4 Planning strategies and action steps—help students to brainstorm, and organize possible actions and provide skill, practice and anticipatory rehearsal.

5. Implementing strategies and taking action—provide specific opportunities for carrying out one's plans either as an individual working alone or as a member of a group.

6. Reflecting on actions taken and considering next steps—guide students into considering the consequences of the actions taken for others, oneself, and in relation to the problem; also, guide students into thinking about possible steps.[65]

Roles of Student and Teacher. Students are to take a very active learning role. They are active not only in the classroom environment but also in the community. Instruction begins with a problem or issue which is meaningful to the student. Once students properly identify problems they are required to identify the conflicting values involved, analyze the significant information, plan strategies for taking action, and take appropriate action to cause social change. Finally, they must reflect upon an action to determine whether further action is necessary or if a different "plan of attack" should be adopted. Students, from this perspective, determine whether they will develop, learn and become responsive and responsible to themselves and their community.

The teacher's role within this approach is that of a leader and an assistant, a person who is engaged in mutual interaction with students. The teacher must be sensitive to the direction the student wants to go and must structure the learning experiences along the lines indicated by the student. If the student has stopped progressing, the teacher must provide stimulus and try to determine the goals the student is trying to achieve. The teacher is required to help students define the social issue and clarify their values in relation to the issue. The teacher must provide students with, or direct them to, significant information, assist them in gathering and analyzing this data, and advise the students on appropriate social action. In some cases the teacher provides some supervision and guidance when the action is taken. Finally, the teacher must plan activities which would cause the students to reflect on the action that was taken.

Although the student initiates specific activities, the teacher chooses topics or areas of study and, through suggestions, may influence the specific activities. Above all, this approach demands that the teacher is in close interaction with his students.

Characteristics of Materials. Since students have such an active role in determining the activities in action learning, classroom materials embodying this approach are characterized by their diversity in both topics and activities. Materials often contain a list of suggested projects that students may attempt. These projects in many cases do not suggest specific activities but are used as a stimulus for students to develop their own action learning activities. Examples of four action learning projects that have been developed by Newman are:

1. Group A wishes to protect land surrounding a glacial pond from development into a high-rise apartment complex. The developer, who has already purchased the land, has requested that the city council change the zoning from single family to high-rise apartments so that construction may

begin. Group A decides to do all it can to prevent this change in zoning.

2. Group B wants to help students in trouble with the law. After visiting various juvenile detention facilities, it decides to make weekly visits to a state detention centre for boys, spending an hour playing cards, dancing, and talking.

3. Group C wants to form a Black Students' union to increase communication and a sense of community among Blacks scattered in four different high schools. They decide to publish a student newspaper and to promote a cultural festival. They want to attract more Blacks into their organization and to learn of their heritage through films, speakers, and books which have not been previously available in school.

4. Mike, a high school student, wants to learn something about the courts and the legal profession. He arranges an internship with the clerk of a local judge. Mike spends several hours each week observing courtroom procedures, discussing this with the clerk, and occasionally with the judge. The clerk helps to explain the operation of the system and reasons for the judge's decisions.[66]

Materials may take forms very different from those suggested by Newman. Kirschenbaum, for example, has developed what he terms "sensitivity modules." These activities are designed so students can have short experiences to increase their awareness of social issues. Some of the suggested activities are:

1. Wear old clothes and sit in the waiting room of the state employment office. Listen, observe, talk to some of the people sitting next to you. Read the announcements on the bulletin board, etc.

2. Go to an inner-city elementary school and read a story to a child in kindergarten or first grade. The child must be held in your lap.

3. Live for three days on the amount of money a typical welfare mother receives to feed a son or daughter closest to your age.[67]

Barr suggested an even broader range of activities which would encourage teachers and students to move beyond the classroom to school-based and community-based learning activities.

1. Outdoor Learning Programs: with emphasis on rigorous programs of hiking, back-packing, canoeing, etc.

2. Cross-cultural Exchange Programs: which enable students to have in-depth "immersion" experiences in cultures different from their own.

3. Service Programs: which enable students to provide volunteer service to local community agencies.

4. Internship Programs: which enable students to have extended experiences with leaders in private business, government, social agencies, cultural agencies, etc.

5. Travel Programs: which enable student to combine academic study with on-site visitations and experiences. These often involve cross-cultural experiences, historical studies, and scientific investigations.

Approach No. 6: Emotional-Rational Approach

Rationale and Purpose. The emotional-rational approach to values education attempts to help students understand and adopt a lifestyle based on care and consideration for others as well as self. McPhail, perhaps the leading proponent of this approach, sees its aim neither as increasing the

Ways of Teaching Values

students' capacity to argue morally nor their ability to say "good thing," but rather as their capacity to know what "love in action" is, to act with love and affection—act warmly and caringly. This approach is strongly based on Wilson's idea that moral decisions are arrived at by a variety of both affective (emotional) and cognitive (rational) processes.

The rationale for this approach is based on the assumption that one can extrapolate the "ought" from the "is." To quote McPhail:

> ...if you want to know what people need and how to meet that need, the first step is to ask them to identify and articulate their problems as they see them and not to tell them what their problems are. The boys' and girls' own use of "good" and "bad" in the survey showed us how the "ought" of morality should come from the "is" of reality. To a large extent, the rational, the emotive, and the moral converge on the question of reciprocal behaviour, which is seen to have a universal rather than a merely individualistic or subjective quality.[68]

The emotional-rational approach, like the action learning approach, perceives humans as interactive. Humans do not totally fashion their environment nor are they totally fashioned by it. For McPhail, students create (from their needs) the values and beliefs they wish to live by. He says, however, that "we all know that we cannot separate ourselves at any time from the world we live in".[69]

The emotional-rational approach differs from action learning in that it stresses feelings or the emotional side rather than the rational side of human nature. The approach does not reject rationalism, nor does it advocate unbridled expression of one's emotion. Rather, humans are viewed more as feeling beings rather than reasoning machines. People co-create with their environment, but in an emotional-rational rather than in just a rational manner.

For students, the more specific purposes of the emotional-rational approach are:

1. to improve their ability to recognize their own and others' needs, interests and feelings;

2. to improve their ability to interpret accurately the messages, both verbal and non-verbal, which other persons are sending;

3. to improve their ability to predict the possible and probable consequences of actions;

4. to improve their ability to see things from another's point of view;

5. to develop a strong sense of identity and see themselves as people who have contribution to make in their community;

6. to identify the various legal and social rules of our society;

7. to identify the various expectations and pressures put on them by society;

8. to learn to choose, to decide in a particular situation, what they will do so long as it is consistent with the needs, interests, and feelings of others as well as their own.[70]

Valuing and Values. Proponents of the emotional-rational approach view valuing in much the same manner as do those who favour the clarification and action learning approaches. Valuing is a process of self-actualization in which students consider alternatives, make choices, and prize, affirm, and act upon those choices. The emotional-rational approach differs, however, in that the valuing process has both an emotional and a rational aspect. The emotional aspect means that valuing is seen as a process of experiencing and expressing one's own intense personal feelings of good and evil. The rational aspect means that valuing is seen as the process of choosing and acting on one's values only if these values are consistent with the needs, interests, and feelings of others.

Values, according to this approach, are personal emotions or feelings that indicate moral approval or disapproval. Values are caused by putting into action one's needs, emotions, and feelings. From this perspective values are means of measuring one's emotional state. McPhail states that the basic aim of this approach is for students to know, feel, and experience "love in action".[71] "Love in action" is the term used to describe students' behaviours when they exhibit care, affection, toleration, understanding, responsibility, sensitivity, compassion, concern, or respect towards other people as well as themselves. These behaviours would fulfil, according to McPhail, "the fundamental human need to get on with others, to love and be loved."

Teaching Methods. McPhail has listed a variety of methods that can help students know and experience "love in action." Each method should involve small groups, ideally not larger than ten or smaller than four. These methods include:

1. expressive and communication techniques such as speaking, writing prose, poetry and plays, painting, modelling with clay, and photography

2. discussion techniques, such as small group and entire class discussions. This method should be limited in its use, however, since few members of the class are good at it.[72]

3. drama techniques with students writing and acting in their own plays

4. role-playing based on situations common to students' experiences

5. simulations involving family, school, or community problems

6. real life involvement such as helping individuals within the community.[73]

Instructional Model. McPhail and his associates have not developed a specific instructional model for the emotional-rational approach. However, they have made a number of suggestions on how to organize activities depending upon which teaching method is employed.

The materials used in the emotional-rational approach are characterized by their format. They start with situations which are immediately personal and sensitive in nature and move towards less personal situations concerning dilemmas involving the community, the country, the world. This format can be broken down into five sections:

1. Sensitivity - designed to improve the students' ability to recognize their own and others' needs, interests, and feelings, and to help them understand why individuals behave as they do.

2. Consequences - designed to improve the students' ability to predict the possible and probable consequences of actions.

3. Points of view - designed to help students decide on action after

Ways of Teaching Values

considering the other individuals involved.

4. Proving the rule - designed to help students find solutions to problems involving the community at large.

5. What would you have done - designed to help students understand real, historical, world problems.[74]

McPhail has stated that students must also develop the four abilities of "moral communication."

1. Reception ability, meaning the ability to be, and remain, "switched on" to the right wavelength, to listen, to look, to receive the messages sent out by others.

2. Interpretative ability, meaning the ability to interpret accurately the messages which another person is sending, what he really means, what he really wants.

3 Response ability, meaning the ability to decide on and adopt appropriate reactions - to meet anothers' needs. It involves decision-making, evaluation, the use of reason as well as psychological knowhow.

4. Message ability, meaning the ability to translate appropriate reactions into clearly transmitted unambivalent messages.[75]

The following instructional model has been inferred from the various organizational suggestions made by McPhail. It is flexible; any of the various teaching methods suggested by McPhail may be used at any point.

1. Sensitivity - students recognize their own and others' needs, interests and feelings.
    1.1 Reception ability - what are the persons' needs, interests and feelings in the situation?
    1.2 Interpretive ability - what is each person saying, both verbally and non-verbally, in this situation?
    1.3 Response ability - how are they reacting to each other in the situation?
    1.4 Message ability - how can they express what each person's needs, interests, and feelings are?

2. Consequences - students predict the possible consequences of the actions in the situation.
    2.1 Reception ability - what are the probable consequences of the situation?
    2.2 Interpretive ability - are the probable consequences going to achieve what the people in the situation really want?
    2.3 Response ability what are the other possible consequences? What is the most desirable consequence? Is the most probable consequence the most desirable consequence?
    2.4 Message ability - how should the people in the situation act differently to bring about the most desirable consequence?

3. Points of view - students decide on action after considering the other individuals involved.
    3.1 Reception ability - what is each person's point of view in the situation?
    3.2 Interpretive ability - what is each person saying, both verbally and non-verbally, to express his point of view?
    3.3 Response ability - are there other responses they could have made to express their points of view? Was the response they

made the most appropriate one to express their points of view?

    3.4   Message ability - are they communicating their points of view clearly and unambiguously?

4 Proving the rule - students examine the legal and social problems involved in the home, in the school, or in the neighbourhood.

    4.1   Reception ability - what are the legal or social problems of the groups of people represented in this situation?

    4.2   Interpretive ability - how are these problems expressed in the situation? What are the symptoms of each problem?

    4.3   Response ability - what reaction could each of the groups have to solve their problem? What reaction should they have?

    4.4   Message ability - how should each group carry out their decision from reaction to action?

5. What would you have done? - students examine what has happened in specific situations in the modern world.

    5.1   Reception ability - what actually happened in the situation?

    5.2   Interpretive ability - what have the various people or groups of people involved said about what happened in the situation? How do they feel about what happened in the situation?

    5.3   Response ability - what would your reaction be in the situation if you were each of the people or groups involved? What should it be?

    5.4   Message ability - can you express how you would have felt in the situation? Can you express what you would have done in the situation?[76]

Roles of Student and Teacher. Students are to take an active learning role. Their personal needs, feelings, and emotions make up the actual subject material for this approach. The situations examined are selected by the student groups on the basis of interest and relevance. Students are actively involved in the classroom environment, expressing their emotions and opinions, making decisions, and developing and acting in a caring and loving manner.

The emotional-rational approach demands that students observe and develop the ability to recognize various verbal and non-verbal cues which other individuals give about their needs, interests, and feelings. Students must develop the ability to predict the consequences of actions and acquire knowledge of both the legal and social rules of their community. Finally, students must practice many forms of creative expression including writing, painting, photography, and acting.

The teacher's role is to act as a facilitator to free students to accept and express a basic concern for the welfare of others. McPhail has indicated that morality is not taught but caught. Therefore, the teacher must take a modelling role, demonstrating care and consideration for each student. The teacher is also required to create a trusting classroom atmosphere where students can express their real and uncensored feelings about issues without fear. This classroom climate requires that teachers work with students to remove blocks to communication, and work again with students to build "moral communication" abilities. Finally, the approach dictates that the teacher must select classroom materials which are of interest and

Ways of Teaching Values

relevance to students, must provide detailed information (if any) required by the students, and must direct the students' work so that they will put their values and attitudes into practice.

Characteristics of Materials. Materials embodying the emotional-rational approach contain a large number of situational readings. The materials have seven specific characteristics:

1. The readings are brief to encourage students to make the situation their own by adding their own personal details.

2. The readings usually contain two or three characters.

3. The situation in the readings demands a reaction from the student, if he identifies with one of the characters.

4. The reading is in the form of a dilemma; that is, it is not immediately apparent what the student should do in a given situation.

5. Situations are derived from the topics identified by McPhail's 1967-1968 student survey which asked students to identify incidents in their lives which made them happy, sad, frustrated, or angry. The topics students identified as relevant to their needs were: sexual attitudes, problems with adults including those in school, economic class attitudes, and racial, cultural, religious, political and psychological conflicts.[77]

6. Questions relating to the readings are generally concerned with doing rather than theorizing.

7. The materials are open-ended in nature allowing a number of follow-up creative activities such as classroom dramas, simulations or role playing sessions, drawing, photography, or creative writing.[78]

Summary

We have attempted to identify the characteristics of the six value education approaches. These six approaches represent distinctive but not totally unrelated efforts to develop values in students. The distinction between the six approaches might be clarified by identifying the kinds of choices a student educated in each approach would most probably make.

The following chart presents the values education approaches and the corresponding types of choices:

One educated in:	would make a:
inculcation approach	positively reinforced and socially acceptable choice
moral development approach	morally developed choice
analysis approach	rational choice
clarification approach	thoughtfully self-actualized choice
action learning approach	rational, personal-social growth enhancing choice
emotional-rational approach	emotional-rational, personal choice

1 D.P. Superka, "A Typology of Valuing Theories and Value Education Approaches," unpublished doctoral disseration, University of California, Berkeley, Cal., 1973, p. 37.

2 D. Krathwohl et al., *Taxonomy of Educational Objectives: The Classification of Educational Goals, Handbook II: Affective Domain* (New York: David McKay, 1964).

3 D. Oliver and J. Shaver, *Teaching Public Issues in the High School* (Boston: Houghton Mifflin, 1966), p. 26.

4 B. Joyce and M. Weil, *Models of Teaching* (Englewood Cliffs: Prentice Hall, 1972); D.P. Superka, P. Johnson and C. Ahrens, *Values Education: Approaches and Materials* (Boulder, Col.: ERIC Clearinghouse for Social Studies/ Social Science Education, 1975).

5 D.P. Superka, et al., *op. cit.*

6 D. Krathwohl et al, *op. cit.*

7 B. Sulzer, *Behavior Modification Procedures for School Personnel* (New York: Dryden Press, 1972).

8 D.P. Superka et al., *op. cit.*, pp. 10-12.

9 B.K. Simpson, *Becoming Aware of Values: A Resource Guide in the Use of Value Games* (San Diego: Pennant Press, 1972), pp. 14-15.

10 L. Kohlberg, "A Cognitive Developmental Analysis of Children's Sex Role Concepts and Attitudes," in E. Maccoby (ed.), *The Development of Sex Differences* (Stanford: Stanford University Press, 1966), p. 19.

11 D.P. Superka et al., *op. cit.*, p. 19.

12 J. Piaget, *The Moral Judgement of the Child* (New York: The Free Press, 1965).

13 Ontario Ministry of Education, *Moral Education Project : Year 4: Annual Report* (Toronto: Ontario Ministry of Education, 1976), p. 116.

14 E. Turiel, "Stage Transition in Moral Development," in R.M. Travers (ed.), *Second Handbook of Research on Teaching* (Chicago: Rand McNally, 1973), pp. 732-758; and M. Blatt, "The Effects of Classroom Discussion Programs upon Children's Level of Moral Development," doctoral disseration, University of Chicago, Chicago, Ill., 1969.

15 D. P. Superka, " A Typology of Valuing..," *op. cit.*

16 L. Kohlberg and E. Turiel, "Moral Development and Moral Education," in G.S. Lesser, (ed.), *Psychology and Educational Practice* (Glenview, Ill.: Scott, Foreman and Co., 1971), p. 447.

17 *Ibid.*, p. 461.

18 F. Simon, "Moral Development: Some Suggested Implications for Teaching," *Journal of Moral Education* 5:2 (1976); and R.P. Craig, "Education for Justice: Some Comments on Piaget," *Contemporary Education*, winter 1976, pp. 69-73.

19 R.E. Galbraith and T.M. Jones, *Moral Reasoning: A Teaching Handbook for Adapting Kohlberg to the Classroom* (Minneapolis: Greenhaven Press, 1976), p. 20.

20 S. Beyer and K. Barry, "Conducting Moral Discusssions in the Classroom," *Social Education*, April 1976, pp. 194-195.

21 *Ibid.*, p. 198.

22 D. P. Superka,*et al.* , *op. cit.*, pp. 24-25.

23 D. Oliver and J. Shaver, *op. cit.*, p. 10.

24 J. R. Coombs, "Objectives of Value Analysis," in L.E. Metcalf (ed.), *Valuing Education: Rationale, Strategies and Procedures* (Washington, D.C.: National Council for the Social Studies, 1971), p. 19.

25 D. J. Bond, "An Analysis of Valuation Strategies in Social Studies Educational Materials," unpublished doctoral dissertation, University of California, Berkeley, Cal., 1971, p. 81.

26 J.R. Coombs, *op. cit.*, p. 20.

27 D. Oliver and J. Shaver, *op. cit.*, pp. 23-28.

Ways of Teaching Values

28 F. Newmann and D. Oliver, *Clarifying Public Controversy: An Approach to Teaching Social Studies* (Boston: Little and Brown, 1970), pp. 293-296.

29 M.P. Hunt and L. E. Metcalf, *Teaching High School Social Studies*, 2nd ed. (New York: Harper and Row, 1968).

30 B.G. Massialas and C.B. Cox, *Inquiry in the Social Studies* (New York: McGraw-Hill, 1966).

31 D. Oliver and J. Shaver, *op. cit.*

32 J.P. Shaver and G. Larkins, *Analysis of Public Issues Program: Instructor's Manual* (Boston: Houghton Mifflin, 1973).

33 J. A. Banks and A.A. Clegg, *Teaching Strategies for the Social Studies*, 2nd ed. (Reading, Mass.: Addison-Wesley, 1977).

34 H. Taba, *A Teacher's Handbook to Elementary Social Studies: An Inductive Approach* (Menlo Park, Cal.: Addison-Wesley, 1971).

35 M. P. Hunt and L. E. Metcalf, *op. cit.*, p. 134.

36 *Ibid.*

37 J. A. Banks and A.A. Clegg, *op. cit.*, pp. 412-413.

38 B.G. Massialas and C.B. Cox, *op. cit.*, p. 166.

39 J. A. Banks and A.A. Clegg, *op. cit.*, pp. 418-420.

40 D. Oliver and J. Shaver, *op. cit.*, p. 166.

41 J. A. Banks and A.A. Clegg, *op. cit.*, pp. 433-441.

42 *Ibid.*, p. 433.

43 D. Oliver and J. Shaver, *op. cit.*, p. 115.

44. L. Raths, M. Harmin, and S. Simon, *Values and Teaching* (Columbus, Ohio: Charles E. Merrill Publishing, 1966).

45 D. P. Superka *et al.*, *op. cit.*, p. 31.

46 F. Simon, *op. cit.*, p. 40.

47 *Ibid.*, p. 41.

48 *Ibid.*, p. 42.

49 *Ibid.*

50 L. Raths, *et al.*, *op. cit.*, p. 259.

51 *Ibid.*, p. 27-37.

52 D. P. Superka, *et al.*, *op. cit.*, p. 32.

53 L. Raths, *et al.*, *op. cit.*, pp. 165-183.

54 *Ibid.*, pp. 63-65.

55 D. P. Superka et al., *op. cit.*, p.35.

56 F. Newmann, *Education for Citizen Action* (Berkeley, Cal.: McCutcheon Publishing, 1975), p. 7.

57 *Ibid.*, pp.19-20.

58 M. Bigge, *Positive Relativism: An Emergent Educational Philosophy* (New York: Harper and Row, 1971), p. 40.

59 F. Newmann, T. Bertocci, and R. Landness, *Skills in Citizen Action* (Madison, Wisc.: University of Wisconsin Publications, 1977), p. 6.

60 J. Dewey and J. Tufts, *Ethics* (New York: Holt, Rinehart and Winston, 1932), pp. 318-319.

61 M. Bigge, *op. cit.*, p. 64.

62 *Ibid.*

63 *Ibid.*, p. 50.

64 F. Newmann, *op cit.*, p. 14.

65 D. P. Superka *et al.*, *op. cit.*, p. 37

66 F. Newmann, *op. cit.*, p. 1.

67 H. Kirschenbaum, "Sensitivity Modules," in D.A. Reid and S. Simon (eds.), *Humanistic Education Sourcebook* (Englewood Cliffs, N.J.: Prentice-Hall, 1975), p. 316.

68 P. McPhail, J. Ungoed-Thomas, and H. Chapman, *Learning to Care -- Teacher Guide* (London: Longman, 1972), p. 30.

69 *Ibid.*, *Lifeline: Moral Education in the Secondary School* (London: Longman, 1972), p. 82.

70 *Ibid.*, pp. 63-125.
71 *Ibid.*, p. 5.
72 P. McPhail, D. Middleton, and D. Ingram, *Startline: Moral Education in the Middle Years* (London: Longman, 1978), p. 137.
73 *Ibid.*, pp.137-139.
74 P. McPhail *et al.*, *op cit.* (1972), pp. 101-125.
75 Ibid., p.63.
76 P. McPhail *et al.*, *op. cit.* (1972), pp. 125-133; and (1978), pp. 134-151.
77 P. McPhail *et al.*, *op. cit.* (1972), pp. 23-49.
78 *Ibid.*, pp. 80-150; and P. McPhail *et al., op. cit.* (1978), pp. 119-158.

Theories and Attitudes Towards Political Education

Marshall W. Conley
*Department of Political Science,
Acadia University, Wolfville, Nova Scotia*

DURING the last decade and a half there has been more interest in political education in countries such as the United Kingdom, the United States and the Federal Republic of Germany. In Canada the call for a fresh look at political education came in 1978 with Hodgetts and Gallagher's *Teaching Canada for the '80's* and their recommendations for "a distinctively Canadian civic education."[1]

In one sense, all of this is nothing new. From its beginning education has had a political purpose. It was intended to train the young to take their place within a particular society, to give them the skills, knowledge and values which were thought necessary for the continuation of their society. This, of course, ignores the divisions within society and the role of education in enabling one group within a society to control or manipulate others. As Susan Houston has observed, "A common school system was an institution established and supported by one group of people not for their own children, but for the children of others."[2] Nonetheless, it makes its point: public education is and has been inevitably political. Its mandate is to train citizens, in the widest sense of the term.

Despite this long tradition, the recent interest in political education represents something new. If nothing else, it is giving new emphasis and directing renewed attention to the citizenship role of education. It is trying to define - or redefine - more precisely the nature of that citizenship and to

> C'est en général pendant les cours d'histoire que les élèves absorbent l'éducation politique. L'auteur analyse les parti-pris qu'ont acquis les manuels d'histoire au cours des ans, il étudie comment on s'est servi des écoles pour promouvoir le chauvinisme canadien et il décrit le regain d'intérêt des dernières années pour les études canadiennes. Selon lui, l'éducation politique ou la politisation ne se limite pas à l'instruction civique ou aux études sociales; elle est plutôt le résultat de toutes les expériences des enfants à l'école. Il termine en indiquant que l'obéissance est la leçon la plus importante qui soit enseignée aux enfants à l'école et que les enfants y apprennent la dépendance et la conformité; il paraît assez rare en effet que l'école fasse valoir l'indépendance, la créativité et l'autonomie.

suggest ways by which the schools can contribute more effectively to it. It is raising to conscious awareness and prompting deliberate planning many assumptions that have long been taken for granted and unexamined. In doing so it is turning primarily to the academic discipline of political science for many of its concepts and frameworks and, at least by implication, is turning away from history, which has long been assigned the main role in citizenship training in Canadian schools.

There can be little doubt that recent interest in political education is a response to developments which characterize western industrial societies generally. In particular, it is a response to what the Trilateral Commission prefers to describe as the "crisis of democracy" with all its suggestions that the liberal democratic system has become ungovernable.[3] A 1975 ten-nation survey reported that "nowhere has the system proved capable of producing the ideal goal of a well-informed citizenry, with democratic attitudes and values, supportive of government policies and interested in civic affairs."[4] The inclusion of the phrase "supportive of government policies" in this list is intriguing. It does not fit with the others. Obviously, a well-informed, democratic and interested citizen need not be at all supportive of government policies. One wonders if the research team was simply cataloguing all the various aims of civic education, regardless of logical consistency, or whether it saw some correlation between civic education and support for government. In any event, it may indicate that civic education is intended to produce citizens who will be more supportive of their governments or, at least if not of their governments, then of their political systems. Certainly, the fear of "youth alienation", and the lowering of the voting age, runs through much of the literature on political education. Supporters of the movement see it as making youngsters who are future voters more understanding of the potential and limitations of politics, leading them to participate in and become committed to a particular political system (or regime). At the same time, they tend to ignore those structural forces which are bearing most heavily on the young, and, in particular, those forces producing high levels of unemployment. Political education is in danger of treating the victims while ignoring the causes of their disease.

Political Education vs Civics

Just what is political education? How does it differ from civics or citizenship education? All education is political and, to some extent, the phrase "political education" is a tautology. However, it also carries a more specific meaning: the attempt to teach people, in this case school children, about politics and the political system of which they are a part, with a view to making them more politically aware and to getting them to participate more effectively and more readily in the political arena. To use Milbrath's terms, it is an attempt to turn spectators and apathetics into gladiators.[5] Thus, Crick and Porter have coined the term "political literacy":

> To have achieved political literacy is to have learned what the main political disputes are about, what beliefs the main contestants have of them, how they are likely to affect you and me. It also means that we are likely to be predisposed to try to do something about the issue in question in a manner which is at once effective and respectful of the sincerity of other people and what they believe.[6]

Theories and Attitudes Towards Political Education

The three-fold process of political literacy therefore includes imparting essential information, building up needed skills to react to or solve problems that arise day-to-day while using the knowledge acquired, and cultivating the needed interests, attitudes and values. Political education consists of knowledge, skills and values which all citizens must have in order to enable them to become intelligent, effective and responsible participants in the political system. All three of these elements are significant and have to be developed together, each conditioning the other. Mere knowledge does not serve the objectives of political education, which requires effective participation based upon appropriate skills. Similarly, unreflective or ill-informed participation is equally undesirable, and neither knowledge nor participation will lead to the realization of socio-economic objectives unless they are both governed by a proper value system. The three components of political literacy can be defined as follows:

Knowledge - The basic information which is prerequisite to understanding the political dimensions of a given context, including the knowledge of what information was lacking and how it may be discovered; a knowledge of basic political concepts; and the knowledge of how to construct analytical frameworks within which to judge political questions.

Skills - Information processing skills; that is, the capacity to critically analyse and evaluate political information, and to reveal any underlying prejudices or ideologies behind arguments; and action skills, which go beyond analytical and verbal skills and lead to positive action, and the capacity to participate in, and change, political situations.

Attitudes - A politically educated, or literate, person can take a critical stance towards political information. (Within the Western tradition it is usual to stress such procedural values as 'freedom, toleration, fairness, and respect for truth and reasoning', which include a capacity to try to see things from the point of view of other groups and persons.) [7]

However, as Karen Dawson rightly points out:

Political Education is a lifelong process and takes place both within formal institutions of education and within other sectors of the community - such as the home, workplace religious institutions - and through mechanisms such as parent-child and peer group relationships, voluntary group associations, and media influences. [8]

In a similar vein, a U.S. statement declared that:

...the goals of civic education should be knowledge of the political system and how it really and ideally works, development of the skills of participation in civic life, improvement of civic competence, commitment to values compatible with the principles which underlie democratic institutions and a capacity to analyse the consequences of these values, and development of self-esteem so that all individuals feel that their participation in civic life can make a difference. [9]

This represents a very ambitious agenda - far more, one suspects, than the schools can possibly achieve - but it is notable that both definitions speak of political knowledge, of skills and of values. The emphasis, more or less explicit, is upon what might best be described as civic competence.

There are two strands to this view that political education should lead to a more highly political citizenry. One sees it as a way of saving the system. Alarmed by the persistent findings of alienation, apathy and cynicism among sections of the population, and especially by the antipathy felt by many people for politics and for politicians,[10] some people hope that through more effective programs of political education, the system can be saved. Hodgetts and Gallagher made a similar point when they noted that "manifestations of social dislocations and dangerously high levels of tension in Canada are readily apparent" and when they described the "many signs of stress and discontent in Canadian society," concluding that "there can be little doubt of the continuing need...to recognize the possible disruption of democracy by internal stress; and to give more intensive consideration to the contribution civic education might make to society." [11] This view sees political education as valuable for maintaining, and indeed improving, the political system, and perhaps even the political community itself, although it may well also include a concern for the individual citizen.

The second strand takes no position on whether the system should or should not be preserved. It concentrates upon the individual citizen and sees a more broadly based and active political involvement as a matter of simple justice. If this results in radical political change, so be it. The first approach sees a wider citizen involvement in politics as a way of reducing alienation and cynicism and so preserving the system. The second sees it as simply worthwhile for its own sake. It accepts the premise of classical democratic theory that participation serves to educate and to humanize those who participate. There is no necessary contradiction between valuing citizen participation and valuing the maintenance of the political system of liberal democracy. One apparently leads to the other.[12] There is, however, a difference in emphasis upon each of the two strands in the political education movement: some projects and writers emphasize the one, some the other.

Some see political education as a means to redress some of the inequities of the political system. It is well known, for example, that in most liberal democracies, political participation and activism is heavily class-based. In Canada,

> although lawyers, doctors, businessmen, and other professionals constitute fewer than ten per cent of the Canadian work force, they occupy almost three-quarters of the seats in the House of Commons and two-thirds of the offices in local party organizations. Blue-collar workers, in contrast, compose nearly half of the population but hold fewer than ten per cent of the positions either in local parties or in parliament.[13]

Hodgetts and Gallagher draw a further conclusion from all this, "the government is in the hands of people who are fairly satisfied with the status quo."[14] There is, of course, a tradition in modern democratic theory that sees virtue in the passiveness of the majority, arguing that too much political involvement would politicize every issue and, so to speak, overload the system: "... extreme interest goes with extreme partisanship and might culminate in a rigid fanaticism that could destroy democratic processes if generalized throughout the system."[15] The wording is revealing: extreme, rigid, fanaticism - the words are hardly neutral. In addition, interest is too narrowly equated with partisanship and partisanship with fanaticism. This is another argument, however. The point being made here is that there is a tendency within political education to reject the theory of elite democracy and support instead a much more participatory form of politics both as good in its own right and as a way of achieving greater social justice.

All this is to say that political education is itself highly political. It is the application in educational terms of a political philosophy. The same cannot be said, or not to the same extent, of another term which is often heard: "civic education" or "civics." It is true that the term is being used nowadays with something of the same meaning as political education, but it has overtones that suggest a rather different approach.

In the past, civics meant little more than a factual knowledge of governmental and political institutions with a sprinkling of desirable social virtues. It was normative rather than analytical. Students, for example, were taught that a bill becomes a law by moving through three readings in both houses and by receiving royal assent; nothing was said about how a bill becomes a subject for legislation in the first place, nor about how people work to further their interests. Civics portrays a consensus view of politics in which questions of conflict and power play little part.

This approach is still very much alive and seems to be especially popular with teachers of younger children. Thus, a 1979 text written for grades 5 and 6 defines government as "you and others working together to meet some of your needs."[16] In reality, of course, government cannot meet everyone's needs. Not all needs are, in any case, valid, legitimate or desirable, hence the recurrent controversies about such problems as abortion or censorship. Government may, in fact, act to prevent people from meeting their needs. Again, different people's needs may conflict, so that government has to make decisions which satisfy some groups but not others, or try to avoid making decisions at all in order to avoid possible crises. Stradling reports similar problems in political education courses taught in the United Kingdom:

> It is apparent from the findings that teaching about the structure and functions of political institutions still predominates in many schools. Only a small proportion of provision focuses on political issues and processes or the politics of everyday life.[17]

There is a further refinement, as we are finding these days in connection with the free-trade question. There are needs which government claims to see more clearly than do the people, so it sets out to deal with needs that people do not even know they have. Beyond all this, there exists a well-defined and coherent political philosophy that argues that government should not be meeting any but the most minimal needs anyway, since this is best left to individual initiative. Civics, however, generally ignores all this, probably because it raises questions about conflict and the exercise of power which, it is thought, are at best too controversial for the schools to handle or at worst will make youngsters unduly cynical. What happens when children see, as they inevitably will in this age of instant information, the contrast between what they are taught and what really goes on? Some years ago Hodgetts suggested that "the lack of realism in civics classes might help to develop unfounded cynicism."[18] Given the latest national poll results on public attitudes towards government in Canada, Hodgetts is probably correct.[19]

In all this, the classic Lasswell definition of politics as "who gets what, when and how" (to which one ought to add, "and why") has no place. One is tempted to say that civics or civic education is political education without the politics.

The third term often used - citizenship education - is even more apolitical. Cary has distinguished between "state citizenship," which he sees as an "individual's relation to the political system," and "social citizenship" which describes "an individual's relationship to the social system, a system not necessarily coterminous with the political system."[20] Most proponents of citizenship education espouse the latter rather than the former, so that citizenship education embraces the whole range of socially useful and desirable qualities that youngsters should acquire. Thus, a recent *Handbook of Basic Citizenship Competencies* categorizes the goals of citizenship education under seven headings: acquiring and using information; assessing involvement; making decisions; making judgements; communicating; co-operating; promoting interests.[21] Clearly, there is much here that is "political," but there is no specific reference to politics or the political system. It is true that politics is not to be equated with government, that one can legitimately speak of the politics of the classroom, the family and so on, but the fact remains that these seven "basic citizenship competencies" will not necessarily entice people to become active beyond, say, the confines of the parent-teacher association or the community club.

All three approaches - politics, civics, and citizenship - can often be found in recent discussions of political education, which contain a varying mixture of concern for political efficacy and participation, for greater civic knowledge and commitment, for a heightened sense of community and social obligation, and for the improvement of the political system. It is usually assumed that all this can be done within the political system as it is. Nearly all the discussions of political education accept the political system as a given and aim at teaching students to play their part actively and effectively within it. To this extent, at least, political education may be more accurately described as political socialization. Most discussions, for instance, see politics as an arena in which all are potentially free to compete on more or less equal terms, with government serving as a neutral arbiter whose main concern is to enforce the rules of the game.

Hodgetts and Gallagher point out that "a great many Canadians, particularly those who might gain from change, sit on the sidelines, exerting little influence over government yet being subject to a multitude of its decisions."[22] The game is there for playing; all that is needed is to become involved, to become a player rather than a spectator. This, of course, is the standard liberal view of the state and certainly students should be familiar with it, although it would more accurately be taught as ideology rather than fact. What rarely appears in all the discussions is the view that sees the state not as the impartial umpire between competing interests, but as a player in the game. The concept that the state is concerned with the promotion of a particular set of interests to the exclusion of others is not a popular one in political education. At times the state is portrayed not even as neutral, but as downright benevolent: "more than anything else they (i.e., governments) try to produce equality of opportunity for all people."[23]

Political Education in Canada

It is very difficult to generalize about Canadian education because of its great diversity. Within Canada's system, education is a provincial responsibility and one which the provinces guard with particular dedication. Not only the ten provinces, but also the two territories operate their own distinct systems of education and patterns of curricula. It is even more complicated, since large cities such as Toronto, Montreal, Winnipeg, or Vancouver, although technically subject to provincial control, often tend to go their own way. Further, teachers throughout Canada possess a good deal of autonomy. Thus the description of political education in Canada which follows must necessarily be highly general.

Only a few Canadian students actually take courses in politics during their school careers, although almost all of them will study at least one topic or unit dealing with a political theme. Most often this will consist of a more or less descriptive treatment of government and political institutions combined with some attempt to explain Canadian federalism, parliamentary democracy and constitutional monarchy - although this last generally gets short shrift: impressionistic evidence suggests that most school students think of Queen Elizabeth as the Queen of England rather than of Canada. In addition to this, most students will get some grounding, either formally or otherwise, in current events.

Nonetheless, although most students do not study politics in any formal way, they do receive a great deal of political education, with particular emphasis on civics and citizenship as defined previously. In particular, Canadian schools have long been concerned with promoting a sense of Canadianism and, more generally, a sense of citizenship, of what it means to be a good or "responsible" (to use a favourite word of curriculum documents) citizen.

The use of the schools to promote a sense of Canadianism is not surprising, given the particular historical context of Canada. Canada is of vast size, regionally divided, inevitably multicultural, peopled largely by successive waves of immigrants. Canada's unity is not something which can always be taken for granted. Thus, the schools early came to be seen as a means of promoting either Canadian unity or, at the very least, a Canadian identity. As one prominent Canadian, Vincent Massey, put it in 1926: "To our schools we must look for the good Canadian."[24] In this, he was reinforcing an already accepted tradition, perhaps best stated by the Winnipeg School Board in 1914:

> ...on the school, more than upon any other agency will depend the quality and the nature of the citizenship of the future;...in the way in which the school avails itself of its opportunities depends the extent to which Canadian traditions will be appropriated, Canadian national sentiment imbibed, and Canadian standards of living adopted by the next generation of the new races that are making their home in our midst.[25]

In all this, Canadian schools were following the course already charted by the other new states created in the 19th century, and indeed by many old ones. The 19th century was, after all, the age of the nation-state and the nation-state demanded not simply external loyalty and outward conformity but an inner commitment. Furthermore, the nation-state demanded unity and even uniformity. Regional loyalties, languages, dialects and identities had to be replaced by a belief in the nation. In all of this, education was crucial, for it was through the schools that national identity would be created. This was a concern not only in Europe but in North America where both the United States and Canada were committed to assimilating the large numbers of "foreign" immigrants who arrived annually. Thus, when the Winnipeg schools staged a celebration to honour the 60th anniversary of Queen Victoria's accession to the throne in 1897, the school board noted of the students that "diverse in origin, diverse in speech and differing in faith, they are one in learning the lessons of loyalty to the empire on whose flag the sun never sets." [26]

One can see the nationalist bent of Canadian civic education most conspicuously in school history courses and textbooks. Naturally enough, history was seen above all as a vehicle for implanting national ideals and thus overcoming both regional divisiveness and immigrant loyalties. As George Ross, Ontario's Minister of Education, put it in 1884:

> ...*the history of the community and nation to which we belong...shows the young the springs of public honour and dishonour; sets before them the national feelings, weaknesses and sins; warns them against future dangers by exhibiting the losses and sufferings of the past; enshrines in their hearts the national heroes; and strengthens in them the precious love of country.*[27]

To this end, in 1892 a competition was launched to find a history textbook that would be satisfactory to all groups and regions in the country, a book that would unite rather than divide and which would provide a truly national view of Canada and Canadianism. It should, perhaps, be added that, when such a book was published in 1898, it was rejected by various provinces as not doing justice to their particular areas.[28] One of the peculiarities of Canadian nationalism, then as now, is that to talk of national unity can itself be divisve.

However, despite the problems, Canadian history textbooks never gave up their nationalist emphasis, even though it was not shared in all parts of the country at the same time. There grew up a long tradition in textbook writing in Canada that nation-building is the most important theme to expound to youngsters. In the 1940s texts carried such titles as *Building the Canadian Nation, Colony to Nation, Canada: A Nation and How it Came to Be*. It seems that textbook titles mirror social concerns. These early titles clearly indicate a confidence that Canada was, indeed, a nation. By the late 1960s this was no longer so certain and it is indicative of something that the most widely used textbook of that period was entitled *Challenge and Survival*. It is perhaps even more indicative that the 1970s revision was called *In Search of Canada*. The old confidence had gone it seems. Nonetheless, the overriding concern of textbooks has been to describe how Canada attained its geographical and political shape with the main actors being explorers and politicians. This emphasis has meant that internal conflict is dealt with very cautiously, since it detracts from the message of national unity with which the textbooks have been so preoccupied.

Admittedly, as early as 1886 a textbook suggested an alternative framework. Pursuing the ideas of the English social historian, T.H. Green, this book declared that

> "*History is part politics.*" *This may be accepted as a fairly*

Theories and Attitudes Towards Political Education

> *correct definition if we enlarge the ordinary conception of "politics" so as to comprehend all the facts connected with the moral, intellectual and social life of a community. History deals with something more than the struggles of contending princes.... It aims to reveal to us the joys and sorrows, the triumphs and defeats, the virtues and vices, of the different classes that make up a nation.*[29]

This remained very much a voice in the wilderness. In fact, even this text, despite the bow to social history in its preface, dealt exclusively with political constitutional topics.

This emphasis can be seen quite clearly in a 1907 text which included a preface by C.W. Colby of McGill, one of Canada's first professors of history. Colby wrote, "But, above everything else, the writer of a school history is compelled to be terse. This means that he must confine himself almost wholly to politics...."[30] For Colby apparently, for most people in the textbook field and for those who drew up curricula, political history had no rivals. When priorities had to be established and choices made on what to include and what to exclude it was axiomatic that political and constitutional themes should predominate.

This emphasis was not modified until a shift took place in 1929, although it proved to be more apparent than real. In that year George Wrong, Chester Martin and Walter Sage, three prominent Canadian historians, co-authored a text which contained remarkably little political history. The book's preface, signed not by the authors but by "The Publishers," explained that the new approach was intended to arouse students' interest, which apparently was flagging badly. The preface noted that "there is something radically wrong when so many students in our schools dislike Canadian history." Its explanation for this state of affairs was that youngsters were being taught political history before they were able to understand it: "many of the most vital issues in the development of Canada are quite beyond students of 13 or 14 years." Worth noting here is the assumption that "the most vital issues" are political or constitutional. The book offered not a new synthesis of Canadian history but rather was an attempt to solve a practical pedagogical problem. The solution was that "Constitutional problems are given a minor place, along with wars, bills, acts and party politics, while stress has been laid upon personalities and events of romantic interest."[31] Thus, the book was intended not so much as social history, but rather as an interesting story-book. Presumably, it filled a need; it was reprinted for the 10th time in 1945.

Despite this, textbooks remained heavily political in their emphases. A.R.M. Lower, for instance, in 1948 co-authored a text with a Winnipeg teacher, J.W. Chafe. Despite Lower's interests and reputation as a social historian, the book's preface stated that:

> *Above all, if we forget the long struggle by which our institutional heritage of government by consent of the governed and the reign of law was built up in England over the centuries, our industries and our forests, our fields, our mines and our stern northern temperaments will avail us nothing.*[32]

Although by the 1940s textbooks came to include increasing amounts of social history, their overwhelming emphasis was, and is still, on the political and constitutional narrative of nation-building.

Marshall W. Conley

All history textbooks have a unit or a section on government. Obviously, the achievement of Confederation in 1867 is a major event and textbooks give it a good deal of attention. The charter document of Confederation, the *British North America Act*, remains a fundamental part of the Canadian constitution. Thus, when textbooks describe Confederation, and the *British North America Act*, they go beyond strictly historical discussion to describe such topics as federalism, the parliamentary system, and responsible government. Here, then, albeit in rather descriptive fashion, history textbooks describe important components of the political system. They also tell students a good deal about Canada as a political community, or at least their authors' perceptions of it. This is true also of French language textbooks in Quebec, although in their case the political community is Quebec rather than Canada. The English-French dichotomy is as much a feature of political education as it is of Canadian society generally.

In both French and English language textbooks, a pervasive theme is that of nation-building. They describe in great detail the ways in which missionaries, fur-traders, explorers, railway-builders and others overcame the hardships of the physical environment. They also describe the demographic shaping of the country through successive waves of immigration and today, at least in anglophone Canada, take the opportunity to extol Canada's official policy of multiculturalism. Thus, for example, one recent textbook, having described the contribution of Chinese labourers to the building of the Canadian Pacific Railway, goes on to editorialize:

> *Over the years Chinese people have contributed much to Canada's growth. As well as their work on the railway, they started a market garden industry in British Columbia and have started thousands of businesses all across the country. Many Chinese Canadians have become important members of the community. In 1972, Dr. George Pon of Toronto, the grandson of one of these early railway workers, became vice-president of Atomic Energy of Canada.*[33]

There are several interesting features in this paragraph, which is typical of recent textbooks. One is the very fact that it was thought worthwhile to include it in a historical description of the building of the Canadian Pacific Railway. Obviously, school history is intended to serve a socializing and moralizing purpose with clear political overtones. The second is the implicit criterion of what makes one an important member of the community. Textbooks, at least in Canada, are incorrigibly hierarchic and deferential in their sympathies. The third is the trouble taken to point out the evidence of social mobility: from unskilled immigrant to corporate vice-president in three generations. A fourth is the change that this passage marks in the message and values of textbooks. After decades of trying to anglicize immigrants, textbooks now promote the virtues of multiculturalism, which has become the official policy of the federal government.[34] Older textbooks simply ignored the Chinese. Textbooks of a few years ago were ambivalent. It is hard to miss the unwitting condescension in this 1970 passage, for example: "Still, these men of the Orient added character to the Canadian Pacific region. When they left the employment of the railroad, many became excellent cooks and restaurant operators."[35]

This switch from assimilation to multiculturalism indicates another political function of history textbooks and courses: they present an idealized

Theories and Attitudes Towards Political Education

view of the Canadian way of life and of the Canadian political culture. Canadian historians have written a good deal about the Canadian identity, or identities, as some would insist. A former president of the Canadian Historical Association told his colleagues in 1978 that "our task is to help people understand their time, their society and themselves."[36] This kind of commitment has been and is so common that a British historian, asked to comment upon the state of Canadian historiography, noted that the task now is "how to write about Canadians without being constantly preoccupied with the mystery of what is Canada."[37] Given this academic tradition, it is hardly surprising that textbooks and courses are infused with the same sense of mission.

Textbooks seem to go out of their way to describe the hardships Canadians have faced - and overcome. Part of the political message of textbooks is that hardship is a natural part of life and that with hard work, patience and determination, it can be overcome. From the pages of Canadian textbooks emerges a picture of the ideal Canadians: people who intend to better themselves, who will work hard without complaint, who can make a virtue out of necessity, who are moderate, self-reliant, respectable and temperate.

One must not think that the paucity of courses labelled "politics" means that students are not receiving a political education. What they are not getting, is any systematic study of or insight into political realities. Where Canadian history courses deal with the political system, they do so within a legal-historical-institutional framework.

In recent years, Canadian history has been supplemented by another subject in the school-curriculum - Canadian Studies. Most provinces now include this subject. Not suprisingly, some eyebrows are being raised at what is seen as an over-emphasis on things Canadian to the exclusion of the rest of the world — a world that includes Central America, the Middle East, South-East Asia and other regions about which no one can afford to be ill-informed.

This growth of interest in Canadian Studies is not new, for Canadians have long pondered their country's prospects. As Joseph Levitt has recently reminded us, "For at least a century thoughtful Canadians have reflected on their country's destiny. What would be the outcome of its political development? Would it remain a British colony, become part of the United States or somehow turn into an independent country?"[38] Despite this long tradition, there is something new about the attention being paid to Canadian Studies in the last 15 years or so. The term itself is new, at least as a more or less accepted academic designation. Also, greater attention is being paid to institutionalizing Canadian Studies in courses and programs. Despite the problems faced by Canadian publishers, there is a greater output of Canadian writing, research and scholarship, if only because of the university expansion of the late 1960s.

What Culture? What Heritage? appeared in 1968; it was a report on the teaching of Canadian history in schools across the country and was a devastating indictment. It found the content of history curricula to be outmoded, dull and even dangerous. The textbooks were worse but even they were better than the atrocious teaching that was said to exist in the great majority of Canadian history classrooms. The report, however, dealt with more than just history teaching and, as a result, had an impact on many people besides teachers. For one thing, it blamed a wide range of institutions for the depressing state of affairs it described: faculties of arts, teacher training institutions, departments of education, school boards, publishers — all took their lumps. If the schools were bad, it was not their fault alone. For another, the report linked the state of history teaching to questions of citizenship, to the "quality of civic life." In Hodgetts' words: "The majority of English-speaking high school graduates leave the Canadian Studies classroom without the intellectual skills, the knowledge and the attitudes they should have to play an effective role as citizens in the present day Canada."[39]

These findings, and the alarm they created, led directly to the creation of the Canada Studies Foundation in 1970, an organization which devoted itself to the production of better Canadian Studies materials and curricula in schools and which sought to involve university scholars working co-operatively with teachers to this end. This is not the place to review the role and record of the Foundation but its influence has been profound in putting Canadian Studies on the agenda of discussions about schools and curriculum reform.

What *What Culture? What Heritage?* did for the schools, the Symons Report, *To Know Ourselves* (1975), did for colleges and universities. Symons was commissioned by the Association of Universities and Colleges in Canada to investigate what was and was not being done in Canadian Studies in post-secondary institutions. Though more diplomatically worded, his report was just as devastating. He concluded, more in sorrow than in anger, that Canadian universities and colleges were simply not devoting enough time and energy to the study of the society that sustained them.

Reference should also be made to a third report, published in 1978, *Teaching Canada for the '80's.* (One of its authors was Birnie Hodgetts who earlier wrote *What Culture? What Heritage?*) In that book he indicated what was wrong; in *Teaching Canada* he (and his co-author Paul Gallagher) suggested what should be done to put it right. It suggested an overall framework for a Canadian Studies curriculum designed to enhance what it described as "pan-Canadian understanding" and to produce "the skilled and sensitive public opinion needed to resolve deep-seated difference in the Canadian political community before tension levels became dangerously high"[40]

And to indicate how seriously Canadian Studies as a subject is being taken at least by some people, it is worth noticing a 1979 position paper issued by the Science Council of Canada, and called, interestingly enough, *A Canadian Context for Science Education.* Even the allegedly international, or at least a national, sphere of science has to be to some extent redirected, for, in the words of the Science Council, "adequate recognition of a Canadian context for science education ought to be a basic educational objective."[41]

In any event, the study of Canada became a matter of some importance: either to investigate where Canadians were and where they might be going; or to hold on to what they had and prevent erosion; or to promote some particular vision. Some conservative intellectuals felt that it was already too late: in this spirit George Grant wrote his *Lament for a Nation* and Donald Creighton pointed to *The Forked Road*, arguing that we had taken the wrong turning. Others felt there was still a chance: "For the members of a country, of a culture, shared knowledge of their place, their home, is not a luxury but a necessity."[42] On this, everyone agreed;

Canadians simply did not know enough about themselves and "without that knowledge we will not survive."[43]

There are some, though only a few, who argue that Canadian Studies is or should be directed to the pursuit of Canadian unity. One suspects, for example, that one reason why the federal government supports Canadian Studies arises from its understandable commitment to Canadian unity. At the time of the Quebec referendum debate in 1980, it established an Office of National Unity. The *National Broadcasting Act* speaks of it explicitly. The problem is, of course, that to speak of unity smacks of uniformity and, given the strength of regionalism in Canadian society and given the historical tensions, implies an assimilating homogenizing impulse. As Cole Harris has put it: "Canada is sustained by nationalism based on experience and destroyed by nationalism based on cultural belief."[44]

More widely acceptable, and in fact more generally accepted, than national unity as a goal of Canadian Studies is the concept of national identity, a phrase much used by Canadians. The problem is that there is nothing beyond the most general agreement concerning what the Canadian identity is or should be. Many are concerned about it, but there is no agreement on what it is. Further, it is not completely clear what it means to have an identity anyway. Armour distinguishes between two meanings. On the one hand are those common beliefs, traditions, assumptions, conventions (often not consciously thought about) shared by people in a given society. On the other, are those things which people think about when they think of themselves as Canadian; for instance, flags, constitutions, anthems.[45] Proponents of Canadian identity have usually thought in terms of the second rather than the first.

It is obvious that there are many contenders for the title of Canadian identity. There are still those, for example, who think in terms of a unitary and probably unilingual nation-state in the classic 19th century sense. There are also those who favour the existing bilingual and multicultural society, or some variation of it. There are those who prefer the vision of two nations within a single state and there are those who want not only two nations but also two states, with whatever association may be created between them. And there is the vexed and complex question of the extent, implications and desirability of regional identities in Canadian society. Besides national unity and national identity (or identities), proponents of Canadian Studies advance another argument, based upon "self-knowledge." In the words of the Symons Report:

> ...the most valid rationale for Canadian Studies is not any relationship that such studies have to the preservation or the promotion of national identity, or national unity, or national sovereignty, or anything of the kind. The most valid and compelling argument for Canadian Studies is the importance of self-knowledge, the need to know and to understand ourselves.[46]

A number of studies have attempted to identify attitudes and levels of knowledge in Canada. In 1975, publisher Mel Hurtig organized a national "Canadian Awareness Study" of students in their last year of high school.[47] During this period two other studies of school children ranging from ages 8 to 17 were completed in Nova Scotia.[48] These three studies discovered that most Canadian students knew very little about their heritage and the workings of the Canadian government. Hurtig described the results of the study as, "simply appalling."

In his pamphlet, *Never Heard of Them...They Must Be Canadian*, Hurtig stressed that in the interest of producing intelligent and politically aware students who would be prepared to enter into a democratic society, political studies should be included as an integral part of secondary school education. He was concerned primarily with increasing students' awareness of the political process so that they would be able to participate effectively in that process as they grew older. He stressed teaching the theories of the democratic system and contrasting them with the way democracy works in actual practice. Hurtig felt very strongly that it was the role of the educational system to teach political awareness and that such awareness, if not picked up in school, would not be acquired later. He wrote,

> *If a similar study were conducted today among adult Canadians, I would bet my last dollar that the result would be even more appalling.*[49]

He wanted the educational system in Canada to produce politically aware Canadians who had developed the civic consciousness to intelligently participate in the political process.

In June 1981, the *Canadian Awareness Project Report*[50] was published by the Alberta Department of Education. This 200-page report on the level of knowledge of 3,500 Alberta school children was similar to Hurtig's study but far more comprehensive in the questions asked. Unfortunately, it appears that little progress had been made in Alberta since the 1975 Hurtig study. Putting as positive a face as possible on their conclusions, the authors indicated that, except for a minority, "young citizens should be encouraged to aspire to that higher level of awareness," and "more young citizens should have a higher level of Canadian awareness than was demonstrated in this project."[51] Indeed, the means scores for the citizenship (knowledge) test were 34%, 39% and 49% for grades 6, 9, and 12 respectively.[52]

In the report of a 1982 study, *A Survey of Elementary and Secondary Pupils: Their Knowledge and Attitudes Regarding Canada*,[53] Kirkwood and Nediger state that there has been an improvement. In this study of over 10,000 students in grades 7 and 10, they indicated that "students do indeed possess a basic level of knowledge about Canada and do possess positive attitudes."[54] Unfortunately, their claim of "basic level of knowedge" would not be popularly conceded. "The mean score for grade 7 students (on the knowledge scale) was 24.88 out of 60 (41.4%) and 32.76 out of 60 (54.6%) for grade 10 students."[55] What is even more disturbing, however, is the fact that on the attitude sub-scales, the grade 7 students outscored the grade 10 students on four of the six items which could be considered to be tolerance questions (i.e., items dealing with rights of ethnic minorities).[56]

The most recent study, *A Survey of Secondary Pupils: Their Knowledge and Attitudes Regarding Canada*,[57] is a replication of the Kirkwood and Nediger project, and surveys 3,200 grade 12 students across Canada. The authors report that there was a mean score of 60% (36 out of 60 items) on the knowledge scale. Once again the authors suggested that "Canadian grade 12 students possess a *good* [my emphasis] basic level of knowledge about Canada."[58] Perhaps the textbook title, *In Search of Canada* is an appropriate one when we have to consider 60% as constituting a good

Theories and Attitudes Towards Political Education

basic level of knowledge about Canada!

Whatever its form, be it through history, Canadian Studies, science or some other subject, an important goal of political education in Canadian schools is to cultivate a sense of nationhood, to strengthen students' attachment to the political community, to use Easton's phrase.

Besides this concern for nationhood and national sentiment, the schools also promote a sense of general citizenship, emphasizing particular attitudes and virtues over others. Ironically, many teachers do not see this as political at all, subscribing, as they do, to the widespread Canadian myth that education is not political in any sense.

In reality, of course, the curriculum is not neutral. It is designed to present a particular view of the world to youngsters. It is obvious, for instance, that not everything can be included in one curriculum, that the curriculum represents a selection from the culture, as Raymond Williams has put it. What is perhaps not so obvious is who makes that selection and for what purposes.

An analysis of Canadian history textbooks, for example, reveals a remarkable series of omissions and value judgements, even in the most recent publications.

(1) Textbooks say little about ordinary working Canadians, although they say a good deal about political and economic elites.

(2) They transmit a clear and consistent moral message, emphasizing the values of perseverance and determination of individualism, hard work, moderation and restraint.

(3) They consistently minimize - to the point of total omission - the existence of social conflict both past and present.[59]

Textbooks ignore conflict — as do many teachers—by often failing to point out the conflict of ideas, of interpretation, of hypotheses that are at the heart of intellectual inquiry, even in the elementary school. The majority of textbooks are written as a series of factual statements, sliced up into chunks, each with its own subheading, and arranged to imply that all one has to do is to learn their contents and thus become educated. As one cynic once put it, they give student answers to problems they did not even know they had.

Curricula and textbooks, emphasizing learning what the "authority" prescribes, preclude any attempt to get students to investigate or to inquire. They forestall all those kinds of activities that would facilitate and enhance students' development and empowerment.

In this they are reinforced by what we have learned to call the "hidden curriculum." Brophy and Good, for example, in reviewing and summarizing the various investigations of what actually happens in classrooms in the United States, concluded that:
- *Teachers monopolize communications in the classroom.*
- *Teachers' emphasis has been placed on obtaining student response to short factual questions.*
- *The quality of teacher-child interaction varies with the achievement level of the student.*
- *There is evidence indicating that students are not as free to act as teachers believe them to be.*[60]

There is abundant evidence to indicate that this kind of pattern holds true in Canada. In 1968, for example, Hodgetts reported that 68% of classes observed stuck closely to the textbook and could only be described as "desk-bound" and bored listeners.[61] A 1977 assessment of social studies in British Columbia found that only a small minority of teachers wanted the right to choose their own textbooks, preferring that such decisions be made at a higher level. This study also found "class-discussion" and "audio-visual presentations" to be the most reported methods of teaching, although, as the report notes, both methods are "frequently characterized by a high degree of student passivity."[62] Similar evidence can be found in the 1975 social studies assessment done in Alberta. At that time the social studies curriculum recommended three "instructional modes": (1) the designative (what is); (2) the appraisive (what should be); and (3) the prescriptive (what should be done) — and found that only the designative (i.e., the descriptive) was thoroughly taught. The report found an 80% emphasis on the designative; 20% on the appraisive and "no orientation whatsoever" to the prescriptive.[63] Indeed, 40% of the teachers rejected the whole open-inquiry, no-textbook approach — a finding borne out recently in Quebec where it was found that a majority of history and social studies teachers chose not to deal with political issues in their classrooms, and indeed declared themselves opposed to such discussions.[64]

From all this, it seems reasonable to conclude that teaching continues to be predominantly didactic, expository and authoritarian. It socializes students and does little or nothing for their sense of efficacy, either generally or politically.

The broad socio-political impact of the school has been described and explained by sociologists such as Talcott Parsons and Robert Dreeben. For them, schools function to internalize in the students' commitments to and capacities for future adult roles. Parsons described the school as a sort of half-way house which moves children out of the personal, emotion-laden atmosphere of the family to the impersonal, objective world of public life. In his terms, schools move youngsters from status based upon *ascription* to status based on *achievement.* Dreeben makes the same point. He describes work in an industrial society as being characterized by (i) a distinction between the worker as a person and the position that he occupies; (ii) a physical separation from the household; (iii) individual accountability for tasks which are assessed by prescribed standards; (iv) being carried out increasingly in large bureaucratically run organizations. This kind of work demands certain attitudes and habits. They may be adopted as a role for convenience's sake or they may be internalized as an ideology, but, nonetheless, they are necessary. Here, says Dreeben, is an important function of the school. It is the institution that trains youngsters for this kind of work and behaviour. To quote him:

> *One answer to the question "What is learned in school?" is the pupils learn to acknowledge that there are tasks they must do alone, and to do them that way. Along with this self-imposed obligation goes the idea that others have a legitimate right to expect such independent behaviour under certain circumstances.*[65]

In Philip Jackson's words:

> *...schools are a place where things happen not because students want them to but because it is time for them to occur.... The distinction between work and play has far-*

reaching consequences for human affairs, and the classroom is the setting in which most people encounter this distinction in a personally meaningful way.[66]

At this level, then, the essential function of the school (far more essential than its concern for teaching knowledge and skills) is to equip students with appropriate dispositions, attitudes, and knowledge for the world of work in an industrial society — a world in which work is an increasing source of dissatisfaction, according to survey after survey of worker alienation — and particularly to encourage the growth of passivity, conformity and obedience.

Thus, overall, most children are taught to be dependent rather than autonomous. They define the teacher's role as one of keeping order, giving instructions and evaluating. An English study noted that:

Primary school children...don't like teachers who shout at them, or who are sarcastic, impatient, or uninterested in their work. Popular teachers are kind, tactful, approachable, and apparently competent. But what is soon clear is that most of these children expect the teacher to act as the boss; to direct, initiate and control learning; to be judge and jury of work and conduct; and to act according to his status in the school. It is these expectations, rather than likes or dislikes which are most apparent...[67]

This can be seen in another way. In recent years political scientists have been paying a good deal of attention to political socialization: what and how children learn about things political. One of their findings is that one cannot confine political learning to the civics or social studies program. Rather, it occurs as a result of all the experiences that children have in school and, consequently, begins at a very early age. The anthropologist Lawrence Wylie made this observation about a French infant school when the teacher remarked of her pupils that "there is nothing serious they have to learn for a year or so":

The Children, however, do learn important lessons. They learn to sit still for long periods. They learn to accept the discipline of the school. They even learn about learning—that is, they are impressed with the fact that to learn means to copy or to repeat what the teacher tells them.[68]

A general finding of the political socialization research is that obedience is one of the most important political lessons that children learn in school. In Hess and Torney's words, "Compliance to rules and authority is a major focus of civics education in elementary schools."[69] There is some evidence that the political messages—both hidden and overt—we teach to children vary according to social class. In brief, with working class students, schools emphasize conformity, duty and obedience; with middle-class students the emphasis is upon participation and efficacy. Obviously, students do not always internalize these messages. What the school teaches is not necessarily what the students learn and Paul Willis has shown how a group of English working class students resist their school's teaching.[70] Nonetheless, the fact remains that schools, often without realizing what they are doing, emphasize a particular cluster of values and behaviours. Their overall message is one of dependency, of conformity, of obedience: in a word, the task is seen as one of socialization.

153

Marshall W. Conley

There is evidence to suggest that independence, creativity, autonomy are not highly valued in schools. Few report cards contain such categories as "thinks for himself/herself"; "autonomous"; "creative"; "asks interesting questions." The usual headings are (to quote a typical Canadian example): "gets along with others"; "uses time to good advantage"; "completes assignments"; "works quietly and independently"; "listens well"; "dependable"; "produces neat work"; "takes criticism and disappointment well." It is difficult to imagine a list of qualities that better describe the loyal, dutiful worker.

Social control is also maintained through the tracking or streaming function of the school. All industrial societies are characterized by social and economic inequalities and Canada is no exception. How then are people led to accept—more or less — these inequalities and rationalize them? Here again schools are important. In awarding credentials—and in their own streaming practices—they serve to legitimize inequality. They make it seem that those who have "made it" have done so because of natural ability. We now know, however, that the best predictor of a child's educational performance is socio-economic position. This holds true in England, Sweden, the U.S.A. and Canada. Jencks has recently argued that school makes no difference to anything. One need not, perhaps, be this pessimistic, but there is nothing very controversial in the corollary that school alone is unable to redress the inequities within society. More disturbing is the realization that it seems to entrench them.

---

1 A.B. Hodgetts and P. Gallagher, *Teaching Canada for the '80s* (Toronto: O.I.S.E., 1978), p. vi.

2 S. Houston, "Politics, Schools and Social Change in Upper Canada," *Canadian Historical Review* LIII:3, (September 1972), p. 256.

3 M.J. Crozier, S.P. Huntington, J. Watanuki, *The Crisis of Democracy* (New York: New York University Press, 1975).

4 J.V. Torney and A. Oppenheim, *Civic Education in Ten Countries* (New York: Wiley, 1975), p. 21.

5 L.W. Milbrath and M.L. Goel, *Political Participation: How and Why Do People Get Involved in Politics?* (Chicago: Rand McNally, 1977).

6 B. Crick and A. Porter, *Political Education and Political Literacy* (London: Longman, 1978), p. 13.

7 Ian Lister, "The Aims of Political Education in Schools", *Teaching Politics*, Vol. 6 (1977), p. 5.

8 Karen Smith Dawson, "Political Education - A Challenge", *News for Teachers of Political Science*, No. 20 (Winter 1979), p. 4.

9 *Education for Responsible Citizenship* (New York: McGraw-Hill, 1977), p.9.

10 As illustrated, for example, by these remarks: ...a majority of Canadians simply do not like politics or politicians...the general comments on politics were 33% positive and 52% negative. The general comments on politicians were a staggering 78%, negative in tone. Politicians tend to be seen by Canadians as "terrible", as "crooked", as "doing a bad job", as "out for themselves", as "wasting the money we pay in taxes", as "serving the big interests", as "generally ineffectual". Government has the same image; attitudes towards it are 75% negative. Similarly, the general comments on parties are 78% negative". H.D. Clarke, J. Jenson, L. LeDuc, J.H. Pammett, *Political Choice in Canada* (Toronto: McGraw-Hill-Ryerson, 1979), p. 10.

11 A.B. Hodgetts and P. Gallagher, *op. cit*, pp. 4-5.

12 This is nicely put by Hodgetts and Gallagher: "A democratic society that tolerates such a situation (i.e., cynicism and apathy) for long takes unwarranted risks with its own stability, and does a disservice to students whose lives will be so

pervasively influenced by governments and the total political system." A.B. Hodgetts and P. Gallagher, op.cit., p. 54.

13 W. Mishler, *Political Particpation in Canada* (Toronto: Macmillan, 1979), p. 95. See also D. Olsen, *The State Elite* (Toronto: McClelland and Stewart, 1980).

14 A.B. Hodgetts and P. Gallagher, op. cit., p. 60.

15 B.R. Berelson, P.F. Lazarsfeld, W.N. McPhee, *Voting* (Chicago: University of Chicago Press, 1954), p. 314.

16 E. Marchand, *Working for Canadians* (Scarborough: Prentice-Hall, 1979), p. 4. For an analysis of the consensus orientation of history textbooks see K. Osborne, *"Hard-working, Temperate and Peaceable": the Portrayal of Workers in Canadian History Textbooks,* University of Manitoba Education Monograph 4, 1980.

17 Quoted in Alan Reid, "An Outsider's View of Political Education in England: Past, Present and Future," *Teaching Politics,* Vol. 14, No. 1 (1985), p. 9.

18 A.B. Hodgetts, *What Culture? What Heritage?* (Toronto: OISE, 1968), p.79.

19 The annual *Maclean's* magazine poll indicated that only 30% of the population was satisified with the performance of Brian Mulroney as Prime Minister and that 44% considered the performance of the federal government to be only average. See, *Maclean's,* 5 January 1987, pp. 32-35.

20 C.D. Cary, "The Goals of Citizenship Training in American and Soviet Schools," *Studies in Comparative Communism,* X:3 (Autumn 1977), p. 282.

21 R. Remy, *Handbook of Basic Citizenship Competencies.* (Washington: A.S.C.D., 1980), p. vii. For another formulation, see J.S. Gibson, "Citizenship Education: Academic and Pragmatic Perspectives," in I. Morrissett and W.W. Stevens (eds.) *Social Science in the Schools: A Search for Rationale* (New York: Holt, Rinehart and Winston, 1971), pp. 45-57.

22 A.B. Hodgetts and P. Gallagher, op. cit, p. 60.

23 E. Marchand, op. cit., p. V. For the alternative view of the state see R. Miliband, *The State in Capitalist Society* (London: Weidenfeld and Nicolson, 1969); and L. Panitch (ed.)., *The Canadian State: Political Economy and Political Power* (Toronto: University of Toronto Press, 1977), esp. pp. 1-27.

24 Cited in E. Milburn (ed.) *Teaching History in Canada* (Toronto: McGraw-Hill-Ryerson, 1972), p. 100.

25 "Report of the School District of Winnipeg", 1914, p. 14.

26 *Ibid.,* 1897, p. 23.

27 Cited in A. Chaiton and N. McDonald (eds.), *Canadian Schools and Canadian Identity* (Toronto: Gage, 1977).

28 See G. Laloux-Jain, *Les manuels d'histoire du Canada au Quebec et en Ontario 1867-1914* (Quebec: Les Presses de l'universite Laval, 1974), pp. 80 ff.

29 G.M. Adams and W.J. Robertson, *A Public School History of England and Canada* (Toronto: 1886), pp. iii-v, *passim.*

30 Preface to I. Gammell, *Elementary History of Canada,* (Toronto: 1907), p.i.

31 G.M. Wrong, C. Martin, W.N. Sage, *The Story of Canada,* (Toronto: 1929).

32 J.W. Chafe and A.R.M. Lower, *Canada: A Nation and How It Came to Be* (Toronto: 1948), p. xiii.

33 J.B. Cruxton and W.D. Wilson, *Flashback Canada* (Toronto: Oxford University Press, 1978), p. 221.

34 See H. Troper, "Nationalism and the History Curriculum in Canada," *The History Teacher,* XII:3, (November 1978), pp. 11-28.

35 D. Willows and S. Richmonds, *Canada: Colony to Centennial* (Toronto: McGraw-Hill-Ryerson, 1970), p. 275.

36 D. Morton, "History and Nationality in Canada: Variations on an old Theme," *Canadian Historical Association Papers,* 1979, p. 2.

37 H.J. Hanham, "Canadian History in the 1970's," *Canadian Historical Review,* LVII:1, (March 1977), p. 22.

38 J. Levitt, *A Vision Beyond Reach: A Century of Images of Canadian Destiny* (Ottawa: Deneau, 1983), p. i.

39 A.B. Hodgetts, *op. cit.*, p. 116.
40 A.B. Hodgetts and P. Gallagher, *Teaching Canada for the '80's* (Toronto: O.I.S.E., 1978), p. 11.
41 Science Council of Canada, *Science in a Canadian Context* (Ottawa: Science Council of Canada, 1979), p. 10.
42 M. Atwood, *Survival* (Toronto: Anansi, 1972), p. 19.
43 *Ibid.*
44 C. Harris, "The Emotional Structure of Canadian Regionalism," *Walter L. Gordon Lectures* (Toronto: Canada Studies Foundation, 1981), p. 15.
45 L. Armour, *The Idea of Canada and the Crisis of Community* (Ottawa: Steel Rail, 1981).
46 T.H.B. Symons, *To Know Ourselves* (Ottawa: A.U.C.C., 1975), p. 13.
47 Mel Hurtig, *Never Heard of Them...They Must Be Canadian* (Toronto: Canadabooks, 1975).
48 M.W. Conley, "The Political Socialization of Nova Scotia School Children, Grades 4 Through 8," Acadia University, 1973; J. Jabbra and R. Landes, *The Political Orientations of Canadian Adolescents* (Halifax: St. Mary's University, 1976).
49 Hurtig, *op. cit.*, p. 11.
50 Minister's Advisory Committee for the Canadian Awareness Project, *Canadian Awareness Project Report* (Edmonton: Alberta Education, June, 1981).
51 *Ibid.*, p. 228.
52 *Ibid.*, p. 220.
53 Kristian John Kirkwood and William G. Nediger, *A Survey of Elementary and Secondary School Pupils; Their Knowledge and Attitudes Towards Canada* (London: Faculty of Education, University of Western Ontario, 1982).
54 Reported in R.M. Anderson, K.J. Kirkwood and W.G. Nediger, "Canadian Studies in 1982: A Progress Report," *CONTACT* 56 (December, 1982), p. 1.
55 *Ibid.*, p. 6.
56 K.J. Kirkwood and W.G. Nediger, *op. cit.*, pp. 25-26
57 K.J. Kirkwood, R.M. Anderson, S.B. Khan, *A Survey of Secondary Pupils: Their Knowledge and Attitudes Regarding Canada* (Toronto: The Canada Studies Foundation, 1984).
58 *Ibid.*, p. 26.
59 K.W. Osborne, *"Hard-working, Temperate and Peaceable" The Portrayal of Workers in Canadian History Textbooks*, Education Monograph No. 4 (Winnipeg: University of Manitoba, 1980).
60 J. Brophy and J. Good, *Looking In Classrooms* (New York: Harper and Row, 1973), pp. 22-37.
61 A.B. Hodgetts, *op. cit.*
62 T.T. Aoki, et al., *British Columbia Social Studies Assessment: A Report to the Ministry of Education* (Victoria: B.C. Ministry of Education, 1977).
63 L.W. Downey, *The Social Studies in Alberta, 1975: A Report of an Assessment* (Edmonton: Alberta Department of Education, 1975).
64 C. Trottier, "Les enseignants comme agents de socialisation politique au Quebec," *Canadian Journal of Education*, 7:1 (1982), pp. 15-43.
65 R. Dreeben, *On What Is Learned In School* (Reading: Addison-Wesley, 1968).
66 P. Jackson, *Life in Classrooms* (New York: Holt, Rinehart and Winston, 1968).
67 D. Hanson and M. Herrington, "Please Miss, You're Supposed to Stop Her," *New Society*, 10 June 1976, p. 568.
68 L. Wylie, *Village in the Vaucluse* (New York: Harper and Row, 1957).
69 R. Hess and J.V. Torney, *The Development of Political Attitudes in Children* (Chicago: Aldine, 1967), p. 110.
70 P. Willis, *Learning to Labour: How Working Class Kids Get Working Class Jobs* (Farnborough: Saxon House, 1977). See also J. Anyon, "Educational Equity and School Instruction," *Social Education*, April 1981, pp. 227-281.

Thoughts on Education for Global Citizenship

Patricia Schuyler
Atlantic Regional Director,
Save the Children Canada
and
George W. Schuyler
Director, International Education Centre,
St. Mary's University, Halifax

> *We are bound together by our belief in a citizenship which is based on the enduring principles of equality, diversity and community...*
> David Crombie, Secretary of State of Canada, 1987

CANADA'S citizenship education emphasizes local and national perspectives at a time when the world is already interdependent and becoming more so. Economic activity has been internationalized through the creation and

À l'heure où les activités économiques, la sécurité dans le monde et l'environnement exigent une perspective globale, l'instruction civique au Canada porte sur des perspectives régionales et nationales. Les auteurs font état de la nécessité d'avoir des citoyens et des citoyennes qui pensent à l'échelle mondiale et ils décrivent les avantages de l'enseignement du développement international. Ils présentent des modifications qui pourraient être apportées au contenu des cours et au processus d'apprentissage de même qu'à la formation du personnel enseignant et au programme d'études. Les éducateurs et éducatrices qui prônent l'enseignement universel souhaitent que le gouvernement canadien et ses citoyens et citoyennes prennent leurs responsabilités dans la communauté mondiale, c.-à-d. qu'ils soient actifs. Pour cela, l'éducation doit stimuler les passions, l'imagination et l'intelligence des élèves pour les amener à contester les forces politiques, sociales et économiques qui perpétuent l'inégalité. La participation, la justice, la tolérance et l'égalité sont des facteurs essentiels au civisme canadien.

swift exchange of information. Global producers search out cheap labour, unprotected natural environments, and markets throughout the world and use cheap transport to profit from them. Politics become the interaction of different peoples, states and systems operating within a global environment, an environment that we are responsible for preserving for all of humankind. The loss of rain forests or the thinning of the ozone layer are international political issues as well as environmental crises. World security and the definition of friend or ally may have less to do with political competition or military strength and more to do with co-operation. Our problems, whether poverty, nuclear warfare, or pollution, demand international solutions. "Whether we like it or not," writes Palestinian scholar Munir J. Fasheh, "we share one globe, one set of basic problems, and, the *only* way we can save this home of ours is by international co-operation to solve the serious threats we face."[1]

Canada needs people who think internationally. The test of citizenship in the 21st century will be to respond to problems and opportunities that affect all countries and that can only be met at the world level. The test of education will be to empower students to understand, think and act as citizens of both Canada and the world.

What kind of education is necessary for global citizenship? Can Canada build a global "civic culture" that shares common space, common resources and common problems with the five billion strangers who occupy the earth? Can we remain rooted in our local communities and national values and still create the co-operative strategies necessary to meet human needs everywhere?[2]

This essay explores relationships between citizenship education, global issues and the relevance of development education in building a global civic culture. Our intent is to probe and question, but we focus on directions that we believe are essential for responsible citizenship. We argue that citizenship education must include a global dimension and that values such as equality, diversity, respect for others and co-operation support global citizenship.

Canada and the World

Canadian citizenship values spring partly from the kind of society that we have become since World War II. Canada is a multicultural nation, enriched by the contributions of new immigrants whose family ties and cultural traditions link us to communities throughout the world. Equality, tolerance, and similar values, however imperfectly applied, make this multicultural society possible.

Such principles also influence Canadian foreign policy. Our economy, limited population, and modest military strength do not permit a commanding role in international affairs. Canada has, however, established a reputation for promoting world understanding, friendship and peace. Lester B. Pearson received his Nobel Prize for leadership in establishing a United Nations Emergency Force in the Middle East during the 1956 Suez Crisis. In 1988 the United Nations Peacekeeping Force won the Nobel Prize for its forty-year effort to maintain peace in areas of international conflict. Canada also benefits economically from peace and co-operation. We are a trading nation, heavily dependent on the production, processing and export

Thoughts on Education for Global Citizenship

of raw materials and finished goods. Like other small and middle-size countries, we rely on international rules to protect our interests.

Canadian education, however, does not reflect our complex involvement with the rest of the world. We are concerned about issues that have captured world attention - famine, poverty, the environment or Central America[3] - but our public education, and thus its preparation for citizenship, remain inwardly-focused. The 1967 centennial celebrations brought a surge of national pride and interest in things Canadian that was long overdue. During the next 20 years curricula, educational publishing and "most aspects of public education" centred on Canada.[4] This emphasis overshadows global concerns, particularly Canada's involvement with less developed nations.

The media, rather than our schools, shape student views of the developing world. A December 1987 Decima poll indicated that a) television and daily newspapers are the primary sources of information on developing countries; b) religious organizations and television news are the most believable sources of information. Although 52% of the respondents agreed with the statement "I think the Canadian school system does a good job teaching our children about poor countries and the people who live there," those who disagreed most were aged 16-19 and those currently in school.[5] Non-governmental organizations and learner centres play an important role in educating Canadians about global issues but their audience is limited. A national effort to equip Canadians for global citizenship is yet to come.

Global Citizenship

Throughout history, citizenship has been linked to specific boundaries - the city-state in ancient Greece and Rome; the nation in France, Canada or other modern states. *Le Petit Robert*, a French dictionary, defines a citizen as an "individual considered to be a civic person, particulary a national of a country that is a republic." But acid rain or nuclear contamination do not respect national frontiers. Drugs, debt, or the flight of manufacturers to cheap labour zones link the developed and developing nations. Citizenship defined within a single nation is inadequate to deal with international problems.

Gross disparities between rich and poor, within and between nations, encourages thinking about the meaning of both national and global citizenship. Urban planner John Friedmann calls for a "charter of political and economic citizenship rights at all levels," to enhance participatory decision making, basic rights and access to the bases of social power. Friedmann sees citizenship as not only political rights but also "citizenship in an economic community where rights to a decent livelihood must be staked out...."[6] Friedmann's "economic community" is now worldwide, a fact dramatically illustrated by the October 1987 stock market collapse and the debt crisis. Moreover, the wealth of the overdeveloped, industrial North is one cause of poverty and underdevelopment in the marginalized South. Mexico pays U.S. $27 million daily to foreign creditors while an estimated 40% of its citizens are malnourished.[7] Global citizenship implies recognition that the Mexican slum-dweller merits the "rights to a decent livelihood" as much as the affluent Torontonian.

Author Benjamin Barber argues that people need two things to create genuine citizenship: institutions in which their input makes a difference; and access to information to inform their decisions. Not until people have power will they be motivated to learn about critical issues.[8] Vaughan Lyon, who teaches political studies at Trent University, carries the empowerment/learning issue into the education system: "...when our well-being is so dependent on good government at all levels, there is virtually no political education in the schools, and what little exists promotes a passive-observer role for students. People who are uninvolved in politics have no incentive to be well informed, and the politicians can appeal to them at only a superficial, emotional level."[9]

The challenge of global citizenship, then, is to engage Canadians in ways that are persuasive and to enlist their involvement in constructive change. The global citizen is informed, critical and active in community affairs, whether local, national or global. He or she understands that in any community the dominant groups convey what it means to be a citizen, and he or she is willing to confront the power of those groups. Education for global citizenship must prepare people to participate more effectively in political and economic processes and to influence public policy; to overcome what Professor Lyon describes as elections that are "cynical exercises in mass manipulation."[10] It helps Canadians to see themselves, their community and their country as contributors to social change rather than as bystanders.

Citizenship Education

In closing a 1977 conference, J. King Gordon, president of the United Nations Association in Canada, remarked that conference delegates "gave some attention [perhaps not enough...] to our role as citizens, not only of Canada, but of our world society."[11] Other conference participants spoke of the need to view the world as a single community. They urged a better understanding of the limits (or increasing irrelevance) of the concept of sovereignty and the adversary system of international relations, and called for a "planetary bargain" arising from more enlightened notions of interdependence.[12] But a decade after the United Nations Association conference, we still define citizenship almost exclusively in terms of Canada:

> If the well-being of Canada and the health of our democratic institutions are dependent on the informed and active participation of all citizens, then active citizenship may be defined as a process in which citizens participate in Canadian life at the individual, community or societal level, by acquiring and acting on the knowledge, skills and attitudes (or values) which will enable them to exercise their rights and responsibilities as Canadian citizens.[13]

Canadian and global citizenship are inseparable. If equality has any meaning for Canadian citizenship, it is the elimination of poverty not only in Canada but throughout the world. Interdependency demands, in the words of Pierre Elliott Trudeau, "an equitable distribution, worldwide, of resources and opportunities."[14]

Despite such insights, economist Gerald Helleiner warns that inequality divides us into two worlds, one rich, one poor, one grossly consuming, the other wretchedly suffering: "...world poverty is the issue of

Thoughts on Education for Global Citizenship

our times.... We may watch, in the comfort of our living rooms, as people starve before us on colour television, what C.P. Snow has described as the 'ultimate obscenity.'"[15]

Education for global citizenship must encourage Canadians to think, reflect and act in ways that help to eliminate the "ultimate obscenity." The schooling process which helps children to form their identity should include the world. The world's people are more alike than they are different, sharing common yearnings for ourselves and our families. Can we teach children to strive for greater equality and citizen participation in Canada and ignore it elsewhere? If our federal government exhorts us to "speak up for equality" in Canada, should we also speak out against blatant disregard of international law or inequality in the international economic system? What would this imply for the refusal of the United States to recognize the jurisdiction of the World Court when it condemned the U.S. mining of Nicaragua's waters? Does citizen participation on behalf of equality imply action that may challenge Canadian policies and politicians - or its schools and teachers? Like the ancient Greeks, should we strive to give our citizenship education an ethical underpining? Should Canadians question the morality of a world system overflowing with food while some 15 to 20 million people die annually from hunger-related causes? In short, what does global citizenship imply for the kind of education that we impart to our children?

Education for citizenship has always been a central mission of the school curriculum in Canada. This often has meant the study of national government institutions and the relationship of the individual to those institutions.[16] The Greeks, on the other hand, linked the relationship between the individual and society to a continuing struggle for a more just and decent political community. Global citizenship requires this broader vision, rooted in Kant's advice to educate "not for the present but for a better future condition of the human race."[17] It means understanding that the United Nations, the World Court, or international agreements such as the Law of the Seas represent steps toward limiting national sovereignty and increasing international co-operation. It means cross-cultural learning - "grasping what is alien and unfamiliar" - and sharing the wisdom and experience of our global neighbours.[18] Most important, it means learning to use our minds, imaginations, and skills in new ways to construct a healthier, more egalitarian world society.

Canadian students, however, learn little about world institutions or international agreements. They worry about nuclear war, are shocked by famine, and deplore environmental destruction, but feel powerless to do anything. Faced by the complexity and vastness of such problems, people flee from them.

Apathy and impotence, of course, are not confined to global challenges. We tend to measure citizen participation in terms of voting every few years rather than the degree to which people can understand and influence public issues. Our schools and classroom practices do not encourage students to challenge authority, question policies or advocate alternatives. Thinking is often circumscribed, driven by procedures and narrow requirements, rather than the goal of unleashing the imaginative, creative capabilities of students to deal with problems. Students seldom acquire the sense that they can make a difference on issues that directly affect them.

Global Education

Global education is a fuzzy concept. In North America it is often broadly defined to include international exchanges, cross-cultural awareness, learning about linkages with other countries, or development education. The relationship between citizenship and global education depends on what words like democracy, citizenship, interdependence, and development really mean - and what values they imply. In an essay on global education in the United States, Willard M. Kniep and Carrol Joy write that:

> ...being a good American citizen means being a good global citizen too. Such an individual will recognize that our very future rests upon a willingness to relate to the rest of the world on the basis of equity, co-operation, and the determination to satisfy mutual interests rather than solely self-interests. And this citizen of the future will participate intelligently and widely in the democratic processes of this country to ensure that public leaders and public policies benefit Americans by contributing to the well-being of that diverse universe of peoples and systems with which we are inextricably linked.[19]

The words sound wonderful. A critical thinker, however, might question whether the acquisitive, driving force of corporate capitalism can be sufficiently bridled to ensure greater equity and co-operation worldwide. When the ideology and values of the "free market" and uninhibited individualism dominate the world economy, are Americans - or Canadians, Europeans, or Japanese - willing to opt for a more equitable distribution of resources, wealth, and power with the developing world? Do we Canadians have the patience and the will to educate ourselves and our children about seemingly intractable problems?

Of the several strands of global education, development education seems particularly relevant to building global citizenship. In Canada it has evolved during the past 20 years among non-governmental agencies seeking to raise awareness of development issues. In North America and Europe, it focuses on the central crises of extreme poverty and inequality. Much of its activity takes place outside the formal school system, in churches, community centres, public libraries and homes.

Development education reflects important goals and values of citizenship education and prepares people for global citizenship. "The beginning point of analysis," writes former Oxfam-America executive Joseph Short, "is the world and the welfare of its four billion human beings. Much of the education establishment's thinking and pedagogy is still shackled by interstate and nationalist perspectives."[20] Development education, on the other hand, "...stresses the one-world values ideal, against which national values have to be considered, and argues that it is as wrong for a Bangladeshi child to die of hunger as it is for the child next door."[21] It examines political and economic relationships. It hypothesizes that productive resources and power must be broadly shared for real development to occur. It urges people to act, both individually and through networks and coalitions. And it seeks to change the conditions that cause poverty at home and in the world, rather than simply doling out assistance year after year.[22]

Because development education is concerned with the causes of world conditions, and with action for change, it stresses a *critical* process of learning that probes beneath the surface. In 1985, the Live Aid concert raised millions of dollars by conveying simple messages to large numbers of people who wanted to feel involved. The public did not (and does not) understand the causes of hunger. Three years later, famine again stalks Africa but funds are more difficult to raise. Famine funds are essential but they are not sufficient - they alleviate short-term emergencies but do little to change policies, whether internal or external, that perpetuate poverty and hunger within a country. And, writes Larry Minear, of Church World Service/Lutheran World Relief, "There is a growing feeling that public policies and [the] understanding of policy implications are as essential in eliminating poverty as development assistance programs themselves."[23]

In a democratic society, good citizenship requires citizens who understand public policies - whether we are talking about energy, free trade, agriculture, or the environment, in Canada or abroad. Development education seeks to create that competence. It describes a given condition - such as the destruction of the Amazon rain forest - analyzes the factors that shape that condition, and encourages people to act: "The process of development education within communities seeks popular involvement in decision-making at all levels, public accountability and recognition of the legitimacy of dissent."[24] Such qualities are essential for good citizenship and global survival.

Critical Thinking

> *Criticism is the examination and test of propositions of any kind,...to find out whether they correspond to reality or not....The critical habit of thought, if usual in a society, will pervade all its mores, because it is a way of taking up the problems of life...[people] educated in it cannot be stampeded by stump orators...They can wait for evidence and weigh evidence uninfluenced by the emphasis of confidence with which assertions are made on one side or the other. They can resist appeals to their dearest prejudices and all kinds of cajolery. Education in the critical faculty is the only education of which it truly can be said that it makes good citizens.*
>
> William Graham Sumner, 1906[25]

In an age of media and image-making, responsible citizenship demands critical thinking. Ira Shor, of the City University of New York, defines it much like Sumner: "the habit of analyzing experience and questioning received knowledge." A "critically literate" person understands that knowledge is influenced by the values of those who produce it.[26] Critical thinking helps to cut through competing arguments and assertions that surround controversial issues. It enables people to question inequality, to see the links among economics, politics, and hunger or human rights; and it helps them to gain a measure of control over the barrage of information to which they are subjected. Responsible citizenship is critical, asking whether society should be changed in a particular way or left as it is.

The critical questions we ask about any issue, local or global, depend upon our values. Equality, fair play and justice have long been ideals of Canadian citizenship. One of the goals for Public Education in Nova Scotia, for example, is "to provide opportunities...for students to develop civic, social, and moral responsibility and judgement."[27] In recent decades, such values, strengthened by religious convictions, have begun to shape a moral perception of development. They are reflected in issues such as ethical investing, indigenous rights - and criticism of a world community with hideous extremes of wealth and poverty, in which "a hunger holocaust claims twenty million human lives every year...."[28]

Moral values, however, often clash with other powerful values. Is education a ticket to income and elite status or a force for social justice? Should we strive for critical citizenship education that helps to lessen inequality - or accept the fact that traditional education often reproduces inequalities inherent in our local, national and world communities? Cautious, control-oriented and hierarchal public educational institutions are unlikely to provide environments that favour critical thinking or the challenge of authority. Although justice and lessening inequality may be in the interest of everyone, this assumption immediately confronts the issue of power. A redistribution of power whether within the school, within Canada, or globally, faces immense challenges.

A Pedagogy for Global Citizenship

Education for global citizenship requires a pedagogy that challenges the status quo and applies egalitarian values in Canada and throughout the world. Analytical skills and an orientation toward action are particularly important and consistent with a main theme that runs through Canadian citizenship education - citizen action and participation. Author David McConkey suggests that children need to grow up thinking globally, to be comfortable raising questions about how wealth and power are distributed in the world, how conflicts are resolved, or how we interact with the environment. There would be a more active learning process, with fewer predetermined "right" answers in a social studies class, for example, and more scope for curricula and teaching styles that empower students by involving them in decisions about what they learn.[29] It would help students move from descriptions of distant Third World countries to analysis; from seeing and hearing politicians to understanding that the ability to project an image on a television screen does not necessarily mean the competence to govern; from learning about the world's apparently overwhelming problems to acquiring a sense of being able to do something positive through individual and collective efforts.

Discussion of values, not simple fact-giving, should be the mode of instruction in dealing with controversial issues. Facts and information are not value-free and students need to be able to make informed - rather than uninformed - value judgements. They must know what the value in question really is and what social forces define a given situation.[30] Appropriate experiential techniques can assist students to reach such informed judgements. We must, as educators, help them to acquire the skills to deal with emotional, controversial, planetary issues that will affect them for the rest of their lives.

Part of our responsibility in creating a pedagogy for global citizenship is to reformulate the role that teachers play in the classroom. In discussing development education, Jean Christie, of Inter Pares, sets forth the reasons:

> *Education must be participatory and active, and is more than simply giving information. It must be a process of learning for all concerned, one which generates critical thinking...What we think about development defines the content and what we think about education to a large extent defines the methods we use. Central to both of these is the notion of power. If we are trying to create educational processes which are respectful, the notion that as teachers we know everything and as students we know nothing must be transformed. In the method itself, the question of power is important.*[31]

The implication is a less hierarchal classroom, with students moving from passive recipients of a fixed body of knowledge toward challenging and questioning the form and substance of the learning process, clarifying their values, and challenging social inequities. This suggests that teachers must understand their own values and beliefs and how these influence students.

Ethical and social considerations are essential in a pedagogy for global citizenship. They can be related to the student's own experience and thus make the need for action intelligible. Through understanding their own frame of reference and their own values, students recognize how these factors organize their view of the world and can begin to think more critically. Professor Donald C. Wilson makes a related point in discussing a "pedagogy of issues":

> *[It]...must go beyond the 'information about' an issue and the 'instructional strategies' for the classroom. Emphasis on such concerns often obscures an understanding of the social and ethical meaning of the issue itself. What is needed is a quality of mind that will help us to use the information to develop in ourselves and in our students an understanding of what is happening in society....One must be conscious of one's own experiences and realize the importance of the issue by relating a personal perspective to the larger societal structure. It is the relationship between oneself and the social context that is central to establishing a pedagogy of issues.*[32]

Finally, a pedagogy for global citizenship would stress co-operation over competition in the classroom. Scores of studies show that co-operation yields better results than competition - that superior performance usually requires the absence of competition in areas ranging from education (grade point averages) to business (salaries), from employment agencies to journalism.[33] Canadians receive much of their global information from the media, but competitive journalism lowers the quality of information and analysis. Researchers at Georgetown University have attributed the "distorted and excessive coverage of terrorist incidents" to "the highly competitive nature of network television" in the United States.[34] In the classroom, researchers David and Roger Johnson found that "the discussion process in co-operative groups promotes the discovery and development of higher quality cognitive strategies for learning than does the individual reasoning found in competitive and individualistic learning situations."[35] Such research has implications for global citizenship education. First, inside and outside the classroom, co-operation appears to pay bigger dividends than competition. A recent article by consultant David A. Teiger stresses the business success that flows from encouraging co-operation, mutual support, independence and creativity - a collaborative process in which *everyone* wins.[36] Second, co-operation is more likely to strengthen values like equality and justice than is competition. Third, environmental and other crises are pushing humankind in a co-operative direction. The Bruntland Report *Our Common Future* indentified "the gap in power and resources" as our planet's main environmental and main development problem.[37] Co-operation is the key to bridging this gap and ensuring planetary survival.

Conclusion

This essay is descriptive rather than analytical but it does suggest some of the possibilities for change in both the content and process of learning. We believe that Canadian citizenship education should be placed within a global context. The major aim is not to "fit" students into the existing world community or to transmit a fixed body of beliefs and information - it is to stimulate their passions, imaginations and intellects to challenge the political, social, and economic forces that perpetuate gross inequality.

Our strategy for citizenship education is straightforward - educate students to understand and to act upon those values embedded in federal and provincial statements about citizenship and education. Its content would extend the notions of justice, fair play and equality beyond the limits of Canadian national sovereignty. Such an education would help students to understand that no child, anywhere, should die from starvation. It would help them to recognize that the polarization of the world into a wealthy, well-fed minority and a hideously impoverished, hungry majority is morally and ethically unacceptable. Its ecological goal would be economic and social systems that sustain, rather than destroy, the world's air, water and soil. Its process would be participatory, critical, action-oriented and empowering. It would, in the words of Douglas Roche, Canada's Ambassador for Disarmament, educate "young people in a newly invigorated and enlightened manner so that they can, with enthusiasm, optimism and driving hope, become the stewards of the planet in the future."[38] Schools are not the sole answer to hunger or environmental destruction, but education can set a framework for understanding the causes of such crises and how to deal with them.

Teacher education and curriculum change are high priorities for global citizenship education. Teacher education would include content about global issues and citizenship but recognize that content alone is insufficient. A pedagogy that stresses critical thinking, values, and co-operation, and uses participation and discussion is vital. The goal is to help students to think critically about information they receive and to act on the basis of their analysis.

"I see my role as an educator," says peace activist Dr. Helen Caldicott. "If you inform a democracy, it functions in a responsible fashion."[39] Global educators want Canadian democracy and its citizens to function responsibly within the world community. This implies a much broader and deeper understanding of both democracy and citizenship.

Thoughts on Education for Global Citizenship

Education for global citizenship, of the kind that we are discussing here, insists that responsibility within a democracy includes active involvement in the processes of decision-making rather than simply placing our future welfare in someone else's hands. Former Multiculturalism Minister David Crombie emphasizes that participation, justice, equality, and tolerance are vital to Canadian citizenship.[40] These are precisely the qualities which, if widely accepted and acted upon, will improve Canadian democracy. These are the qualities that characterize education for global citizenship.

---

1 Munir Fasheh, "Talking About What to Cook for Dinner When Our House is on Fire: The Poverty of Existing Forms of International Education," *Harvard Educational Review* 55:1 (February 1985), p. 122.

2 Elise Boulding, *Building a Global Civic Culture: Education for an Interdependent World* (New York: Teachers College Press, Columbia University, 1988), p. xix.

3 Decima Research, *Report to CIDA: Public Attitudes Toward International Development Assistance* (Hull: CIDA, 1988).

4 Project in International Education, *"They Want a Better Life" What Canadian Children Are Supposed to Know About the World: A Review of Canadian Social Studies Curriculum Guidelines*, Paper Three (Halifax: International Education Centre, Saint Mary's University and the School of Education, Dalhousie University, September 1988), p. 6.

5 Decima Research, *op.cit.*, p. 21.

6 John Friedmann, "From Social to Political Power: Collective Self-Empowerment and Social Change," paper D875, Graduate School of Architecture and Urban Planning, University of California at Los Angeles, 1987.

7 Susan George, *A Fate Worse Than Debt* (London: Penguin, 1988).

8 Benjamin Barber, *Strong Democracy: Participatory Politics for a New Age* (1984), cited in Elizabeth Nielsen, "The Public Sphere: Nuclear-Freeze Posters in a Commodity Culture," *Monthly Review* 40:2 (June 1988) p. 50.

9. Vaughn Lyon, "Why Canada is Selling Democracy Short," *Globe and Mail*, 29 September 1988.

10 *Ibid.*

11 *Canada and the United Nations in a Changing World* (Ottawa: United Nations Association in Canada, 1977), p. 140.

12 *Ibid.*, p. 32.

13 Vandra I. Masemann, "Citizenship Education in Canada," pre-conference report, Department of the Secretary of State of Canada, Ottawa, September 1987, p. 2.

14 Quoted in *Canada and the United Nations*, *op.cit.*, p. 37.

15 *Canada and the United Nations*, *op.cit.*, p. 78.

16 See Vandra Masemann, "Citizenship Education in Canada," *op. cit.* p. 9. Ontario curriculum units on citizenship, for example, include topics such as living in a community with people, the rights and duties of citizenship, why individuals should vote, processes women went through to get the right to vote and hold office, and ways in which an individual can participate in the political system.

17 Quoted in Henry A. Giroux, *Theory and Resistance in Education: A Pedagogy for the Opposition* (South Hadley, Mass.: Bergin & Garvey Publishers, 1983), p. 174.

18 Elise Boulding, *op. cit.*, p. x.

19 *Access*, Number 76, Special Issue on Development Education, New York, February 1988, p. 7.

167

20 Joseph Short, "Learning and Teaching Development" *Harvard Education Review* 55:1 (February 1985), p. 36.

21 *Ibid.*, p. 40.

22 For a superb explanation of what development education is, and does, see Joseph Short, *op.cit.*, pp. 38-41.

23 Larry Minear, "The Other Missions of NGOs: Education and Advocacy," *World Development*, Vol. 15, Special Supplement, (Autumn 1987), pp. 201-202.

24 Tim Broadhead, "NGOs: In One Year, Out the Other?", *World Development*, Vol. 15, (Autumn 1987), pp. 1-6.

25 William Graham Sumner, *Folkways: A Study of the Sociological Importance of Usages, Manners, Customs, Mores, and Morals* (New York: Mentor, New American Library Edition, 1940), pp. 523-524.

26 Ira Shor, "Equality is Excellence: Transforming Teacher Education and the Learning Process" *Harvard Educational Review* 56:4 (November 1986), pp. 415, 420.

27 Vandra Masemann, *op.cit.*, p. 3.

28 Joseph Short, *op.cit.*, p. 35.

29 David McConkey, *Choices: A Family Global Action Handbook* (Brandon, Man.: The Marquis Project, Inc., 1987), p. 26.

30 Donald C. Wilson, ed., *Teaching Public Issues in a Canadian Context* (Toronto: OISE Press, 1982), pp. 3-4

31 Jean Christie, Keynote Address, Together in Education Workshop, Saskatchewan Council for International Co-operation, 1985.

32 Donald Wilson, *op.cit.*, pp. 3-4.

33 Of 122 studies conducted in North America between 1924 and 1981 that considered achievement or performance data in co-operative, competitive and/or individualistic classrooms, 65 showed that co-operation promotes higher achievement than competition, eight showed the reverse and 36 showed no statistically significant diffrences. Alfie Kohn, "How to Succeed Without Even Vying," *Psychology Today*, September 1986, pp. 22-28.

34 A. Kohn, *ibid.*, p. 24.

35 *Ibid.*, pp. 26-27.

36 *Globe and Mail*, 12 December 1988.

37 Gro Harlem Brundtland, Chairperson, *Our Common Future, The Report of the World Commission on Environment and Development* (New York: Oxford University Press, 1987).

38 Quoted in McConkey, *op.cit.*, p. 97.

39 Quoted in Sam Totten, "Activist Educators," *Teachers College Record* 84:1 (Fall, 1982), p. 201.

40 David Crombie, "A Message From the Secretary of State of Canada," materials prepared by Secretary of State for National Citizenship Week, April 17 - 23, 1988.

Role-play and Citizenship Education

Moira Fraser Juliebo
Faculty of Education, University of Alberta
Edmonton

CITIZENSHIP education necessarily involves the analysis of complex controversial issues. These issues can, of course, be addressed through lectures, publications, media and critical debate. In most of these ways, the majority of participants play a passive role. This passivity can best be combated through the use of drama as a teaching-learning medium. Despite the fact that drama has had a legitimate place in schooling for many years, it is perhaps one of the least used learning mediums. Drama is, of course, a term that is used to describe a wide variety of activities ranging from dramatic play to theatre. This article will focus on one dramatic technique, that of role-play and its potential for providing a milieu for citizenship education.

Role-play as a creative medium has the potential for helping students to acquire, learn or refine facts, skills and value-laden concepts.[1] Simulation situations can put participants in touch with their own feelings about a particular event, for example, voting, and as a result, clarify their understanding of that event. In role-playing, students are asked to stand in someone else's shoes and respond in an imaginary setting. Participants are required to assume attitudes and opinions that may be quite different from their own. In order to make a role as authentic as possible, students are required to research certain areas; the responsibility for learning lies with the learner who has to examine issues from many different points of view. For example, if you are to be a judge presiding over a court hearing for a juvenile offender, then you must become knowledgeable about Canadian court procedures and points of law for this type of case. Examining

> *Si, comme le suggère le professeur Juliebo, la citoyenneté est un processus actif, alors les méthodes pédagogiques qui sont actives, comme la simulation, sont particulièrement efficaces. Elle explique comment utiliser la simulation et donne des exemples et des lignes directrices à suivre avec des élèves du primaire ou des élèves plus âgés.*

citizenship issues in a human context extends students' understanding of such issues and affects learning more powerfully and directly than any textbook or lecture. The dramatic mode involves students in talking and moving in real life situations and this combination of sensory input and language are, according to Vygotsky, "both indispensable parts of concept formation."[2]

Role Play

Here the term "role-play" is used to mean "an action-spontaneity procedure that takes place under contrived circumstances."[3] Role-playing provides students and teachers with a medium through which they can safely practise many complicated human relationships. By doing this, students develop a better understanding of the role of themselves and others in our society. Role-play can inform them, for example, about court proceedings or can train them how to act in a certain setting, for example, voting in an election. It can also provide scenarios which can be critically evaluated and can provide opportunities to teach students how to behave in certain circumstances, for example, how to initiate a complaint.

Many teachers are reluctant to use this medium as they fear failure and a lack of classroom discipline. Stanford[4] suggests the following strategies to promote successful role-playing activities:

1) Students should know each other well and be comfortable working together.

2) Older students often exhibit inhibitions and self-consciousness. The teacher must introduce activities that reduce anxiety and promote risk-taking.

3) Students may lack necessary skills. The teacher must provide drama experiences that will promote students' ability to pretend and react to the subtle behaviour changes in others.

4) Students should be warmed up before enacting scenes.

5) The teacher must be prepared to play an active role in the drama to make enactment more effective.

6) Students must strive for reality rather than comedy.

Role drama proceeds through five main stages. The first is choosing a relevant social issue. The choice may be made by the students or by the teacher. Now preparation for the drama takes place and the people, the situation, and the role of the facilitator must all be considered. The students should be involved as much as possible in planning and implementing the role-play. The teacher should know the students well and be aware that feelings and tensions are often "let go" in role-play. The teacher must create an atmosphere where trial and error and expressive behaviour are handled sensitively and students participate voluntarily, commit themselves to authenticity and show care and respect for others. The physical setting should be a suitable size, be private and should not have fixed furniture.

There are two basic frameworks for role-play — structured and unstructured. In structured role-play a specific purpose and behavioural objectives are formulated. Materials are designed before the session. Instructions for players are formulated in advance and a format for discussing key issues is designed. In contrast, in unstructured role-play, key relationships are developed by the group members. The structure emerges from the drama rather than from a structure predesigned by the facilitator/teacher. The teacher must avoid imposing relationships and opinions on the group. The teacher as facilitator must be able to judge situations quickly, handle people sensitively, and make rapid decisions. She may participate in role or she may prefer to observe and lead reflective sessions. The role-play itself will involve setting the climate, interacting between group members in role, engaging in post-enactment discussions, and reflecting on role-playing. This helps learning and the preparation for the next stage. During discussions generalizations may also be formulated.

Single-Group Structured Role-Play (Primary Students)

Following is a description of how a teacher might conduct a structured role-play with the whole class using the story of the Pied Piper.

Objective: To examine responsibility when entering into a written or verbal contract.

Climate-setting: Have the students sit either in a circle or a crescent shape and tell the story of the Pied Piper of Hamelin.

Additional Warm-up: Engage the class in a discussion of the key issues in the story. Break into small groups to share personal instances of "breaking promises." Return to the large group setting and discuss how individuals felt when verbal agreements were broken. Discuss what steps might be taken to redress the breaking of a verbal contract.

Role-play: Divide the class into family groups. These are the families who have just lost their children. They are about to attend a town council protest meeting where they will try to persuade the council to redress its decision not to pay the Pied Piper 1000 guilders. In role they will discuss strategies for the meeting (10 minutes). Four students are selected to play the roles of Mayor, Doctor, Treasurer, and Merchant. Each student is given a written description of their role as follows:

Each player is instructed not to reveal his or her motives.

MAYOR: You are at heart a politician whose main concern is getting votes to stay in office. You do not take a strong stance on any issues but prefer to straddle the fence. When in a tight position you find a scapegoat.

CITY TREASURER: You have been embezzling city funds for years. Your biggest fear is an audit by the citizens. You have always advocated low taxation to keep the taxpayer happy.

MERCHANT: You own the biggest general store in Hamelin and recently have made enormous profits from the sale of pesticides and rat traps. You still have a great deal of stock to sell and would be quite happy if the rats came back.

DOCTOR: Since the rats appeared you have been making a great deal of money from the fees you charged to treat people for rat bites and infection from vermin. You succumbed to public pressure and voted to hire the Pied Piper.

The meeting is called to order by the teacher in role as chairperson and the council introduce themselves to the irate citizenry. The floor is open to discussion and the distraught parents attack the council for breach of contract and demand the return of their children.[5]

On another day, the drama could change direction and the teacher, in the role as the Pied Piper, sets the scene for a role-play in a dark cave far away from Hamelin. "I will allow you to write a letter to your parents, asking that they do all they can to get you back. You must not reveal this hiding place." This activity facilitates a good writing experience and provides a milieu for students to discuss how they feel when separated from their families. Thus they develop deeper understanding of their inner feelings and the feelings of others and they reflect from different perspectives on the disapperance of the children.

Unstructured Multiple-Group Role-Play (Junior/Senior High Students)

Objective: To develop group consensus around a key issue and to examine this issue critically through unstructured role-play. In this lesson, drama will be used to enliven current events, lead to group problem-solving, and to value clarification.

Climate-Setting: Each student is given a copy of the following newspaper article which they will read silently.

Six Charged in Bus Theft

GRANTFORD, ONT. (CP) — *Six persons were charged Wednesday after an $80,000 Canada Coachlines bus was taken from the Grantford bus terminal and driven about seven miles northeast of the city and abandoned. Police said damage to the bus was about $1,700. The teenagers have been charged with possession of a stolen automobile valued at more than $200.*

Role-play   Day 1

The class breaks into groups and is encourged to decide who they will be in a drama about this article. Choices would include a teenager, parents of the teenager, the bus driver, passengers on the bus, law enforcement officers, etc. The group must also decide where they will be for the role-play. Choices would include a teenager's home, a cafe, the bus station, on the bus, a lonely road outside of town, a police station, etc. The time has also to be decided, for example, before the theft, while it is going on, immediately after, a month later, etc. The students then go into role for about 10 minutes. The teacher as facilitator may move in role, in and out of groups. The teacher then calls time out and group by group share what happened in their group. This would be one day's work.

Days 2, 3 & 4

For this role-play, the teacher assigns roles to the students as follows: father, mother, daughter/son or (4 sets of these) single parent, daughter/son, arresting officer, social worker, school principal, passengers from the bus, bus station manager, school counsellor, lawyer (defence), and lawyer (prosecution).

The teacher in role as judge conducts a preliminary hearing to decide if there is sufficient evidence to go to trial. The purpose of this hearing is not to establish guilt or innocence but to provide a wide variety of background information about the accused and the theft. The prosecutor first calls witnesses who are then cross-examined by the defence lawyer. Then the defence calls witnesses and the procedure is reversed. After each hearing, the families are asked to wait in the ante-chamber and the judge makes a decision about the teenager. Once the decision is made the family is called back in and told the recommendations. Role is then dropped and an articulation period is held. Hearings will be held over several days. This "living through" of current events facilitates opportunities for discussion that no other medium is able to do[6]

When the hearings are over the drama need not end. Extensions of the role-play could include:

- **New scenes**: in a newsroom, a teenager's home after the hearing, the bus station, in the school, etc
- **Newspaper articles**: reporting on the hearing, the trails, interviews with parents, law officers, etc.
- **T.V. interviews of friends**, families, teenagers, law enforcement officers, social workers, etc.
- **Diary entries** revealing how the teenagers felt after the hearings, what they learned, etc.
- **Reading research** focusing on what probation does to young people, the concept of parenting, and the upswing of crime in this age group.

From these two examples we see that role-play is an easily accessible drama strategy which can operate in any normal classroom. In role-play the students have the opportunity to use language in ways that are quite different from their everyday lives. Language is extended in meaningful contexts and the teacher can observe oral communicative competence in terms of fluency, communicative range, management skills, range of vocabulary, pronunciation and grammatical accuracy.[7]

In anthropology, researchers often try to understand situations by attempting to view them from the perspective of the participants. Citizenship education can best be learned by facilitating experience from within situations through role-play and improvisation. In this way, drama provides the students with many opportunities for affective, psychomotor and cognitive growth. It takes time and patience to create dramatic experiences in which make-believe situations clarify or modify what the student already knows or feels about something. Early sessions may be characterized by artificiality and action that simply reinforces what children already know.[8] Do not despair. Through reflective discussions and careful restructuring, the role-play will move to higher plains and reach the pinnacles of learning where drama can truly be called a learning medium.

---

1 G. Bolton, "Emotion and Meaning in Creative Drama," *Canadian Child Drama Association Journal*, February 1976, pp.13-19.

2 L.S. Vygotsky, *Thought and Language*, E. Hansmann and G. Vakar eds. (Cambridge, Mass.: MIT Press, 1962), p. 52.

3 M.E. Shaw, R.J. Corsini, R.R. Blake, and J.S. Mouton, *Role Playing* (San Diego: University Associates Inc., 1980), p.1.
4 G. Stanford, "Why Role Playing Fails," *English Journal* 63:9 (1974), pp. 50-54.
5 G.B. Lipson and B. Morrison, *Fact, Fantasy and Folklore* (Illinois: Good Apple, Inc., 1977).
6 T. Craig, "Using Drama as a 'Tool' to Make Real Current Events," unpublished paper, University of Alberta, Edmonton, 1987.
7 C. Evans, J.M. Gaudin, and F. Raveau, "Testing Advanced Communicative Competence through Role-play," *The British Journal of Language Teaching* 25:2 (1987). pp.104-108.
8 G. Bolton, "Creative Drama and Learning," *Children's Theatre Review* 26:2 (1977), pp.10-12.

Horizon Canada:
Une collection unique
de l'histoire du pays

Benoît Robert
*Département de didactique,
Faculté des Sciences de l'Éducation, Université Laval,
Québec*

HORIZON CANADA une nouvelle façon de découvrir l'histoire du Canada, Horizon Canada, A new way to discover the history of Canada est l'aboutissement d'un long processus en études du Canada. En effet, la Fondation d'Études du Canada (1970-1985) a joué un rôle important dans le développement des études canadiennes interrégionales pour les niveaux primaire, secondaire et collégial. La Fondation a produit plus de 200 publications, manuscrits et prototypes et a suscité des dizaines de séminaires et de colloques. Son impact dans toutes les provinces a été très important, particulièrement pour les divers programmes d'enseignement de géographie, d'histoire et de sciences sociales au Canada.[1] Dès 1984, à la FEC, nous avions la conviction que notre mission était accomplie, compte tenu du mandat que nous avions. L'essentiel de notre travail se faisait en collaboration avec les divers milieux d'éducation du pays : Conseil des ministres de l'Éducation (Canada), ministères de l'Éducation, conseils scolaires, divers regroupements d'enseignants, facultés d'éducation et bien sûr, les élèves et étudiants.

Mais le grand rêve qui avait présidé à la création de la Fondation ne s'était pas encore tout à fait réalisé. En effet, suite à une enquête portant sur l'enseignement de l'histoire à travers le Canada[2], on découvrit (et on s'en doutait) que l'une des causes de la méconnaissance des Canadiens entre eux et des préjugés qui en découlent, vient en partie d'un enseignement de

> The author describes the creation and production of Horizon Canada, a bilingual series giving the social history of Canada, produced by the Centre for the Study of Teaching located at Laval University. It was launched in February 1985. Each issue is written in a clear and lively style with many illustrations and drawings. It will cover, over an expected life of some 15 years, numerous themes such as Canada's business and industry, communications and transport, explorations, the people of Canada, politics, natural resources, science and technology, sports, leisure and the military.

175

Robert Benoît

l'histoire du Canada inadéquat, partiel, et souvent partial, périmé ou quelquefois inexistant dans plusieurs milieux. Il ne manquait pas de recherches universitaires savantes en histoire du pays, mais leurs résultats ne semblaient pas influencer outre mesure les milieux scolaires et le grand public en général. La Fondation, à la suite de cette enquête, se devait de corriger cette situation très particulière au Canada. Malgré beaucoup d'efforts, elle ne réussit que partiellement dans cette entreprise.

En 1984, il n'existait toujours pas d'histoire sociale du Canada qui soit la même pour tous (anglophones, francophones, allophones, autochtones) respectant les régions constituantes du pays, écrite dans le deux langues officielles et adaptée à tous les niveaux de la société canadienne. Nous avions remarqué que plusieurs autres pays avaient déjà réalisé leur histoire sociale (populaire). C'était le cas des États-Unis, de l'Australie, de l'Espagne, de la France et de l'Angleterre. Pour nous lancer dans le développement des études du Canada, il nous fallait franchir une autre étape, c'est-à-dire prendre tous les moyens souhaitables pour bâtir ce genre d'histoire pour notre pays.

Le Centre d'Études en enseignement du Canada/Centre for the Study of Teaching Canada, situé à la Tour de l'Éducation de l'Université Laval, avec un conseil d'administration[3] composé de spécialistes venant de diverses régions du pays, lance *Horizon Canada* sous forme de fascicules, en février 1985. Cette première phase se termine en septembre 1987 après la vente de plus de 15 000 collections au grand public et dans les écoles (la collection comprend 120 fascicules de 28 pages chacun). À la fin de décembre 1987, nous réalisons et complétons la deuxième phase du projet qui comprend 8000 collections *reliées de luxe* (chaque collection contient 10 volumes)[4]. Cet ouvrage historique et social est publié simultanément en anglais et en français.

Qu'est-ce qui fait l'originalité de cette collection?

Nous avons voulu agrandir le concept d'histoire traditionnellement enseignée dans nos écoles et collèges, qui s'est caractérisé surtout par des suites d'événements purement chronologiques où de grands héros (surtout des hommes) venaient par leur courage et leur détermination sauver la patrie du danger. L'histoire enseignée et apprise au Canada anglophone était fort différente de celle des francophones; souventes fois les interprétations étaient contradictoires, et chaque école de pensée cultivait ses préjugés à l'occasion. Heureusement, aujourd'hui beaucoup d'efforts de la part d'historiens et d'éducateurs tendent à renverser ce courant. Le travail de la Fondation d'études du Canada et de l'Association des études canadiennes est exemplaire dans ce renouveau de l'enseignement de l'histoire du pays. Les responsables d'*Horizon Canada* se devaient de pousser encore plus loin leurs efforts dans ce sens. Voici une illustration des points originaux de cet ouvrage. Ce que nous décrivons plus bas est loin d'être exhaustif.

Les grands thèmes choisis

Horizon Canada comprend plusieurs thèmes qui couvrent les réalités socio-historiques du pays. Il y a bien sûr, l'*histoire chronologique* qui

Horizon Canada

débute avec les Vikings pour se terminer avec le rapatriement de la Constitution. Cette histoire chronologique se retrouve tout au long des dix volumes et comprend 118 articles.

Une attention toute particulière a porté sur *l'histoire thématique*. Nous l'avons divisée comme suit : *Affaires et industrie*, comprenant plus de vingt articles traitant à la fois de sujets aussi diversifiés que ceux de l'industrie automobile en Ontario et des ranches de l'Alberta. *Arts et littérature* est couvert par trente études allant du Groupe des Sept au rock'n'roll. La partie *Communications et transport* touche une dimension essentielle du Canada; si c'est un pays avec une histoire, c'est encore plus un espace géographique nordique de près de dix millions de kilomètres carrés. Quarante-cinq chapitres composent cette rubrique dont plusieurs sont fort originaux. La partie *Explorations et découvertes* constitue une dimension importante pour un pays neuf et peu exploré. Des noms comme Frobisher, Hudson, Bernier, Franklin et bien d'autres viennent enrichir le contenu de ces thèmes. *Peuples du Canada* couvre à la fois l'aspect multiculturel du pays et l'apport important des premières nations. Une cinquantaine de sujets sont traités sous cette rubrique (Amérindiens, Inuit, Italiens, Allemands, Juifs, etc.). Nous pensons avoir rendu justice à tous les groupes qui apportent au Canada une diversité très enrichissante sans laquelle le pays ne serait pas ce qu'il est. *Politique*, voilà un sujet qui passionne les Canadiens, surtout quand il met en question l'intégrité du pays ou bien quand nos politiciens font l'objet de « scandale » ou de petites histoires un peu croustillantes. Les *Ressources naturelles* constituent pour le Canada une richesse immense dont les habitants retirent un bien-être qui ne se dément jamais (ressources minérales, pétrolières, agricoles, marines, etc.). *Science et technologie* nous démontre que le pays ne repose pas seulement sur ses richesses naturelles mais aussi, et surtout, sur sa richesse humaine qui fait du Canada un des pays les plus évolués technologiquement. *Sports et divertissements* sont une réalité omniprésente pour tous. Plus d'une vingtaine d'articles couvrent ce thème. Dans *Vie militaire*, ceux qui s'intéressent à cette dimension découvriront que malgré un taux de population faible, le Canada a joué et joue toujours un rôle important sur le plan international, surtout depuis le deuxième conflit mondial; 25 sujets sont présentés sous cette rubrique.

L'histoire sociale du pays tient la place essentielle dans *Horizon Canada*; en effet, près de 90 chapitres décrivent cette dimension qui se divise en sous thèmes : *affaires juridiques, éducation et travail social, famille, médecine, population et colonisation, religion, travail et loisirs*.

Le Canada est devenu au début du siècle un pays majoritairement urbain; il nous a semblé important d'étudier la vie urbaine en décrivant la plupart des grandes villes du pays (Toronto, Montréal, Vancouver, Ottawa, Calgary, Winnipeg, Québec, etc.)[5].

Le cadre de présentation
L'iconographie

L'une des principales caractéristiques d'*Horizon Canada*, c'est son aspect de *qualité et de diversité visuelles*. La recherche iconographique a été très poussée, et nous n'avons négligé aucun effort pour toujours trouver le bon document où qu'il soit. Cette œuvre comprend près de 10 000

Robert Benoît

illustrations. Les documents d'époque viennent des meilleurs musées du pays et le l'extérieur, la plupart de ces documents n'ont jamais été vus par les lecteurs. Des centaines de photographies évocatrices, réalisées par nos meilleurs photographes, donnent beaucoup de couleur et de force au texte. Des centaines d'encarts mettent un accent tout particulier sur un fait, un personnage ou tout simplement donnent le résumé d'une situation; ces encarts permettent aussi de tracer des séquences chronologiques et de faire ressortir les dates importantes. Des dizaines de caricatures d'époque nous font découvrir l'humour des gens du moment. L'aspect cartographique n'a pas été négligé; chaque fois qu'une carte de localisation ou une carte thématique était nécessaire pour mieux comprendre ou illustrer le texte, elle était dessinée à cette fin par des spécialistes.

Afin de démontrer ce qui a été dit plus haut, allons voir l'index thématique, à la fin du volume 10. (On peut utiliser aussi l'index alphabétique qui est fort complet.) Prenons comme exemple *Politique indienne et Trudeau* (pp. 902-907, vol. 4.), par Tony Hall. La première page nous montre deux images clés : a) Le titre éveille l'intérêt : *Les Indiens ne jouent plus*. Sous ce titre cinq lignes en caractères gras donnent le ton à l'article : « *Entre 1968 et 1984, sous les gouvernements successifs du premier ministre Pierre Elliott Trudeau, les nations autochtones mènent une lutte de plus en plus âpre pour faire valoir leurs droits. Elles ont marqué des points, mais la victoire continue à leur échapper.* » b) Une photo (10 x 17 cm) nous fait voir une Indienne signant un traîté sous l'oeil « bienveillant » des fonctionnaires et d'un agent de la gendarmerie royale. Le titre de la photo: *Une légalité douteuse*. Sur l'autre page nous pouvons lire la *Déclaration des Premières Nations*, inscrite dans un encart (11 x 18 cm). Les pages suivantes (904-905) comprennent un encart, trois photos, une caricature (un porc bien gras illustrant l'Alberta Heritage Fund, tandis que l'Indien, à l'arrière, a les mains vides) et une carte géographique originale portant sur les *Réclamations territoriales des autochtones au Canada*. Tout cela vient décrire visuellement l'importance des revendications des Premières Nations. Les deux dernières pages sont illustrées de quatre photos : celle d'une affiche publique déterminant le territoire des Dénés; celle d'un Indien faisant face à un agent de la gendarmerie royale; puis, celle de M. Trudeau portant un chapeau indien et une dernière montrant une vue panoramique d'un village Déné.

Les 472 chapitres de la collection sont tous aussi évocateurs que celui que nous venons de décrire. Nous avons essayé de toujours garder l'équilibre entre les photos d'époque, les encarts, les croquis, les caricatures et les cartes. Tous ces efforts de présentations iconographiques et visuelles avaient pour but de donner plus de vie au texte en l'illustrant abondamment. Il en est résulté une histoire vivante et captivante du Canada.

Le texte

Les articles ont été écrits par plus de 300 auteurs venant de toutes les régions du Canada. Ces spécialistes sont historiens et géographes, d'autres viennent des sciences sociales et des sciences exactes. Plusieurs d'entre eux ont rédigé plus d'un texte. Tous les articles retenus par l'équipe de rédaction ont été réécrits par elle afin de donner à l'œuvre un style plus uniforme. Il ne faut pas confondre une certaine uniformité dans le texte et

Horizon Canada

une morosité dans le style. Au contraire, la réécriture de plusieurs chapitres nous a donné un style plus léger et vivant. Étant donné qu'*Horizon Canada* ne devait pas s'adresser uniquement aux universités et collèges mais aussi et *surtout au grand public*, il nous a fallu éliminer un certain jargon technique sans nuire à la qualité scientifique de l'article. D'ailleurs, la plupart des chapitres ont été retournés aux auteurs pour approbation finale. Les textes qui nous arrivaient dans une langue donnée, devaient être rendus le plus exactement possible dans l'autre langue; ceux qui étaient traduits ne devaient pas « sentir la traduction ». L'équipe de rédaction a réalisé un travail de toute beauté avec la collaboration de traducteurs de haut niveau. Nous croyons qu'en général le contenu de la collection répond à trois grandes qualités : la simplicité du style, la clarté de la phrase et la précision du sujet étudié[6].

Beaucoup d'efforts ont été consentis afin de trouver des titres évocateurs et des sous-titres déclencheurs d'intérêt. On a souvent dit que l'histoire du Canada, dans bien des cas, était grise et morose à lire. Nous osons espérer qu'il n'en sera pas de même pour *Horizon Canada*, car les critiques que nous avons eues jusqu'à maintenant sont très élogieuses. En voici deux : « *Ces textes sur les gens et les événements hauts en couleur qui ont fait le Canada offrent le genre de lecture vivante qui a si souvent fait défaut dans les manuels d'histoire du Canada. La formule rédactionnelle, l'intérêt des sujets et la qualité des illustrations retiennent l'attention et forment un ensemble qui incite l'étudiant blasé à d'abord les feuilleter, puis à les lire, découvrant à sa grande surprise que l'histoire du Canada n'est pas ennuyeuse!* » (Linda McDowell, conseillère en sciences sociales, Winnipeg). « *C'est exactement ce dont les Canadiens ont besoin! Et c'est aussi ce dont nous [aux États-Unis] avons besoin!* » (Larry Neal, Université de l'Oregon).

Autres exploitations possibles de la collection

Deux phases importantes viennent d'être réalisées :

La distribution hebdomadaire par *fascicules* s'est faite dans les divers kiosques à journaux à travers le pays. Cette publication s'est échelonnée sur une période de 120 semaines. Aussi, durant cette publication, les gens et les institutions pouvaient s'abonner. On pouvait se procurer des albums (10 albums par collection) pour y insérer les fascicules. Les couvertures 3 et 4 de chaque fascicule illustrent *les Découvertes et Inventions canadiennes* ainsi que les *Chefs-d'œuvre de la peinture canadienne*. Ces deux thèmes ne se retrouvent pas dans la collection reliée de luxe.

La *collection reliée* est vendue aux institutions scolaires et universitaires ainsi qu'à diverses bibliothèques. Les personnes intéressées peuvent toujours se les procurer chez l'éditeur.

Selon les besoins exprimés, nous pouvons réaliser d'autres formes de publications de la collection; ainsi, nous pourrions la publier en livres séparés :

1. *Découvertes et Inventions canadiennes.*
2. *Chefs-d'œuvre de la peinture canadienne.*
3. Tous les textes de l'histoire chronologique canadienne (sans les illustrations). Cette publication prendrait la forme de morceaux choisis. Ce serait un livre particulièrement utile pour les institutions scolaires.
4. Toute une série de livres spécialisés répondrait à des besoins

spécifiques en exploitant les divers thèmes de la collection. Voici quelques thèmes suggérés :
    a. *Les Premières nations au Canada*
    b. *Un Canada multiethnique ou l'histoire de la diversité canadienne*
    c. *Les grands personnages politiques du Canada*
    d. *Évolution de nos grandes villes canadiennes*
    e. *Le sport dans la vie des Canadiens*
    f. *Les grands découvreurs et explorateurs*
    g. *L'évolution du transport au Canada*
    h. *L'évolution des droits des ouvriers*
    i. *La voix des femmes canadiennes ou la conquête des droits égaux pour tous*
    j. *Les grands scandales politiques*
    k. *Les relations entre francophones et anglophones*
    l. *L'évolution du bilinguisme et du multiculturalisme au Canada*

Nous estimons qu'*Horizon Canada* aura une vie active d'au moins quinze ans. Son exploitation sous plusieurs formes répondra à bien des attentes, car la société canadienne est diversifiée et fortement régionalisée. Notre intention n'était pas de faire une histoire à thèse unique, mais au contraire nous avons voulu que cette œuvre reflète ce que nous sommes, surtout pas ce que nous devrions être. Nous laissons le lecteur libre de tirer ses propres conclusions. Les qualités d'un pareil ouvrage sont telles que nous avons la conviction de laisser aux Canadiens de toutes les allégeances un héritage unique[7]. Dans cette collection, nous avons insisté sur le *temps historique* du pays; dans un proche avenir, il nous faudra redécouvrir son *espace géographique et économique*.

---

    1 Pour en savoir plus long sur la Fondation d'Études du Canada, voir : *La Fondation d'études du Canada* (1986), Toronto. Dans cette publication de la Fondation, on retrouve trois sections : *La mission de la Fondation d'études du Canada*, par P. McGreath; *Historique de la fondation d'études du Canada*, par J. N. Grant; et *Les résultats de la publication du travail de la Fondation d'études du Canada*, par R . M. Anderson. Pour ce qui est de la philosophie et du plan d'action en études du Canada, voir : B. Robert (1979) *Perspectives nouvelles en enseignement du Canada*, Toronto, FEC; A. B. Hodgetts et P. Gallagher (1978) *Teaching Canada for the '80s*, Toronto, IÉPO.
    2 Voir les résultats de cette enquête dans A. B. Hodgetts, *Quelle culture? Quel héritage? Une étude de l'éducation civique au Canada*, Toronto, IÉPO (1968). Aussi disponible en langue anglaise.
    3 Benoît Robert est président et directeur général (Université Laval, Qué.) de CEEC/CSTC (société sans but lucratif). Plus d'une quarantaine de personnes ont pris part au projet *Horizon Canada*.
    4 Les éditions *reliées* anglaise et française d'*Horizon Canada* sont distribuées par les Éditions Transmo, 533, rue Deslauriers, Saint-Laurent (Qué.) H4N 1W2. Les collections *en fascicules* sont épuisées.
    5 Le lecteur d'*Horizon Canada* pourra se rendre compte de la diversité de l'œuvre en consultant les index thématique et alphabétique (pp. 2833-2876), vol. 10.
    6 La rédaction : Daniel Francis, directeur; Lucie Desaulniers et Frank Mackey, rédacteurs. Claude Paulette et Sandra Steiman, iconographes. Tout le soutien technique a été assumé par les Éditions Transmo.
    7 Nous tenons à exprimer notre profonde reconnaissance au Secrétaire d'État et au Ministre des Communications du Canada pour leur soutien et leur encouragement. Sans leur appui financier, la collection n'aurait jamais vu le jour.

Co-operative Learning: Active Citizenship Education

Daniel McDougall
*Department of Educational Psychology,
The University of Calgary,
    and*
Karen Annon
*Sundance Elementary School,
Calgary Board of Education*

SOCIETIES are maintained and enhanced by co-operation among their citizens. Moreover, co-operation is fundamental to democracy. An obvious example is the electoral process. Elections are most successful when a large proportion of the citizenry co-ordinate their efforts by establishing election procedures, organizing political parties, setting election platforms and strategies, holding party conventions, electing leaders and candidates, and campaigning for election. Although there is an interesting mix of individual action, competition and co-operation in any election (for instance, when candidates compete for the leadership of a political party but supporters work together for their candidate), the dominant activity remains co-operation.
    The education of young Canadians recognizes the importance of co-operation to Canadian society by emphasizing the theme of co-operation in the social studies and citizenship curricula. In the elementary school, children learn how citizens co-operate to improve their neighbourhoods and

> *Les citoyens ont besoin d'apprendre à unir leurs efforts. L'apprentissage coopératif leur permet d'acquérir les connaissances, les aptitudes et les attitudes qu'il leur faut et constitue une technique pédagogique qui permet aux gens de collaborer pour atteindre un objectif. Les auteurs examinent les différentes stratégies d'apprentissage coopératif, l'enseignement tutoriel, la recherche collective, et exhortent les enseignants à cesser de favoriser la rivalité entre les élèves. Ils étudient aussi les effets et les problèmes reliés à l'apprentissage coopératif.*

communities. During the secondary school years, co-operation in the wider Canadian community is described. Citizenship education stresses the importance of co-operation.[1]

Definition of Co-operative Learning

The skills needed for harmonious co-operative action as citizens are acquired when students learn co-operatively. Slavin writes that co-operative learning means "...techniques in which students work on activities in small groups and receive rewards or recognition based on their group's performance."[2] Further, he claims that co-operative education is primarily a change in the interpersonal reward structure of the classroom from a competitive reward structure to a co-operative one. This situation leads to unavoidable alterations such as a change from whole class instruction followed by individual task completion to small group interaction followed by group projects and group sharing.

Co-operative learning has been referred to as a co-operative social situation in which the goals of individuals are so linked together that there is a positive relationship among their goal attainments. Thus, in a co-operative learning situation a person seeks an outcome that is beneficial to all participants with whom she or he is co-operatively linked. Kail claims that the idea of co-opeative learning is not new, but the fact "that students are being required to work on writing together, commanded to learn from each other; they must collaborate" is new.[3]

Types of Co-operative Learning Strategies

There are various learning strategies that could be classified as co-operative learning or co-operative education. According to Sharan[4] the team-learning methods share the fundamental features of employing small teams of pupils to promote peer interaction and co-operation for studying academic subjects. It is through this small group co-operation that team-learning methods influence the pupil's cognitive learning, attitudes towards learning and school, and interpersonal skills.

How the teacher structures the learning situation greatly affects the nature of the pupil interactions: independent, competitive or co-operative. Moreover, whether or not the task was co-operatively accomplished influences the affective and cognitive instructional products. Through co-operation, students learn that it is unnecessary for others to lose so that they can succeed, and that it is possible to support their peers in achieving objectives.

Two broad types of co-operative learning are student tutorials and group investigation. The jigsaw technique is an example of the student tutorial approach.[5] In this method a class is divided into groups of five or six pupils and each pupil receives a limited amount of information about a topic. In order to fit the segments of the topic together into a unified whole, the students are dependent upon each other. After receiving their topic segment, and studying them independently, the pupils join other classmates who have the same segment and help each other learn the topic. That is, their counterparts, who have the same elements, check comprehension and presentation. Next, the pupils return to their original groups to tutor one another within a specified time limit. Students are dependent upon each other for full understanding of the topic; each student contributes to the knowledge of others and individual performance is dependent upon the assistance of all members. Besides setting broad limits on the curriculum, the teacher facilitates group interaction; positive group study is promoted. The teacher is not the main source of information as may be the case in more traditional classrooms.

The Teams-Games-Tournament system is another tutorial approach. Pupils are assigned, according to their ability, sex or ethnicity, to heterogeneous groups of four or five. Students of approximately equal achievement are assigned to tournament tables in groups of three. Representing their teams, they compete at educational games which test knowledge of the recently studied material. Since the top scorer at each table carries an equal number of points home, and since homogeneous ability grouping occurs, players have the opportunity to achieve the maximum score for their teams. After a tournament, a teacher-prepared newsletter publicizes the names of the top scorers and teams. Team assignments do not change, whereas tournament assignments are based on an equality-of-last performance principle.[6]

Similar to the Teams-Games-Tournament method, the Student Teams-Achievement Divisions uses heterogeneous ability groups. However, the games and tournaments are replaced with 15-minute tests taken after team-supported study. The top six scores (an achievement division) on each quiz are compared. The top scorer receives eight points for his or her team and the next highest gets six points, and so on. The second highest group of six students (another achievement division) are now compared, and so forth. Comparison of any student, then, is within a homogeneous group of six students called the achievement division. This is an important modification because a child is only competing with five other classmates of similar achievement rather than with the whole class. A disadvantage might be that membership in a low-achieving group is sometimes discouraging.[7]

The group-investigation model (GI) is a second broad type of co-operative learning.[8] It has several steps: (a) The teacher describes a general problem, and students choose more specific sub-topics. (b) Small heterogeneous groups are formed. (c) Teachers and pupils jointly plan how to study the topics. (d) Team study begins and the teacher monitors progress and guides the learning. (e) Eventually pupils draw conclusions and create ways of informing the class of their findings. (f) Co-ordinated by the teacher, teams present their ideas to the class. (g) Teacher and pupil assessments of the presentations complete the sequence.

The Effects of Co-operative Learning

The research on co-operative learning has generally been most encouraging. Sharan[9] conducted a field experiment to assess the effects of GI learning on cognitive and social variables. The study involved 1145 students in a lower class neighbourhood in Israel for over two years. The results showed that the pupils involved in small group, co-operative experiences were more co-operative and altruistic and much less competitive and selfish when they could choose spontaneously to work alone or with others on a school task, or when they could select the amount of pay-off they would take for themselves or distribute to group-mates.

Co-operative learning frequently enhances student self-esteem and lowers unnecessary competitiveness. Co-operative learning improves student perception of ethnically different classmates.[10] It produces increased friendships and interactions among students from different ethnic backgrounds.[11] Marked increases in cross-ethnic helping of peers has been recorded.[12] Co-operative learning leads students to prefer ethnically heterogeneous study groups.[13] A co-operative learning environment promotes ego-enhancing pro-social explanations of successes and failures both for individuals and their classmates; whereas competitive situations are conducive to ego-deflating explanations of another person's successes and failures.

In a study by Nevin, Polewski and Skieber[14] it was found that upon changing the classroom into a co-operative learning environment as outlined by Johnson and Johnson[15] many favourable results were noticed. The academic skills increased along with a gain in social attitude scores. However, the teacher reported that the most dramatic outcome occurred in the frequency of appropriate behaviour as compared to disruptive behaviour from three problem students. It appears that successful co-operation affirms the individual and the group.[16] Where they can share and appreciate each other's points of view, children seem to enjoy working together as a group. It was concluded that co-operation promoted greater self-esteem, greater perspective-taking ability, and a general belief that each individual is a worthwhle person.

According to Johnson and Johnson[17] achievement will be higher when learning environments are structured co-operatively. These experiences will promote greater competencies in critical thinking, more positive attitudes towards the subject studied, greater competencies in working collaboratively with others, greater psychological health, and more positive views of the grading system as being fair.

Of the 41 field studies related to the effects of co-operative learning on academic achievement reviewed by Slavin,[18] 63% demonstrated positive results. The strongest effect on achievement was derived from specific group rewards based on members' learning. In addition, the influence of co-operative learning on achievement was primarily motivational.[19]

Johnson and Johnson[20] state that there is considerable evidence that co-operative experiences result in more positive interpersonal relationships characterized by mutual liking, positive attitudes towards each other, mutual concern, friendliness, attentivenes, feelings of obligation to other students and a desire to win the respect of other students. Co-operative experiences within a classroom set the framework for peer tutoring as co-operative learning experiences result in stronger beliefs that one is liked and accepted by other students and that other students care about how much one learns and how much one wants to help.[21] Johnson and Johnson state "...intermixed in both the cognitive and affective domains are the basic social competencies a person needs to develop in order to function effectively in relationships with other persons. Cognitive development, acquistion of facilitative attitudes, and behavioural skills are all needed for the development and maintenance of a psychologically healthy person who lives a productive and fulfilling life."[22]

Problems

Although co-operative learning methods have generally produced positive effects upon intergroup relations, there are problems with measurement, tutorial relationships, competition, duration of episodes and quality of implementation.[23] Measurement of ethnic relationships has not focused on actual behaviour, but has often been by sociometric questionnaires. Slavin[24] has observed off-task helping, but there should be increased scrutiny of out-of-school behaviour in mixed-ethnic situations. Another unresolved question is whether or not minority children are effective tutors of their majority classmates.

The main emphasis is co-operation, but the team competition within the Team-Games-Tournament approach and the tests of the jigsaw technique may diminish effects upon prejudice. Reduced competition exists in the Student Teams-Achievement Divisions, however, which gives this method an advantage over the others. In most studies the actual class time devoted to co-operative learning has been relatively short; with longer applications, what would result? Finally, role changes for the teacher, from instructor to facilitator, may be too demanding so that poor adaptations lower the quality of the co-operative experience. Despite these problems, teachers can be encouraged by the positive results, even with short-term use, and by the fact that co-operative learning is productive alongside other methods.

Competition and Co-operation

Aronson and his colleagues feel that competitiveness is not inborn but it seems to be because it is learned so early. It is apparently fostered by the family and the media, but the classroom is the major place where it is taught. "Whether primarily traditional or primarily innovative, virtually all classrooms share two common aspects: the major process that occurs is highly competitive, and the ultimate goal of the competition among students is to win the love and respect of the teacher."[25] Aronson would like to see the basic process changed so that children could learn to like and trust each other without feeling competition and prejudice.

It should be noted, however, that the negative results from competition are not a necessary outcome. The adverse side effects of competition may be reduced by intelligent, sensitive use as recommended by Kolesnik:

1. Evenly match the contestants so that all pupils have a good opportunity to win.

2. Avoid intense competitions and maintain a spirit of fun.

3. Use individualistic and co-operative methods of achieving goals in conjunction with competition.

4. Maintain the confidentiality of test scores and report card marks.

5. Provide success experiences more often than failure for each student.

6. Since competition among students is essentially an extrinsic motivational process, develop the students' intrinsic motivation towards the subject. The joy of successfully completing a project, or understanding a concept, should be available to each student.

7. Students should compete against their own previous performances. Self-competition is related to criterion-referenced approaches to

evaluation in which the criterion for success is set by the prior achievement of the student. Students could record their test scores and obtain feedback by checking present scores with past test results.

Adherence to the foregoing suggestions will reduce the adverse side effects of competition. When it seems appropriate, teachers will use competition. In general, however, we should lessen our reliance on competition by developing co-operative learning strategies.

Conclusion

Arkin and Shollar state that the importance of co-operative learning is due to the fact that "...the traditional classroom does not serve most students well."[26] They elaborate by noting that the traditional classroom is detrimental to many student's intellectual and emotional development and that it encourages dependence on authority; it fosters a competitive, threatening atmosphere and it makes students bored and depressed about learning. Traditional classrooms are seen as having an interpersonal competition goal structure where students are expected to outperform their peers.[27] According to Arkin and Shollar collaborative learning, meaning learning with others in a nurturing, supportive community that is free of authoritarian restrictions, is needed in our society. "Collaborative learning stresses the group's - and the individual's - contribution to a developing community."[28]

With greater emphasis on co-operative learning, citizenship education in Canadian schools is more likely to reach the goal of creating citizens who use knowledge, skills and attitudes at the interpersonal, neighbourhood or societal level that permit them to best exercise their insights and responsibilities as citizens. Co-operation among individuals in a human society can lead to improved group organizations, family units and school systems. Without a high co-operation there wouldn't be co-ordination on highways, on sidewalks, in stores, or within organizations.[29] The more complex the unit or organization becomes the more co-operation is needed for individuals to function in a positive, productive and worthwhile fashion. Co-operative learning promotes the necessary knowledge, skills, and attitudes for active citizenship.

---

1 V. L. Masemann, "Citizenship Education in Canada," background paper prepared for the Canadian Education Association's Forum on Citizenship and Citizenship Education in Schools and Communities, "Challenges for the Present and Future," Edmonton, Alberta, November 9-11, 1987, p. 2.

2 R. E. Slavin, "Co-operative Learning," *Review of Educational Research* 50 (1980), p. 315.

3 Harvey Kail, "Collaborative Learning in Context: The Problems with Peer Tutoring," *College English* 45 (1983), p. 594.

4 S. Sharan, "Co-operative Learning in Groups: Recent Methods and Effects on Achievement, Attitudes and Ethnic Relations," *Review of Educational Research* 50 (1980), pp. 241-271.

5 E. Aronson, N. Blaney, C. Stephan, J. Sikes and M. Snapp, *The Jigsaw Classroom* (Beverly Hills: Sage Publications, 1978).

6 R.E. Slavin, "Co-operative Learning," *Review of Educational Research*, *op. cit.*

7 *Ibid.*
8 S. Sharan, *op. cit.*
9 *Ibid.*
10 E. Aronson et al., *op. cit.*
11 R.E. Salvin, "Effects of Biracial Learning Teams on Cross-racial Friendships," *Journal of Educational Psychology* 71 (1979), pp. 381-387.
12 R. Weigel, P. Wiser and S Cook, "The Impact of Co-operative Learning Experiences on Cross-ethnic Relations and Attitudes," *Journal of Social Issues* 31 (1975), pp. 219-244.
13 E. Aronson et al., *op. cit.*
14 A. Nevin, J. Polewiski and R. Skieber, "The Impact of Co-operative Learning in a Regular Classroom," *The Pointer* 20 (1984), pp. 19-27.
15 D.W. Johnson and R.T. Johnson, *Learning Together and Alone: Co-operation, Competition and Individualization* (Englewood Cliffs, N.J.: Prentice-Hall, 1975).
16 P. Prutzman, "Creating a Positive Classroom Environment," *Momentum* 14 (1983), pp. 22-24.
17 D. W. Johnson and R. T. Johnson, *Circles of Learning: Co-operation in the Classroom* (Minneapolis: Association for Supervision and Curriculum Development, 1984).
18 R.E. Slavin, *Co-operative Learning* (New York: Longmans, 1983).
19 *Ibid.*
20 D.W. Johnson and R.T. Johnson, "Co-operative, Competitive and Individualistic Learning," *Journal of Research and Development* 12 (1978), pp.3-15.
21 *Ibid.*
22 D.W. Johnson and R.T. Johnson, "Instructional Goal Structure: Co-operative, Competitive or Individualistic," *Review of Educational Research* 44 (1974), p. 11.
23 J. Moskowitz, J. H. Malvin, G.A. Schaeffer and E. Schaps, "Evaluation of a Co-operative Learning Strategy," *American Educational Research Journal* 20 (1983), pp. 687-696; and S. Sharan, *op. cit.*
24 R.E. Slavin, "Effects of Biracial Learning Teams on Cross-racial Friendships," *op. cit.*
25 E. Aronson et al., *op. cit.*, p.21.
26 M. Arkin, and B. Shollar, *The Tutor Book* (New York: Longmans, 1982), p. 7.
27 D.W. Johnson and T.R. Johnson, "Instructional Goal Structure," *op. cit.*
28 M. Arkin and B. Shollar, *op. cit.*, p. 8.
29 D.W. Johnson and T.R. Johnson, "Instructional Goal Structure," *op. cit.*

Selecting a Capital for Canada - An Exercise in Simulations and Citizenship Education

Charles Hou
Social Studies Department,
Burnaby North Secondary School, Burnaby

THE PRIMARY aim of social studies education is to prepare students to take their places as good citizens of their country. In this sense, everything a social studies teacher does can be considered as citizenship education. In teaching such subjects as geography, history, law, archaeology and political science, the basic emphasis is on developing the skills needed to function in society. Such skills include problem-solving, decision-making, interpreting maps and globes, understanding time and chronology, and locating, organizing, evaluating and communicating information. Equally important, though, are projects and lessons designed to build the students' sense of self-worth and to develop their ability to work with others, participate in group discussions and take on the responsibility of leadership.

One of the most successful ways of satisfying these diverse aims involves the use of simulations. Such simulations include historical roleplaying or re-enactments, mock trials, parliamentary style or historical debates, film-making, historically oriented field trips, "Meeting of the Minds" and "Front Page Challenge" panel discussions and "Reach for the Top" type of quizzes.

La simulation peut être une démarche pédagogique efficace en instruction civique. À titre d'exemple, l'auteur décrit un exercice appelé « Choisir une capitale pour le Canada ». La simulation est une méthode populaire; elle demande d'enseigner et d'apprendre un sujet à fond, de participer pleinement; et elle donne aux enseignants l'occasion de répondre aux aptitudes et aux intérêts différents des élèves. Grâce à la simulation, ces derniers acquièrent une vue d'ensemble positive des sciences humaines et de l'instruction civique. Selon l'auteur, lorsqu'ils ont participé à une simulation, les élèves sont en mesure, une fois le moment venu, de participer plus facilement et avec plus d'enthousiasme à de vraies élections, de se joindre à un parti politique, de protester contre une mesure du gouvernement ou d'écrire à leur député. La simulation leur permet d'acquérir l'expérience et la vue d'ensemble nécessaire pour devenir des citoyens engagés.

Charles Hou

Simulations are generally popular with both teachers and students. They usually require teaching and learning a subject in some depth. Instead of superficially surveying information, one is able to bring in details that would otherwise be ignored. This can do much to increase student interest in a topic. Good simulation projects also involve the students very much in the learning process. Rather than sitting passively in their seats, they learn to take an inquiry approach - defining a topic to be investigated or a problem to be solved, researching and evaluating information and communicating their findings. Finally, simulations usually give teachers a better opportunity to provide for the tremendous range of individual differences in interest, ability and talents found in every class. As a result of all this, the students' knowledge, skills and attitude development will often improve dramatically when simulation techniques are used.

A good example of a simulation involving historical role-playing is one based on the 1857 selection of a capital for Canada.[1] From 1841 to 1865, Canadians were divided over the choice of a capital for Canada, then a British colony. The capital was moved over the years from Kingston (1841-44) to Montreal (1844-49) to Toronto (1849-51) to Quebec (1851-55) to Toronto (1855-59) to Quebec (1859-65); then finally to Ottawa in 1865. The final move was made on the decision of Queen Victoria, who studied submissions from the various contending cities and decided in 1857 in favour of Ottawa. (The final move did not take place until 1865.)

Using the survey approach, one might tell the students that Queen Victoria selected Ottawa as the capital of Canada in 1857, and perhaps list a few of the advantages of that site. Using the simulation approach, the teacher or the students choose one member of the class to play the role of Queen Victoria and another to play Prince Albert to assist her. The rest of the class is divided into five groups, each representing one of the five main cities - Kingston, Montreal, Toronto, Quebec and Ottawa - that competed to become the capital of Canada. Students brought up on a steady diet of sports rivalry between cities will immediately start to pay attention, and natural co-operative and competitive instincts will start to take over as each group works to prepare the best case to present to "Queen Victoria." History is no longer static. With hard work and a spirited presentation, any of the groups might be able to "change" history.

As the students search for relevant information, the various elements of these cities will suddenly become intriguing and meaningful. Factors considered may include the various cities' population statistics, growth rate, ethnic mix, centrality, wealth, power, defence capabilities, and distance from the American border. Comparisons may also be made with other capital cities. The wealth of potential information should provide plenty of mental stimulation both when students do the necessary reasearch and later when they make their own presentations or listen to those of other groups.

Having found the relevant information, the students must decide on the most effective way of communicating it. Tables, graphs, sketch maps, reproductions of paintings and drawings, etc., must be prepared and slides, posters, overhead transparencies made. In the actual presentation of the material, a student "mayor" from each group may act as spokesman or several student "aldermen" may speak in turn. Some groups might even decide that a skit, panel discussion, or staged quiz show might be the most effective way of presenting their information. The students who play the parts of the Queen, Prince Albert, mayors and aldermen can even dress in costume for the occasion. It is amazing what a crown and royal robes, a few top hats, and theatrical beards will do to stimulate student interest. The higher the degree of involvement and commitment from the students, the greater is the learning potential, and costumes will always help. (In mock trials one can always get the best students to take on the challenging roles of Crown and defence counsel by offering them a chance to dress up in lawyers' robes.) The promise of an audience also encourages a greater degree of preparation and higher level of perfomance. The presentations may accordingly be made before an audience of other students or at a Parents' Night at the school or in a courtroom, legislative committee room, or city council chamber.

One reason for the success of simulations is that they provide for individual differences. The roles of the Queen, Prince Albert, and the city mayors and aldermen will challenge the brighter or more enthusiastic students, and the rest of the class can participate to the extent of their abilities and interests. Usually the co-operation and competitiveness necessary for an effective presentation will spur students to the highest level of performance of which they are capable - a level much higher than that usually displayed in class. This enhanced degree of interest and effort often spills over into the next unit studied in class.

No other country in the world has experienced such indecisions as did colonial Canada in the selection of its capital. In studying this process, students will learn a great deal about Canada in 1857 (and about the role of political deadlock in bringing about Confederation in 1867), and will come to understand the uniqueness of our bilingual nation. They will also learn a great deal about other nations and cities of the world when the student "mayors" of the different cities refer to other world capitals to strengthen their arguments. Further, they will be sensitized to the location of our provincial capitals and to the location of capitals in other countries such as Brazil (whose capital was moved) or states such as Alaska (where moving the capital was considered). In each case, the city selected as the capital often provides insights into the character of a nation or area. The topic is thus of considerable local, national and international significance.

Students at high school generally relate to people much better than they do to abstract ideas. Although the capital for Canada simulation does not particularly include a biographical aspect, other simulations may be used to exploit the popularity of this approach with students. Suitable examples include a mock trial of Louis Riel, a mock parliamentary debate dealing with B.C.'s decision to join Confederation and a debate dealing with the federal government's decisions to ban and later allow the potlatch ceremony.[2] These simulations involve students in role-playing many of the personalities in our past.

Students learn best when they become involved in the learning process. "I hear and I forget, I see and I remember, I do and I understand." The in-depth study of a meaningful topic, coupled with the uncertainty and suspense of a simulation, will appeal to many students who might not be interested in traditional classroom activities. Students of varying abilities

Charles Hou

can take part to varying degrees, and all can benefit from the experience.

Perhaps even more important than learning about a subject, though, is the degree of satisfaction experienced by the students. If they have enjoyed the learning experience they will have a positive outlook towards social studies and towards citizenship education. When the time comes that they can participate in a election, join a political party, protest a government action, or write a letter to the editor or to a member of parliament, they will have both the experience and the positive outlook that are fundamental to active citizenship.

---

1 Charles Hou, *Selecting a Capital for Canada* (Vancouver: B.C. Teachers' Federation, 1971).

2 Charles and Cynthia Hou, *The Riel Rebellion: A Biographical Approach and Teacher's Guide* (Vancouver: Tantalus Research Ltd., 1984); and Charles Hou and Marlena Morgan, *The Destiny of British Columbia: Confederation or Annexation 1866-1871* (1984) and Charles Hou, *To Potlatch or Not to Potlatch* (Vancouver: B.C. Teachers' Federation, 1969).

Part 3:
Recommendations and Suggestions

Recommendations and Suggestions from the Forum on Citizenship Education

THE FOLLOWING recommendations or suggestions were drawn from the reports of the discussion groups and from the evaluation reports submitted by delegates attending the Forum on Citizenship and Citizenship Education, held in Edmonton, November 1987.

Structures/Policy and Structure
4.8　Citizenship values should be flexible enough to allow for some acceptance or qualification of the values. What makes us strong is a recognition and acceptance of our enriching diversity.
4.9　Establish a set of guidelines for citizenship values that represent at least a majority opinion if not a consensus. There are some values which can be identified as uniquely Canadian.
2.2　All Canadians should go through a Citizenship Court ceremony to gain a feeling of the country.
2.3　Citizenship needs to be taught to all Canadians, not just immigrants, but the method of teaching must be tailored to fit the group.
1.3　The status of French as an official language should not be replaced by multibilingualism, especially in the provinces where francophones are a minority. Canada's bilingualism should be taught in citizenship courses across Canada.
10.21 There is a need for an umbrella organization, either existing or new, to focus on citizenship and carry out the recommendations made at the forum.

Institutions
1.1 & 2 The media should recognize the role they play in shaping citizenship and defining the Canadian identity. We should develop in people a critical mind vis-à-vis the information they receive from the media.
8.4　In advertising and promotion, create an image of what a Canadian looks like; create a sense of sharing among Canada's diverse ethnocultural groups.

8.14 Work with mainstream institutions to develop their sensitivity toward multicultural and multiracial issues, and, in the case of the CBC, to portray same.
4.10 Media, especially the CBC, should be encouraged to emphasize what it means to be Canadian and have pride in the country. An example is the use of vignettes to promote citizenship.
8.3 Explore the possibility of the NFB producing vignettes on the House of Commons, Senate, heroes and contributors to Canada. Participation type of fillers on the same subjects could be produced for the print media.
8.11 Work with cable TV stations to find guest speakers on citizenship topics.

Governments - Federal and Provincial
8.13 Encourage other federal departments and programs to pick up on the Citizenship Week theme of pride in being Canadian.
4.14 Include in the Oath of Canadian Citizenship a statement of allegiance to the flag.
4.13 Appropriate government agencies should promote an awareness of the role of our athletes in showing respect for our national symbols - singing the National Anthem, standing at attention, etc. - at all major sports events.

Community
8.1 At community events, print the words of the National Anthem on the back of the program or run them on the scoreboard.
8.2 Reward and honour good neighbours and community service with an award (a good Neighbour Award) or the Citizen of the Week on TV. The spinoff effects include role modelling as well the encouragement of volunteerism and current volunteers.
8.6 Encourage volunteerism in the schools. Citizenship Court judges could talk about community service and suggest actual opportunities for voluntary activity in their community.
1.6 We should remind politicians of their responsibilities for the images they project to the public.
8.8 Invite political candidates to address school assemblies.
8.12 More follow-up publicity on recipients of the Order of Canada and the Citation for Citizenship so they can serve as role models.
6.3 Citizenship education for immigrants should be different; that is, the content should build on structures learned in another part of the world and begin with the notion of global citizenship.
10.4 Expertise and strategies that are developed for students should be shared with those involved with citizenship education for adult immigrants.
2.9 Cross-cultural relations are not in the world of academe alone, but at the grass roots, street level of society too. Integration is taking place at that level now. Maybe a conference won't be necessary in 20 years as we'll all be Canadians. But we must all work consciously against the bigotry that still exists and keep trying to change attitudes. If people are given the information, they'll generally make the right judgements.

Recommendations and Suggestions

General
10.25 Citizenship education is part of all education, from the youngest to the eldest; it is especially appropriate for adults who went through "citizenship" at an earlier stage.
4.11 Promote better understanding among all Canadians and respect for our symbols and emblems of nationhood - the flag, our anthem, and other traditions.
8.9 Define and promote core values so all Canadians understand them.
4.12 Remembrance Day should be a national holiday.
10.11 An ad hoc committee under the CEA, including regional, ethnic and native representation as well as women, seniors, the disadvantaged and students, should be formed to plan a mechanism for sharing.
10.28 & 8 There is a need for another conference with more time for sharing concerns and ideas about citizenship; it should be followed by annual conferences by region or interest group. Those who attend should assume responsibility for returning home to carry out follow-up activities.

Education and Schooling
Policy and Educational Practice
9.9 & 10 Every jurisdiction and school district should enact a regulation that all school policies must respect the Canadian Charter of Rights and Freedoms. In addition, school policy and practice should reflect mutual respect between staff and students in line with the Charter.
6.4 Schools in Canada should be modelled on a democratic basis.
4.7 Support local student unions and student councils.
4.6 Do whatever is possible to facilitate student involvement in such activities as simulations of local, national and provincial governments and model United Nations.
4.2 Support the continuation and expansion of exchange programs for both students and teachers in the official and heritage languages.
1.5 Encourage meetings between youngsters from across the nation (Forum for Young Canadians, Terry Fox Centre) so that they may learn from each other and become more aware.
8.5 There is a need for more travel and exchange opportunities, expecially one-way programs.
V.5 Although an agenda for the future was not set at the Forum, a direction toward a broader definition of citizenship education did emerge; it now requires focusing.

Education and Schooling
Teachers/Administration
1.7 All teacher training courses and continuing education courses should include a civics component.
8.7 Encourage teachers of all subjects to act as role models and reflect good citizenship. Eliminate double standards in the achool administration and practices.

4.3 Make funds available to teachers to maintain, develop or improve their language and teaching skills in a multilingual as well as a bilingual context.
10.1 Provincial teachers' associations could hold conferences or workshop sessions on citizenship.
8.10 Encourage education organizations such as the Canadian Teachers' Federation, the Canadian School Trustees' Association and the Canadian Education Association to take a more active interest in citizenship education. Get their help in raising awareness through their publications.
v.1 Citizenship educators need a forum or network for exchanging information and ideas on curriculum and methods, materials and resources and future directions.

Education and Schooling
Curriculum and Instruction

V.2 We need to agree on definitions of citizenship and citizenship education. What concepts, issues, knowledge, skills and values are included? Then we need to agree on goals and effective means of achieving them.
6.1 All agreed that citizenship education was important though the approaches to the ultimate goal differed. Some felt there should be a special subject called citizenship that would be taught at various levels. Others felt that the approach should be through a role model. None felt that indoctrination was a desired goal.
6.2 Citizenship in Canada still needs definition but it should be integrated into the whole school experience. If citizenship were taught as a subject, perceived difficulties would be in deciding what gets taught and what gets omitted. Goals must be specified (realizing that some are difficult to attain). The most important goals relate to the skills and knowledge of processes that a citizen needs to function. Vital concepts to be understood are: sharing and interdependence; resolving conflicts and controversy; functioning of the political system.
V.3 Some educators are looking for specific citizenship education curriculum content and a clearly articulated citizenship program.
2.4 The teaching of citizenship must begin early in elementary school - as it's very difficult to bring about a change of attitude in secondary school. Understanding, tolerance, compromise and a sense of belonging must be developed early and expanded as the student matures from local community to a sense of global belonging.
1.4 We must develop good citizens by teaching fundamental values, respect for others and critical thinking in our school system. As we incorporate information on citizenship training, we should consider the developmental stages of children, their tastes, their ages and their levels of maturity. We should develop in the child the ability to examine information with the goal of solving problems and taking wise, thoughtful and bold decisions.
9.1, 2.3 & 8 Citizenship education should include a knowledge of major Canadian political institutions as well as history, geography and social sciences; an understanding of how to become a Canadian citizen; a knowledge of the makeup of Canadian society and of the rights and

Recommendations and Suggestions

responsibilities of people who live in Canada and a knowledge of small-structure organizational patterns throughout Canadian society.
2.1   Schools should teach skills of citizenship - discipline, critical thinking and order which are not transferable or inherent - to enable born Canadians to have the skills necessary to be a citizen of Canada or any nation, skills essential for living with others.
4.5   Stress basic literacy of the official languages as part of being able to contribute to the life of the country. Special emphasis should be placed on "critical literacy" at an early age to become a functioning member of society.
2.7   Most Canadians know little about Canada as a country; they live in their own corner. Schools must instil a feeling of belonging, of being a part of Canada - no matter where one comes from, no matter what one's race or religion.
2.5   Encourage students to learn about Canada and become a part of what is happening. Educate students (and adults via the media) about what they can do - not always stressing what is being done for them.
2.6   Basic to good citizenship is an understanding of humankind.
4.4   Develop appropriate scope and sequencing for the skills, knowledge and attitudes required for citizenship education; begin the process in schools at an early age.
4.1   Funding and support mechanisms, paid for from the public purse, should be developed for teaching heritage languages by such means as immersion programs.
9.6   Develop support materials that have a federal orientation.
10.17 & 8 The annotated list of citizenship materials and services available in the schools needs to be more visible to school boards and educational institutions.
1.7b   We should encourage national meetings between those who develop programs in citizenship in order to clarify concepts and to promote exchange mechanisms and curriculum resources.